PUNK ROCK

PUNK ROCK

Music Is the Currency of Life

Mindy Clegg

SUNY
PRESS

Published by State University of New York Press, Albany

© 2022 State University of New York

For information, contact State University of New York Press, Albany, NY
www.sunypress.edu

Library of Congress Cataloging-in-Publication Data

Name: Clegg, Mindy, author.
Title: Punk rock : music is the currency of life / Mindy Clegg.
Description: Albany : State University of New York Press, 2022. | Includes
    bibliographical references and index.
Identifiers: LCCN 2022002690 (print) | LCCN 2022002691 (ebook) | ISBN
    9781438489377 (hardcover : alk. paper) | ISBN 9781438489391 (ebook) |
    ISBN 9781438489384 (pbk. : alk. paper)
Subjects: LCSH: Punk rock music—History and criticism. | Punk culture.
Classification: LCC ML3534 .C592 2022 (print) | LCC ML3534 (ebook) | DDC
    781.6609—dc23
LC record available at https://lccn.loc.gov/2022002690
LC ebook record available at https://lccn.loc.gov/2022002691

10 9 8 7 6 5 4 3 2 1

There is no document of civilization which is not at the same time a document of barbarism.

—Walter Benjamin, *Theses on the Philosophy of History*

"Punk" by Daquella manera. (Creative Commons CC0 1.0)

Contents

Illustrations

Acknowledgments

Like any book, this volume is a collective effort. My youth was shaped by the kind of popular culture I enjoyed and the connections I made through that culture. Growing up in a small north Georgia town in the 1980s, I had little access to the world of independent music initially. But I did get MTV early on, which introduced me to music I would have otherwise missed. After the alternative boom of the early 1990s, I found my people among the other outsiders in town. I got to know a variety of wonderful and weird folks through Schroeder's New Deli who introduced me to a variety of underground music that still give me pleasure today.

I began studying punk rock in the 2000s as an undergraduate at Georgia State University (GSU). I continued with my master's degree at GSU, working with Michelle Brattain. For my PhD (also at GSU) I especially thank the people who served on my dissertation committee. My dissertation adviser, Alex Sayf Cummings, managed to get me through the process at a particularly difficult time in my life. My endless thanks go to her. John McMillian and Montgomery Wolf offered great advice on various drafts. Montgomery was kind enough to share her wisdom about punk rock early in the process. I'm looking forward to seeing her dissertation finally become a book! Denis Gainty was also on my committee. He unexpectedly passed away at age forty-six just prior to my defense. Denis was a generous person, an excellent scholar, and a wicked awesome mandolin player with his band the Porch Bottom Boys. I can certainly say that I am better off for having known him and wish that he was still with us today. I know many others feel the same.

Dewar MacLeod alerted me to the call for proposals for this new series from SUNY Press. We've never had the chance to meet in person, sadly. But his excellent work is an inspiration for those of us who wish to take punk rock seriously as a topic of academic inquiry. Richard Carlin made this process of creating a book a bit easier. My thanks go to both of them.

I was given permission to reprint covers of several zines. This includes Jack Rabid of *The Big Takeover* (tune in to the radio show, folks!), Dan Sinker of *Punk Planet*, Kent McClard of *HeartattCk*, and Tom Jennings of *Homocore*. Jack allowed me to use a fantastic Even Worse flyer that was originally created by R. B. Korbet. Marek Loub, the "Enfant Terrible" of the Czech Republic hardcore scene, was kind enough to provide scans for *HeartattCk*. I used the zine archive at the Internet Archive to conduct much of the research. I appreciate everyone who took the time to upload their old zines to share with the rest of humanity. I appreciate the hard work of the archivists at the Internet Archive. It could very much be the modern-day library of Alexandria. Several images I used were found in the Creative Commons. I appreciate everyone who freely shared their images with the world. The images I used were either public domain or under an attribution license. I also thank everyone whose work I cite in this book and pretty much anyone else who studies punk, postpunk, or any underground cultures. I certainly stand on the shoulders of giants.

Last are the people who have put up with me the most. My thanks to Anna Baumstark, a wonderful friend who has heard me yap about punk rock for years now. Getting to spend a few hours each week in conversation with you is always a pleasure. I thank my mother, Beth, and my late father, Michael, for putting up with me being a weirdo for years. I thank my sister Michelle and her family, Ron and the kids, Brandon, Kelly, and Jordan, as well as my brother-in-law Jason and his daughters, Emily, Megan, and Lily. I send love to my entire extended family, the Moriarty side, the Howard side, and the Clegg side.

Last is Rome and Fiona. As I'm wrapping this up, Fiona is preparing to enter college. I'm still amazed we've raised such an awesome human. I am humbled to be her mother and love her so much. Rome put as much work into this book as I have. He's an excellent copyeditor! He's been endlessly supportive of my career and I can't thank him enough for his patience and love.

Introduction

Punk Rock and History

Public perceptions of history and what historians actually do have diverged in recent years. Much of the public still thinks of history through the Great Man theory, which dominated the historical field until relatively recently. This approach positions famous individuals at the center of historical narratives. Generally speaking, men (often white men) are considered the primary agents of change over time through heroic individual action. Abraham Lincoln freed the slaves. Winston Churchill and the royal family kept the British public together during World War II. Elvis Presley created rock-n-roll. Dr. Martin Luther King Jr. ended segregation in the United States. Ronald Reagan ended the Cold War, and so on. The rest of humanity has little agency in affecting change over time; their lives are merely shaped by happenings outside of their control. These historical narratives argue that major events such as wars, politics, or the ends of empires are the primary engine of historical change. Events that happen outside of these history-shaping structures are merely seen as precursors or tangential to "real" historical developments. History written in this manner just becomes "one damn thing after another" for many. It is often dull and dry and has no real connection to our lives. People find it hard to see themselves as people who can make history without becoming one of those "great men." Historical change, good or bad, becomes seen as something that happens to people, not as something that we cause. Because of this, many people believe that history has no real or direct connection to their lives.

Since the 1960s, many historians have come to reject this outmoded understanding. Instead they focus on how everyday people are just as much agents of historical change as the elites whose names we all know. Modern

1

Figure I.1. Even Worse flyer from 1981. (Used by permission of Jack Rabid, created by R. B. Korbet)

historians write bottom-up, complicated histories that rarely offer easy answers to the "so what?" question. Historians in this mode present the reader with the complexity and contingency of events. They refuse to sidestep the difficulty of charting the "why" of historical change. As a result of this shift, modern historiographies are filled with more than just great men in stuffy rooms. Ordinary people in pedestrian locations help drive historical change just as much (if not more) than elites. The historical field has become more democratic. The topics historians investigate have also changed. Politics and important men still make their appearance in historical narratives, but so do the mundane days and the ordinary people. Books that explore earth-shattering events share shelf space with books on those smaller, quiet moments that are more relatable. Social and cultural histories have helped us understand that everyday life matters just as much as the big events. In fact, they might tell us more about what really produces change over time. Each big historical moment has a longer trajectory shaped in various ways by numerous individuals—well-known and less so.

This newer approach to history has had its public advocates. Historians like Howard Zinn argued for the importance of writing history aimed at the general public that put ordinary people at the center of the narrative.[1] His years of teaching and engaging with the public helped popularize a more people-centric version of public history, a growing field of history. Journalists have also been part of opening up grassroots approaches to history for the general public. Nikole Hannah-Jones's 1619 Project published in the *New York Times* explored how racism in US society today has roots in the first enslaved people arriving in Jamestown.[2] History that is connected and engaged with the lives of everyday people shows how we all can be agents of change. That resonates, and that resonance can be turned into motion. If people understand that those who came before made change in the world, they might be more inclined to believe that they, too, can make change.

This brings us to the topic of this book: punk rock. Punk evokes strong emotions in people. For years, punks and others have endlessly debated the meaning, origins, and current mortality of punk rock. Although scholars in other fields have been writing about punk since its inception, academic historians have only recently started to focus on punk as a historical phenomenon. The best way to gauge what historians are interested in is by searching for dissertations. If you search on ProQuest's dissertations and thesis database for dissertations in the field of history, you get about 60 hits, a number that expands to over 600 when other fields are included. Some include punk as a part of a larger set of arguments. There are now some dissertations with punk as their central concern. Trailblazer Dewar MacLeod completed his dissertation "Kids of the Black Hole" in 1998. MacLeod used punk as a lens for understanding changes happening during the 1970s. He sought to understand why hardcore punk emerged in locations like Southern California, especially against the backdrop of a shift from suburban communities to exurban. He argued that it "reflected transformation in both the position of young people in American society and the landscape of Southern California."[3] MacLeod has since published his dissertation as a book.[4] Other historians followed in MacLeod's footsteps. Montgomery Wolf completed her dissertation at the University of North Carolina at Chapel Hill in 2007. "We Accept You, One of Us?" took a different focus, on society and self during the 1970s. She said that trying to define punk is "like trying to nail Jello to the wall."[5] She argued that punk was an example of a shift in focus to individualism during the 1970s and 1980s. This meant that it was an "unstable" construct and thus a "moving target."[6] A year after Wolf defended her dissertation, Brock Ruggles defended his at Arizona State University. In "Not So Quiet on the Western Front," he argued that punks organized against the "conservative ascendancy" that began during the Reagan era. This produced a sort of punk "intelligentsia" that influenced the direction of the punk subculture and the political beliefs of many involved in it.[7] More recently, historians have studied punk in other parts of the world. In 2013, Jeff Patrick Hayton completed his dissertation on punk rock in East and West Germany. In the introduction, he discussed a museum to the Ramones found in Berlin. He argued that it made sense for the museum to be there because punk "had a more lasting and deeper cultural resonance on German culture, society and politics than it has in either the United States or Great Britain."[8] This activity means that we will see more historians delve into the field and give their own spin on this topic. This does not even address all the popular histories of punk. Some are more hagiographic—an uncritical celebration of punk rock with little interest in historicizing it. Others seek to wrestle with the meaning of punk and make historical arguments about it. All work to show us why punk matters.

The point of this book is to add to this messy discourse in the hope of clarifying for the punk and nonpunk audience the "so what?" of punk rock. I want to show you why punk matters in the larger historical scheme of things. Punk was and is a genre of music, a social movement, and a set of cultural practices that changed how we think about popular culture and its role in our lives. The critical insights that punks brought to bear on music production are now a regular feature of our cultural life. Punk helped us consume music, literature, and film in a more thoughtful and critical manner. Punk has also become a term that we often positively associate with rebelling against stifling conformity. After the 1960s and 1970s, a new-found cynicism crept into American life with regard to institutions—government entities, corporations, churches, family, and so on. Punks shared in that cynicism. But punk evokes a demand for truth and authenticity via connection with others. Punks built democratic institutions—or perhaps counterinstitutions—to fill that need for connection and structure. Over the years punk has become incorporated into mainstream culture, but it also led to more democratic and less commercial ways of making music and art. More artists across genres are willing to put themselves out there without the structures of the recording industry. Punk has reminded us that music is not just a commodity but a means of building community through a shared understanding of the world. It was a new iteration of the dialectical conversation about culture as a commodity that came with the modern era. The story of punk highlights how we can build new things out of necessity and become deeply resistant to change. It reflects a larger set of changes since the 1970s with regard to how we interact with and understand ourselves via music. Punk illustrates just how people take a commodity created for profit and forge it into a plowshare of community and social sustenance. But it became a divisive descriptor subjected to colonization by corporate interests. The story of punk can be found in these contradictions. This book will show how punk shaped our understanding of the production of popular culture and the role that culture plays in our lives. It has become more than just an amorphous genre of music or an empty exercise in rebellion via consumption. Rather, it is a set of cultural practices—modern invented traditions where participants seek to inject communal values into the production and consumption of music.

The subtitle of this book came from a quote by Ian MacKaye in the zine *Punk Planet*. People had asked him about "the function" of his band Fugazi, which was making music. Perhaps the askers expected something more dramatic given MacKaye's reputation as a political punk. He told Dan Sinker that "music is the currency of life" and argued that music has "been one of the most important forms of communication *forever*."[9] In other words, he felt that music was important not just because it is entertaining or it can generate wealth for some. It matters because it is constructive and communicative. The history of punk music and the social movements that grew around it reveal just how important music can be for communication, community-building, and making changes in our modern, media-drenched society. Punk music is an important form of communication that brought together an imagined community that crossed international boundaries. Punks shared tastes in music and dress, as well as beliefs about how music should be made and shared. They created artist-controlled record labels, alternative distribution networks, spaces for performances and socializing, and their own media. In other words, they created a durable counterpublic to the corporate music culture by what Josh Kun called an audiotopia. Kun called music "an architecture of sound" and argued that music could be a means of imagining alternatives to what exists.[10] Punks imagined the world differently in their songs. They built alternative social structures through their activities. Although it remains an underground phenomenon today and thrives online, the structures that punks built up for more than four decades also had an effect on how mainstream culture thinks about music production. The language and critiques that punks had about the mainstream music industry can be seen in the mainstream media today in discussions about cultural production. Many of today's young pop artists regularly seek a high level of control and independence over the music they make. They are often willing to talk about the political economy of making music, in addition to other issues like racism, misogyny, homophobia, and transphobia. Many music consumers today think more critically about music, too. This partly due to the mode of sharing music online being shaped by the punk underground that predated widespread internet usage. Punk was more than just a brief moment of nihilistic rebellion in the late 1970s that burned bright and flared out. Rather, punk was—and remains—a translocal underground counterculture based on the production and consumption of music. It is translocal in that it is connected across national boundaries but enacted locally. It has made important changes to how we think about music production and consumption. The people who made up the community of punk rockers changed history.

Chapter 1 is a prehistory of punk. We start with the early modern era and end with the postwar youth cultures that developed in the United States and elsewhere. The chapter explores the rise of the modern world-system and how that changed how we think about youth and our relationship to culture. It addresses how the commodification of culture was connected to the rise of a new social category in modern life—the teenager. This became globalized in part because of the cultural Cold War, where the United States promoted American popular culture to gain an edge over the Soviet Union. We see the discussions between artists, philosophers, and young people about mass culture during the twentieth century before punk. Popular music (and other culture) became a contested terrain as it was made into a commodity through sound recordings.

In Chapter 2, I turn to the rise of punk in the 1970s. I begin with what are known as the proto-punk bands (who are identified in hindsight). These are bands that were somewhat out of step with their contemporaries, and they influenced the sound and attitude of punk music. I try to locate the earliest use of the word "punk" as applied to music. From the start, what became known as punk rock was transnational and contested. The first-wave punk bands were not underground as we understand the term. Some of the bands that came out of these first scenes in New York and London had a good deal of mainstream success, and most did not object to that.

In Chapter 3, in the 1980s the first wave of punk gave way to a translocal underground punk scene that continues today. This was shaped in part by late Cold War politics, which came roaring back with a vengeance after the end of detente in the age of Reagan and Thatcher. Punk became more than just a music genre—it grew to a set of cultural practices that included a do-it-yourself ethos. It was in part driven by the sense of mistrust in institutions of the time. By the late 1970s, punk had emerged in the larger public imagination, had been subjected to a public backlash, and influenced a new wave of punks that splintered into several different subcultures. I focus primarily on the second wave of punk rock known as hardcore punk. Hardcore became the primary definition of what people meant by punk rock. Hardcore punks forged a translocal underground, connected via independent labels with distribution networks, globally circulating punk countermedia (such as the long-running zine *Maximum Rocknroll*), and punks traveling the world. A growing hostility toward punk in the form of "punk panics" in the United States, the West, and the socialist countries led to a growing sense of a shared cultural identity that crossed various boundaries. It also politicized punk scenes. Controversies emerged in punk communities, such as violence at punk shows and who should be considered a punk—with white, straight men coming to dominate many scenes.

In the Chapter 4, new divisions emerged out of the controversies of the 1980s. Women and LGBQT+ punks sought greater space and visibility in punk scenes. They embraced punk practices not only to stake their claims in punk itself but to bring awareness to the struggles they faced in a world full of misogyny and homophobia, in addition to other social ills. They objected to how many punk scenes just replicated forms of discrimination found in mainstream society. They worked to make punk communities more reflective of how many imagined themselves—as creating communities that are more democratic and egalitarian. At the same time, many felt like their scenes were being invaded by the increasing levels of attention punk was getting. During the 1990s, the mainstream music industry "rediscovered" punk rock. In 1991, Nirvana's surprise hit album *Nevermind* set off a frenzy among major labels to sign independent artists, although independent music had been making inroads into the public consciousness during the 1980s. After Nirvana, many independent music labels—including some punk labels—ended up being gobbled up by the major labels. This reignited discussions over whether punk was just another genre of music or something more. Several new, nationally distributed zines emerged out of the conflict that arose over the meaning of punk in the wake of corporate interest. Plus, a new wave of punks came into underground scenes because of the higher profile of some punk bands. Some bands on independent punk labels garnered mainstream audiences, which was facilitated by several high-profile "alternative" music festivals that started in the 1990s. Punk panic was waning, but not completely gone. By the end of this period, many punks decided that ignoring the mainstream and reinforcing their own communities was the better part of valor.

In the final chapter, I turn to punk in the 2000s. Punks started to go online as early as the 1980s. Many punk practices made the transition to the internet rather seamlessly. Punks were already used to organizing across vast distances. Zines began to appear online in the late 1990s. By the 2000s, the ways many people used the internet socially was influenced by punk's DIY mindset. Punk as a musical genre splintered further. I use the example of punks who embraced folk music. We look at several "ethnic punk" genres that explored the realities of different ethnic or racial groups. This often came from diasporic communities or those struggling with post-colonial conditions. As such, they were often an attempt to make sense of their lives and connect with others who had the same struggles.

In the conclusion, I show how people seek to embrace the term "punk" for their own purposes, while ignoring the punk underground that exists today. We also look at the punk scene in Myanmar that has gotten some mainstream media attention.

Punk itself never "died," as some are fond of saying. It exists as both a genre of music and a set of cultural practices that have exerted influence outside of popular music. This connection through music and ideas about the role culture should play in our lives can be seen all over the place. The punk DIY ethos has led to new ways of thinking about the production of culture and the institutions that make that culture. Many more people are willing to seek alternatives to mainstream culture industries. Punk went from a marginal subculture to a translocal counterculture that exists today all over the world. This set of invented traditions is shared across traditional boundaries (nation, race, ethnicity, gender, sexual orientation, etc.) and age groups. It tells people that you do not have to wait for an expert to come along and make the culture and community you want to see. Rather, you can make that community yourself, right now, with like-minded individuals. Punk tells us that if you build it, others will come and help you.

Chapter 1

The Roots: Fashion, Art, Politics, and Music in Modernity

Nineteenth Century to 1970

March 5, 150,435 BCE

There on the shimmering horizon stood figures you knew were others, those you'd never met before. You look left and right to your people, who bore the same uncertain unease on their faces. Who were those people? What were they like? What did they intend?

The new group had been spotted a day before by the lake on the far side and none had been back while the appropriate response was formulated by the group. You had all traveled far to find this place, after all. It was perfect—trees, water, shelter of a large cave cleared of animals, plenty of food to gather, game to hunt, and a high vantage point.

After much talk, a course of action was decided upon and they brought you. They could have just sent the men with newly sharpened weapons, but instead those were left with the mothers of mothers, along with the youngest babes.

You leave the group, walk to the water's edge, and seat yourself on a large, flat boulder. You can see the faces of the new people—nervous like your people, suspicious, but also curious. You smile in a way that you hope is encouraging and welcoming. Then you pull out the newly carved bone flute and begin to play. Soon, one of their own slowly begins to circle around to you, sits on the far side of the same boulder, pulls out a small drum and begins to beat in time with your playing.

Thus went history's first concert, which saw the incorporation of new members into your group, a new community built out of a shared love of melody and rhythm.

Romantics	Teddy Boys
Oscar Wilde	Skinheads
Swing Kids	Hippies

For us to fully understand punk, we must establish its prehistory, the chain of events that made the subculture possible. I mean this to be more than just figuring out the earliest use of the term or the earliest bands that we know influenced or were understood as punk, which we'll do in later chapters. Such deep roots will enrich our understanding, as it will reveal social processes that have deeper resonances in the society in which we live—increasingly a globalized, interconnected society where many identify with others who share a particular cultural understanding of the world. Here I will pull together several historical strands that will weave together our the background for the emergence of punk. Punks took a marginal subgenre of rock music and made it into a subcultural community where young people struggling to fit in could find acceptance through a communal experience with music. Punks employed a critical way of thinking about the production and consumption of culture that shaped mainstream discussions about culture. In recent years, punks moved from youthful cultural villains to outsider cultural heroes. Our modern discussions about the political economy of music today stem directly from punk and post-punk subcultures. For now, though, we need to show what made something like punk possible in the first place.

I begin with the human need to make music and tell stories, an ancient instinct, and then explore the historical concept of consumerist modernity. I define the term, its origins in the rise of capitalism, and how it shaped the Cold War. Next I look at how artists, writers, and musicians responded to consumerist modernity and the changing circumstances of making a living as an artist. Then I turn to the concept of the teenager, which many just see as a natural stage of social development. A "teenager" turns out to be a rather new concept, in part related to consumerism. I wrap up with a discussion of youth subcultures that shaped teen consumption and their relationship to musical genres like jazz and rock.

The Rise of Capitalist Modernity

First I want to address human origins. How and when did intelligent primates become the thinking, considering, producing, innovating, imagining beings that we are today? Many have argued that the roots are in the physical tools that made life easier over time: the first axes chipped from stones, the earliest bone needles for sewing clothing, the stone plows combined with domesticated horses to make farmers out of hunters; pottery, bricks, and forged metal followed. Then came what we think of civilizations—in the Middle East, North Africa, China, and India at first, and then all around the world. People everywhere had to have this latest and greatest fad, for all its faults. Technologies played a role in the rise of civilization, but perhaps not the definitive role. Maybe the linchpin to our domination of the planet was the ability to abstract our innermost thoughts to communicate with others. Music, stories, and art are part of our ability to communicate complex emotions and experiences. British author Terry Pratchett called humans "pans narrans," or the "storytelling chimpanzee."[1] Our ability to make the complex emotions and thoughts in our heads understandable to others seems like a remarkable, nearly supernatural ability that might make humans unique.

Music has that same power. The invention of music allowed people to build communities across time and space.[2] Much like storytelling functioned to help us understand our common condition, perhaps music evolved as a means of promoting social cohesion. Anyone who has ever been to a concert understands the power of sharing a moment with others through a love of music. Music works as a form of storytelling, too. A song that expresses a sentiment about the social or political aspect of the world can bring people together in a shared moment. Think about Bad Brains singing about being banned in DC or Bikini Kill celebrating rebellious women.[3] Both convey messages that resonate today. They can be understood and translated into our current context. They unite community across time and space, much as the first stories or the first songs must have done. They create the shared, historically bound community under consideration in this book. Punk music was the glue of a community that creates a common but contested understanding of community. It created an alternative to consumerist modernity in that framework. Even after music became a commodity, people used it to reinforce community.

I want to avoid academic jargon, but "capitalist modernity" is a necessity for understanding the rise of punk. Fortunately, it is a straightforward and an important phrase. Capitalist modernity describes how we produce the goods we need to live and how we obtain them by earning a wage that financially sustains us. Production and consumption are at the center of many of our modern experiences. Our labor makes us producers, and our consumption makes us consumers. Capitalist modernity also hints at how we view ourselves as moving in a historically forward motion, building progressively on the past into an inevitable conclusion of today. It helps define us to ourselves in the modern world—we've become consumers of the goods that some other person unknown to us makes while we produce goods for others. We experience much of our social life through consumerism. It shapes our foundational aspirations and our social relations. Consumerism is an aspect of the capitalist economy that appears to be a natural, ahistorical fact of life rather than a social reality that exists in the flow of history. It emerged, evolved, and will likely one day be replaced by some other means of reproducing the necessities of human life. The concept has a history, meaning we can study it. Punk is part of the longer history of our struggle with consumerism in the modern world.

Let's take on the concept of "modernity" first. The modern world emerged from a shift in power that triggered sweeping, often violent changes in European society and the rest of the world Europeans attempted to conquer. Although a few people from the Old World had already visited the New World (such as Viking Leif Erickson), the voyages of Christopher Columbus signaled a new scramble for resources by Europeans. The expansion of the Ottoman Empire (a Muslim empire that many Europeans viewed with hostility) dried up the pipelines for goods that European rulers enjoyed, such as Chinese silks and Indian spices. First the Portuguese and then the Spanish sought alternatives to dealing with the Ottomans as middle men. The Portuguese moved down the West African coast and into the Indian Oceans, where they established trading colonies in India. The Spanish partnered with Christopher Columbus, who insisted to the Spanish monarchs that he could reach the Far East by heading west. People of the time knew the Earth was round, not flat. But Columbus insisted that the monks, priests, and other educated men had overestimated the size of the globe. Most were unaware of an entire continent across the Atlantic Ocean, which was thought to be filled with massive, ship-destroying creatures. The Spanish monarchs gave Columbus three ships and meager provisions. They might have even forgotten about him, probably thinking he was done for. He hit the Canary Islands and sailed west. Several months later, he cheated one of his sailors out of the bounty for whoever first spied land, proclaimed the first people they saw as "good slave material," and he proceeded to set up a brutal colony on the island of Hispaniola (modern-day Haiti and Dominican Republic). This opened up exploration of what turned out to be a new continent, filled with new people, new flora and fauna, and tons of silver. So much, in fact, that the influx of new silver into the Old World economy caused global economic disruptions for decades.[4]

Other goods were found to be extraditable from this New World, dubbed the Americas after Italian explorer Amerigo Vespucci, who charted the eastern coast. The Dutch, French, and English soon followed suit. They established economic colonies, spreading disease and violence to the Native people across the Americas. Sometimes egalitarian relationships formed between the various peoples of the Americas and Europeans, but this was the exception to the rule. Fur trading, silver, and timber were some early products European traders took from the landscape and sold back home. They were given monopolies in the hopes of making a profit and enriching themselves and their monarch. This is the origin of the modern corporation—a monopoly granted by a monarch to individuals, allowing them to raise funds and create a return on investment for those investors. This also gave new people opportunities to profit from goods extracted or produced in the New World—the origins of capitalism. Soon, especially in the English colonies along the North American coast and in the Caribbean, farming on an industrial scale became the core means of creating a surplus to sell to the motherland. The English settlement in Jamestown nearly dissolved seeking a profitable way forward. The first big hit back home was tobacco, a sacred leaf often used to seal deals in some Native American cultures, such as the Algonquin. Other agricultural goods were grown, such as rice further south. In the Caribbean, sugar was the crop of choice. This blood-splattered, sweet necessity of modern life drove the African slave trade and eventually fueled the rise of the English working classes, historian Sidney Mintz argued.[5]

The wealth created here by the conquest and pillaging of the New World contributed to violent ideological splits in Western Christendom that marked the sixteenth and seventeenth centuries, the Protestant Reformation, and the Catholic Counter-Reformation. The split was long in coming. Through the Reformation, monarchs found new means of challenging the Church buffered by the wealth extracted from the New World. Here lies the roots of the modern nation-state. Soon the Netherlands and some of the small principalities in the Holy Roman Empire embraced the Reformation and broke away from the Church. They could more effectively challenge the power of the Catholic Church in Europe with their new colonial wealth. England also eventually embraced Protestantism as they emerged from a period of internal chaos, though they lagged in joining in on colonialism. Although it was prompted by Henry VIII's desire to set aside his marriage to Katherine of Aragon, a Spanish princess, it was far more about his desire to more tightly control wealth in England.[6] As Europe tore itself apart over questions of theology, the Ottoman Empire secured its position in the Balkans, ensuring that Western Europeans would continue to look west for trading opportunities.[7] Some European powers engaged with the Ottomans and made common cause against their European enemies, such as Queen Elizabeth I of England. This was after the age of exploration had been established.[8] Here we can find the seeds of European overseas imperial empires (that still haunt countries such as the United Kingdom and France today) and of the modern nation-state, the preeminent political structure of the modern world.[9] Historian Alfred Crosby noted that Europeans struggled to incorporate all the new forms of knowledge realized by New World conquests. It affected popular trust in the Roman Catholic Church and the later development of the Enlightenment.[10] New modes of thinking had been prompted by new information and new economic opportunities offered by wealth extracted from the Americas.

If Western European monarchs were empowered thanks to the changes that came out of the Columbian exchange, there were other long-term consequences that empowered a new group of people—the bourgeois. Merchants and bankers were able to accumulate wealth, which bought them a newly empowered position in European society. The wealth and privilege of this new class was underwritten by slavery in the New World. As noted, slavery underwrote changing labor patterns in Europe. Peasants pushed off the land came to depend on "selling" their labor in cities.[11] This was the "proletarianization" of the European peasantry or, in the phrasing of E. P. Thompson, the "making" of the working classes.[12] By the eighteenth century, free trade principles slowly replaced the mercantile mindset, guaranteeing the mass production and consumption of sugar in the British diet going forward.[13] These changes were initially limited to the traditional landowning class of the nobility, but soon nonaristocratic people began accumulating wealth and capitalized new businesses—especially in the British North American colonies. Gentlemen farmers dominated huge tracts of land in the New World that generated vast wealth, and they needed hundreds of workers.

Those running these plantations in the American colonies were also reading Enlightenment thinkers. These were new ideas about freedom, political economy, and governance. Political realities made these men try something new. After supporting the mother country during the North American front of the Seven Years' War, some of the colonial elite felt that Parliament was sticking them with the bill via taxation. They used language from the European Enlightenment, especially from Scotland, Germany, and France. When they revolted against Parliament and the Crown, this kicked off what Eric Hobsbawm dubbed the Age of Revolutions. He noted the critical effect of the English Industrial Revolution and the French Revolution on world history.[14] The American and Haitian Revolutions were critical, too. The American Revolution certainly helped inspire the French Revolution. It also contributed a live experiment in some of the new political ideas that emerged out of the Enlightenment that are still playing out today.[15] The Haitian Revolution firmly put race at the center of the discussion about freedom and citizenship.[16] The Age of Revolutions started changes, some unexpected and unintended. Increased industrialization translated into an increased need for a workforce with some literacy, and not just for the new strata of middle management. All three revolutions put new political ideas into the public consciousness that influenced later generations of political thinkers, building democratic realities onto the eighteenth-century political philosophy that animated these revolutions. By 1848, a wave of popular uprisings known as the Springtime of Nations swept central Europe. Democratic movements roiled France, the German states, Italy, and Poland, challenging monarchies across the continent. The people were increasingly demanding a say in their own governance.[17] Unrest continued into the end of the century resulting in a mass movement of people some of whom landed in the United States, a growing industrial and imperial power.[18] In North America, democracy and industrialization merged into capitalist modernity or a mass society.

"Modernity" refers to the rise of full industrialization, the rationalization of the economy, and the emergence of mass society and widespread consumerism. The average person was transformed in the rise of the modern era, defined by their nationality, their position in the division of labor, and their patterns of consumption. Most influential in this mode of thinking about the modern world might be Max Weber, an early twentieth-century German sociologist known for his theories about the role of the Protestant Reformation in shaping the modern economy.[19] Many aspects of modern life, including how we create art, were turned over to be produce via commercial interests. Because of that, the modern world took on what Guy Debord said was more real than reality. This "spectacle" shaped all aspects of modern life. Debord argued that it was alienating in the extreme, but many found it pleasurable.[20] Economist Karl Polanyi similarly argued that the marketization of everyday life prior to World War I contributed to the rise of genocidal fascism in the 1930s and 1940s.[21] Polanyi argued that these were the perils of social relations mediated solely by a transactional mindset. The roots of this shift were in the United States. Historian William Leach argued that the rise of modern commerce was an entirely new American culture, centered on consumption. By the late nineteenth century, modern corporations transformed US culture into one that was "preoccupied with consumption" and was "a future-oriented culture of desire that confused the good life with goods."[22] By the time of the Cold War, the United States— now one of the two most powerful nations on Earth—worked to extend this culture to the whole world.[23] American-style consumerism became a key weapon in the arsenal for global supremacy, a central element of the argument for American hegemony over Soviet.

Modernity does not just mean American-style consumerism. Instead of a singular modernity, modernities or perhaps competing globalizations might be more accurate. After the death of Joseph Stalin in 1953, the new leader of the Soviet Union, Nikita Khrushchev, promised US Vice President Richard Nixon on July 24, 1959, that the Soviet Union would pass the United States with their own consumer paradise—a bigger, better, more modern one. The pair had just concluded a Nixon-led tour of the American exhibition in Moscow that included an entire modern American home, complete with time-saving gadgets in the kitchen for the housewife. This "kitchen debate" was broadcast on US and Soviet TV and signaled a shift in the Cold War. Culture and consumerism were becoming a major field of competition.[24] The Eisenhower administration inaugurated the Jazz Tours, where American jazz artists were sent on performance tours underwritten by the State Department. This was to promote US culture and counter Soviet weaponization of Jim Crow.[25] Other communist nations sought to bring a socialist consumer modernity to their citizens. In East Germany, often thought of as drab and boring, the government made serious attempts to address consumerist desires of the average citizen. The major difference between West and East Germany with regard to fashioning a new consumer landscape in the aftermath of World War II was that in the communist east, the state had a more visible, direct role in shaping consumerism, argued historian Judd Stitziel.[26]

These competing globalizations created a shared cultural experience for young people in different societies. The increasingly strong focus on the promotion of culture by the United States and the Soviet Union reveal just how far comprehensive Cold War logic extended during this period. It was more than just a set of economic, political, or military confrontations; rather, the Cold War created competing worldviews with all aspects of life up for debate. Both sides sought to champion and impose their systems on each other and the world. Two sides of the same coin, they sought to bring all of humanity along with them, by persuasion if possible and by force if necessary. What matters here was that both sides were advocating for their vision on how to best organize a modern, mass society. At the end of the day, the United States and their allies had an advantage; American mass culture proved popular, as did the privatized means of producing and distributing it.

Culture plays a central role in the construction and experience of modernity. Culture is the glue that holds societies together and might be a defining feature of humanity. How we produce culture reflects the ruling economic norm of every age. For the modern period, that meant the mass production of culture, especially popular culture. Mass production represents the exploitation of working-class producers of art and greater democratization of the production and consumption of the culture. Popular music was a case in point. Sound recording and the mass production of records had a profound effect on how we interacted with music. Davis Suisman argued in his book *Selling Sound* that the ability to record and play back sound revolutionized our relationship to music.[27] Sound recording allowed for greater exploitation of artists. It also opened up new possibilities for how the consumer interacted with music.[28] The expansion of sound recording equipment into ever larger markets (such as the compact cassette tape and later MP3s) eventually allowed artists themselves to take greater control of their output and make more direct relationships with consumers, blurring the line between producer and consumer.

During the Cold War, a transnational community of young people was built around the consumption of popular music. Identity in the modern era is a complicated phenomenon, and consumerism added a new axis to that complexity. All areas of life transformed during the modern era to conform to the capitalist economy for good or ill (depending on your point of view). I would argue that it is a little of both. The means of producing and consuming art—high and low—changed during the modern era. In medieval Europe, elite artists gained support from wealthy patrons, such as kings, aristocrats, or the Catholic Church. Folk artists made art when and how they could in their free time to share with their local communities. In the modern, capitalist economy, this system was replaced by a new set of cultural institutions. First was high-end art galleries where the newly enriched classes that owned factories or other businesses could burnish their status by supporting the arts and displaying expensive works of art in their homes. Modern nation-states supported high art via national or regional art galleries. These also benefited from tax dollars and donations from elites, often in exchange for their name associated with the building or sometimes a wing. The arts were now considered part and parcel of the national project, and as such they received state support.[29] The aspiring middle class could participate by visiting museums and buying prints or reproductions of high-end works of art. Art was transformed into a commodity that was sold in an open market. Prices reflected the prestige and rarity of the art, driven by consumer demand. There was some continuation from the past because in the high-end art world, only the wealthy elite could participate fully in the market original art. Ordinary consumers could buy prints of their favorite elite artists.

Low or popular culture had a different process of commodification. Mass production on the widest possible scale applied here. In the late nineteenth century, a new industry grew up in New York City that became known as Tin Pan Alley. This early forerunner to the recording industry sold sheet music to the public, setting up "pluggers" in department stores to sell them. They employed a variety of songwriters, which Suisman noted included popular songwriters now considered key figures in the modern American songbook, like Irving Berlin and George Gershwin. He argued that "Tin Pan Alley's essential impact, however, lay not in aesthetic innovation but in the relation between aesthetic forms and the industry's modern capitalist structure."[30] In other words, how the industry produced music was what made it revolutionary. Sound recordings soon became the central product sold by the recording industry. This transformed people's relationship with music by turning it into a commodity. At the beginning of the nineteenth century, inventor Emile Berliner developed improvements on Thomas Edison's contraption to capture sound. Edison's machine used a cylinder, and Berliner's machine used a disc. It also projected the sound via a bell-shaped horn, making it more conducive for multiple listeners at once. Another more abstract innovation of Berliner's included "licensed reproductions" of events like speeches or musical performances, which Suisman noted could help artists make a living so long as those copyrights of sound recordings were protected.[31] New companies sought the widest possible audience by embracing the most popular of songs to sell. American record labels promoted a wide variety of music to a broad audience. The spectacle of pop music found an eager audience of young people who embraced a modern identity. By the postwar period, young people were the core consumers of popular music. Later on, some attempted to turn the spectacle of pop music into a more authentic and democratic community. I will return to this question, but first I address how some engaged with these changes taking place in our relationship to music.

Philosophical and Artistic Responses to Consumerist Modernity

To understand how punks engaged critically with the popular culture they created and consumed, we need to understand some of the arguments made by theorists, cultural critics, philosophers, and artists during the rise of this new mass culture. Many of their criticisms and theories found fertile ground in postwar countercultures. Nearly a century or so of discussion, debate, and theorizing would give youth movements in the postwar period new means of thinking about popular culture and how it intersected with their attempts to change the world. This proved to be especially true with popular music. The relationship between artists and the culture industries that were commercializing and democratizing popular music was fraught. Some embraced the new categorization that put mass culture in one box and high art in another. Others embraced mass production. Still others saw possibilities in playing across the artificial divisions modernity imposed on art via mass production.

Philosophers, scholars, and cultural theorists engaged in a robust discussion of culture in modern society. They examined how modern society was changing the production of culture and our interactions with that culture. In his book *Teenage*, Jon Savage quoted Thorstein Veblen, who expressed concerns with the rise of US consumer culture in the late nineteenth and twentieth centuries. Veblen developed some new terminology to describe changes happening in American society. He used the term "conspicuous consumption" in his 1899 book *The Theory of the Leisure Class*.[32] Savage argued that Veblen described a crossover of attitudes between elite class youths "bumming it" and unruly urban working-class youths. Both groups rejected the kind of disciplining of leisure time seen as critical by many business leaders and progressive critics, John Kasson argued.[33] Kasson showed that locations of cheap leisure and pleasure like Coney Island were not what the progressives of the day had in mind. In 1893, Chicago hosted the World's Columbian Exposition. Many of the progressive activists of the day hoped that the masses would embrace the exhibit known as the White City, a sprawling complex of neoclassical buildings constructed just for the exposition.

This massive exhibit was meant to "uplift" the "taste and character" of US "gross materialism."[34] Instead, the masses only dutifully trudged through the White City. The designer of New York City's Central Park, Frederick Law Olmsted, said that the crowds had "a tired, dutiful, 'melancholy air.'" But the masses really responded more positively to the Midway. This mile-long stretch of amusements "formed a colossal sideshow," full of "Barnumesque eclecticism" that had "exciting, cheap amusements and exotic displays."[35] Veblen and Olmsted hoped the public would embrace culture that would uplift and enrich them. But they underestimated the siren song of the new mass culture, produced to turn a profit.

Not all critics viewed mass culture entirely negatively. In her study of immigrant industrial labor in the early twentieth century, Lizabeth Cohen described the relationship between those interested in incorporating the immigrant working class into US society and working-class immigrants themselves in the city of Chicago. The new commercial culture was thought of as a means of "taming" unruly labor and integrating immigrants into the national fabric. This assumption—often found in the pages of popular magazines—was that a combination of good, steady work with adequate leisure time could make immigrants fully American.[36] The popular media proclaimed that the creation of a "homogeneous people" would be on the basis of this shared mass culture.[37] Mass culture found on the radio and in films had a particularly strong appeal to the children of working-class immigrants. It became a means of expressing independence and cementing social bonds with their peers.[38] Cohen argued that "members of the younger generation were more attracted to mainstream mass culture than their parents."[39] Kasson showed much the same about working-class immigrant youths in New York. The new mass culture was understood as being "inclusive" for young people of all ethnic backgrounds.[40] The new mass culture had supporters and detractors early on.

By the interwar period, Europeans were also formulating a critique of the new mass culture. Italian Marxist Antonio Gramsci provided some insight into the shift to mass society, including the dangers and possibilities. Marxists were often enthusiastic about the changes brought by the Enlightenment and the age of revolutions. They saw it as a far-reaching and ultimately democratic set of changes that furthered the cause of human freedom. Writing in 1916, Gramsci called the Enlightenment "a magnificent revolution in itself" that "gave all Europe a bourgeois spiritual International in the form of a unified consciousness, one that was sensitive to all the woes and misfortunes of the common people." He argued that this was an unfinished revolution. He hoped that the proletariat (the laboring classes) would eventually add "another link to that chain" of revolution in the future.[41] Gramsci also tried to come to terms with the rise of mass culture. He expressed concerns about working-class cultural autonomy in the face of the hegemony of the ruling class. David Forgacs noted how Gramsci saw education as central to ensuring working-class autonomy. As a Marxist, Gramsci hoped education would create the conditions for a working class revolution.[42] His biggest contribution to Marxist theory was his focus on cultural hegemony. He argued that rather than pure force, most societies run on a combination of force and persuasion built on the concept of common sense. The ruling class in modern societies seek to tightly control the media to ensure that their ideas about the economy and society are positioned as common sense, rather than as one ideology among many. This process happens primarily via the construction of culture. For example, in Gramsci's dissection of the works of Italian idealist Benedetto Croce, he argued that culture was central to the building of the "conception of the state."[43] Building consensus around a society needed to be "naturalized" through culture. Gramsci argued that the revolutionary working classes need to do much the same if and when they come to power.

Others built on the argument that culture played a critical role in modern society and took a more critical tone. The Frankfurt School philosophers (associated with Institute for Social Research at the Goethe University Frankfurt before the rise of the Nazis) explored popular culture in their works. Theodor Adorno, a German theorist and musicologist, had much to say on the topic of the culture industries and their role in disciplining the new workforce in a mass society. Perhaps most famous of his works on mass-produced popular culture was his essay with Max Horkheimer from 1944, "The Culture Industry: Enlightenment as Mass Deception." Their objection to mass culture rested on how "culture now impresses the same stamp on everything."[44] They argued that "all mass culture under monopoly [was] identical." They said that the structures themselves were obvious to all. That reality reflected the power of the class with the "strongest economic position" in society.[45] Moreover, the culture industries made promises to the consumer that it never really delivered.[46] Most notable about mass culture, they argued, was how it amuses via "entertainment." According to Adorno and Horkheimer, the concept of entertainment was an ideology of the industry. Entertainment for leisure time had emerged in modern society because of the rigors of modern forms of labor as a means of mollifying the working classes. Embracing that kind of entertainment was "to be in agreement" with the modern capitalist society. They argued that "at its root is powerlessness. It is indeed escape, but not from, as it claims, escape from bad reality but from the last thought of resisting that reality." But not all is lost, as "it has become increasingly difficult to keep the public in submission."[47] The products of the culture industries could not fully hide the inequality caused by the capitalist economy, according to Adorno and Horkheimer. "Just as totalitarian society does not abolish suffering of its members, but registers and plans it, mass culture does the same with tragedy. Hence the persistent borrowing from art."[48] Mass culture was a pale imitation of real art, they argued. They saw little space between totalitarian societies like Nazi Germany and the United States, as both deployed culture as a form of social control. Much like certain words or concepts were spread top-down in Germany, the culture industries spread popular fads.[49] American mass society offered up "economic coercion" rather than the more naked use of force found in Nazi Germany.[50]

Walter Benjamin interrogated the changes brought to the production of art via mass production in one of his most famous works, *The Work of Art in the Age of Mechanical Reproduction.*[51] Like many others philosophers of his day, he was deeply concerned with the effects of the capitalist economy on the production of art. He saw some possibilities in mass production of art. He argued that new people were being empowered to define art. In the modern economy, the ability to reproduce art easily put the consumer of the art in the driver's seat. It also expanded who could be a consumer of art. He said that mass production "detaches the reproduced object from the domain of tradition" and allows "the reproduction to meet the beholder or listener in his own particular situation."[52] He argued that the art humans produced always stems from the historical circumstances that shape artistic perceptions.[53] Hinting at the democratic possibilities, Benjamin argued that in the modern age, "mechanical reproduction emancipates the work of art from its parasitical dependence on ritual."[54] He did not assume that mass production was all positive, arguing that the "cult of the movie star" rested on selling a personality as a commodity.[55] Overall, Benjamin argued for the need to understand how the means of production shapes how art is made, understood, and consumed.

These theorists addressed real concerns about social control and consumerism, but debates about consumerism were not just academic. During the first half of the twentieth century, the mass media became a place for discussing these issues. Some of the media narratives were about social control, which included tropes about "youth out of control." Consumerism became one proposed means of creating a less restive and more compliant society. People like Adorno might have had these arguments in mind with their criticism. Several authors were associated with this line of thinking, including Walter Lippman. He argued for the "manufacturing of consent" by shaping public opinion through mass media. He wrote that "we cannot rely upon intuition, conscience, or the accidents of casual opinions if we are to deal with the world beyond our reach."[56] His contemporary Edward Bernays argued that consumerism could be an effective form of social control. His work with advertisers in the twentieth century gave us the field of public relations. Bernays, a nephew of pioneering psychologist Sigmund Freud, embraced some of his uncle's theories in creating public relations. In one advertising campaign, he worked with cigarette companies to convince more women to smoke. He hired attractive young women to light up cigarettes during an Easter parade, telling the newspapers that suffragists were going to be making a high-profile statement about freedom. He called it the "torches of freedom" campaign. The goal was to get more women to take up smoking by associating it with the recent suffragist movement and glamorous young women.[57] The goal of such campaigns was to shape the desires of consumers and by extension channel their concerns about society through a desire for consumer goods. Bernays wrote an entire work on the positive aspects of propaganda in a modern society with mass media. Published in 1928, *Propaganda* became a foundational text for the field of public relations and an oft-cited handbook for the concept of "engineering consent" for the public good.[58] Noam Chomsky and Edward Herman studied this phenomenon, examining how manufacturing consent functioned historically over the twentieth century, especially in the United States.[59]

While Gramsci and Benjamin felt that mass culture could be used to further revolutionary actions, Lippman and Bernays believed that social control was a necessary component of a democratic society. The arguments put forth by critics such as Adorno and Horkheimer came from real concern about social control via mass media. Others built on their critiques, especially the Letterists and the Situationists in France. They merged the theoretical with an artistic response to modernity. Greil Marcus investigated the artistic resistance to modernity that later influenced the first wave of punk music, drawing a direct line between artistic movements like Dada and punk rock. Dada emerged and flamed out quickly during World War I. Hugo Ball, Emmy Hennings, Hans Arp, Tristan Tzara, Marcel Janco, and Richard Huelsenbeck launched Dadaism in Switzerland in early 1916. From the confines of their club, Cabaret Voltaire, they married music and performance with a critique of modernity.[60] The Letterists and the splinter group the Situationists sought to emulate and destroy their Dadaist heroes. The founder of Letterism, Isidore Isou, announced his new movement by disrupting a production of Tzara's play *La Fuit* in 1946.[61] Cofounder of the Situationist International Raoul Vaneigem said of the group that "the Dadaists built the first laboratory for the revitalization of everyday life," which was the focus of his own work.[62] Guy Debord, originally a member of the Letterists, broke away in 1957 to form the Situationists with Vaneigem. This group had a major influence on the counterculture in Europe in the 1960s and 1970s.[63] Debord penned *The Society of the Spectacle*, a pamphlet arguing that modern society was built on artifice and spectacle of mass media.[64] Artistic groups across Europe and North America aligned themselves with the Situationists in France. King Mob formed in Britain in the late 1960s, with Malcolm McLaren (later the manager of the Sex Pistols) counting himself as a member.[65] These groups refused to keep art confined to the gallery or studio. Instead, they staged street actions meant to disrupt "normal" society. They hoped to break people out of the everyday and confront them in a ways meant to get them to rethink their lives. These groups blurred the lines between types of art and insisted that art should not remain in the hands of a chosen few gatekeepers but be undertaken as a daily praxis by everyone. These groups were the original culture jammers. As such, they influenced people like McLaren to do the same through popular culture.

A key question was about the success of shaping public opinion through mass media and culture. Adorno and Horkheimer erred on the side of assuming the effectiveness of such strategies. There was little room in their analysis for how people understood the culture they consumed or how they used it to understand their lives and the world around them. In more recent years, many works have been produced on just that topic. Marcus argued that "modern capitalism was a tricky project: dangerous. Free income and free time might provoke desires the market could never satisfy, and those desires might contain a wish to go off the market."[66] Kasson showed a ground-up perspective on how consumers understood mass culture. People of all classes flocked to Coney Island at the beginning of the twentieth century. He argued that these new amusement parks functioned "as laboratories of the new mass culture" actively embraced by many in American society.[67] As such, "Coney [Island] offers a case study of the growing cultural revolt against genteel standards of taste and conduct that would swell to a climax in the 1920s."[68] Cohen demonstrated that consumers did not just accept the meaning imposed on mass-produced culture by the culture industries.

She argued that "what mattered were the experiences and expectations that the consumer brought to the object."[69] Even the output of various culture industries were not as homogenizing as some have argued. Critics believed that immigrants would Americanize via mass culture. But the various ethnic groups that made up Chicago's working-class communities often bought records that captured modern Italian culture, such as Enrico Caruso's recordings of Italian opera favorites.[70] In other words, "A commodity could just as easily help a person reinforce ethnic or working-class culture as lose it."[71] Radio "had a distinctly grassroots orientation" during the early days of broadcasting. Stations were small, locally operated, and often focused on local content during this period, Cohen argued. Most of these early stations only had at most 5,000 watts until after 1925.[72] These stations would focus on the interests of the local community, including "ethnic nationality hours" and local entertainers.[73] This was true of the next generation as well. For the sons and daughters of immigrants, raised and sometimes born in the United States, ethnic affiliation still dominated their lives during this period. They would go to events that centered on youth culture in various neighborhood clubs, and the people in the clubs often shared ethnic heritage.[74] From the beginning, people made choices as consumers, and their relationship to mass culture was not always what was expected by the industry. Consumers also came to expect some amount of responsiveness from these modern industries built around leisure and entertainment. In the period after World War II, the youth demographic known as teenagers eventually became some of the most demanding consumers of culture.

The Creation of Teenagers and Youth Cultures

We turn to the prehistory of teenagers, which will help us understand the emergence of punk in the 1970s. Many consider the teen years to be a natural stage of life, a transitional period between childhood and adulthood that sets a person's personality for life. Consumption of popular culture is tightly intertwined with this concept. But like many other aspects of human life, the concept of the "teenager" has a history. The development of teenagers as a social category and the broader category of youth subcultures intersect with the rise of the consumer economy. What do we mean when we say "teenager"? It means far more than just a set of years. It has become a stage of life that is highly mythologized in our culture and has a major effect on the production of popular culture—especially music.

Jon Savage argued that starting in the late nineteenth century, "it was no longer adequate to think that adulthood immediately followed childhood." He tied this shift to cultural movements such as Romanticism. But it also came from changes in political and economic structures in the late eighteenth century. These changes "inaugurated a new society based on materialism, consumerism, and mass production."[75] The notion of generational conflict was part of the age of revolutions, inscribed in French revolutionary law as Article 28. It addressed the effect of laws written by older generations on younger people. A democratic ideal aimed at ensuring equal rights for all, it stated that "one generation cannot subject to its laws future generations." These ideals, Savage asserted, echoed down through the nineteenth century, expanding who should be considered citizens with regard to rights under the law.[76] Savage stated that by the 1870s, "hitherto neglected classes like the urban working poor" were getting more attention in politics and in culture. This new culture was gestating in the industrialization of Europe and North America and was marketed to the young across classes, making youth its own class to some degree. Seeing oneself reflected in the culture one consumes ends up having a powerful effect on how people view themselves. One example was mass-produced dime novels, which gave a young people models of youthful behavior to emulate, which then provided a template for further cultural production.[77] The shift to mass culture helped create the concept of the teenager.

Other social structures shaped teenage identity, such as the establishment of compulsory education through high school in the United States and Europe. Moral panics over juvenile delinquency helped drive compulsory educational policies.[78] Sensational stories about youth gangs filled newspapers in Western Europe and North America in the late nineteenth and early twentieth centuries.[79] The problem was blown way of proportion. Newspapers sometimes made up entire street gangs, such as with the Apache gang in the French media.[80] The police were often called to deal with violent youths.[81] But school was also seen as a solution to the problem of wayward youth. Late nineteenth-century psychologist G. Stanley Hall advocated for understanding a new stage of life, the adolescent phase. He insisted that this phase needed to be carefully shaped and monitored to produce productive and mentally sound members of society. Hall maintained that public schools were an important means to achieve that end.[82] He was greatly influenced by the German child study movement.[83] In his work, Hall blamed the psychological problems that youths might exhibit (such as juvenile delinquency) on the emergence of mass society in general. To counter that, he advocated for sheltering young people during adolescence, such as with greater enforcement of school attendance.[84]

Concerns about juvenile delinquency were shared in Europe. Class was part of these discussions in the United Kingdom. Young people from the elite and working classes posed a problem for British critics. Group sports in elite "public" schools (schools for the children of the upper classes) became a means of creating the leaders of the imperial order of the late nineteenth and early twentieth century.[85] David Greenblatt made this argument in his global history of soccer. This was true about young men in the nineteenth-century British public school system. These schools promoted a particular form of colonial ideology known as "Christian masculinity," meant to prepare these young men for moral leadership in the empire. Football (soccer) and rugby (to a lesser degree) allowed these two distinct classes to work out the new hierarchies emerging in British society thanks to industrial capitalism and empire.[86] This embrace of sport as a means of shaping young people into productive members of society trickled down to the rest of British society, with the YMCA doing much of the heavy lifting of spreading the mindset among the working classes.[87]

Literature also offered the elite classes a vision of youth rebellion. French poet Arthur Rimbaud embraced the upheaval of the Paris Commune of 1871, for example.[88] British author Oscar Wilde influenced a rebellious image of youth by embracing socialism and homosexuality. Wilde sought to influence young people. According to Savage, he valued youth over adults, something that also marks consumer culture.[89] The way of life embraced by Rimbaud and Wilde eventually did get the mass production treatment. Savage argued that avant-garde bohemian culture became "diluted and promoted for mass consumption within America" in the twentieth century.[90] By the time of the roaring '20s, the embrace of mass culture by the young grew alongside the rise of compulsory education, which meant an increase in youth literacy. F. Scott Fitzgerald incorporated a celebration and a critique of pleasurable living into his novel *The Great Gatsby*. It showcased hedonism influenced by mass culture but also a kind of bohemianism marked by short-term pleasure-seeking, which some came to see as a model. Savage argued that the embrace of short-term thinking was inherent in these "extreme" lifestyles, but they also proved to be "an alluring but unstable form of mass control."[91] This dialectical process of fringe movements being repackaged for the masses played out over the course of the twentieth century, from margins to center. Even if couched as a warning or in a diluted form, many young people found such cultures alluring. Artistic movements often set the tone for how the general public viewed culture. Movements like the Italian Futurists celebrated the new mass culture and lionized youth. Savage showed how Futurists like F. T. Marinetti embraced youth and technology in their work. They also embraced militarism, which made them allied with the fascists in the 1920s.[92] World War I also shaped the emergence of youth cultures, argued to Savage. In the United Kingdom, during the war years young people found themselves working in jobs previously held by adult men, with about 600,000 young people taking on such industrial work by 1917 (in Germany the number was around 300,000). Young people in rural areas were tasked with maintaining food production. Savage showed that at the same time, there was far less adult control. This drove a wave of "aberrant youth behavior." Many young people in the United Kingdom attacked those with German names, among other delinquent behavior. Predictably, more moral panics over the danger to and of young people followed.[93]

The destruction of World War I was largely borne by young men. The violence of the war drove a new cynicism that shaped interwar youth culture. Savage noted that it "forever destroyed the automatic obedience that elders expected from their children."[94] Before the war, a fringe culture was critical of capitalist modernity. But in the interwar period, popular culture that was critical of society became more widespread, facilitated by the new cynicism of the generation that lived through the war. Savage argued that youth became a powerful social force in US and some European societies. "Youth embodied the headlong flight into the future."[95] This cultural focus on youth found greater expression in the new mass culture. Several goods were aimed at the youth market in the 1920s, "clothes, magazines, cosmetics, movies, phonographs, and cigarettes." Attendance at high schools also doubled during this period, and a growing number of young people began to attend college. As a result, advertisers "began to aggressively target the new, discrete, pan-youth class created by the eventual successful introduction of mass education."[96] Cohen showed how immigrants worried about their children embracing mass culture. But their children wanted to assimilate and express their independence, and mass culture was a way to do both. Cohen argued that there was a growing "peer society" among American youth "that celebrated the most commercial aspects of mass culture" but gave them a space to express their individuality from their parents and to assert their Americanness.[97] This period also saw the rise of flappers, young women who built an identity around consumerism. Zelda Fitzgerald wrote about the mainstreaming of flapper culture in 1921 in "Eulogy on the Flapper."[98] Fitzgerald noted the dynamic of a cultural phenomenon starting with a small group and spreading to the larger culture, playing out through the rest of the century and into the next one. Rather than just illustrating how the culture industries profited off youthful consumers, this shows how consumerism itself was becoming useful for forming a coherent social identity.

Over the century, the struggle to carve out meaningful identity via consumer culture became increasingly fraught. Conventional wisdom dictates that young people often reflexively consume whatever mass culture they are fed. The young are considered the least critical consumers. It is true that young people were on the cutting edge of what Savage called "America's dream economy." They made up a large portion of the audiences for films and radio, influencing what was shown or played. This translated into youth culture being reproduced and disseminated by these new mass media. "The process was so fast, and the sleight of hand so accomplished, that it usually seemed that these media actually set the styles. In fact, they were merely capitalizing on adolescent reality."[99] This chicken-and-egg problem between youth culture and mass culture vexed many who studied it. Which comes first, the underground or the exploitation of the underground? Historian and journalist Thomas Frank came down firmly on the side of exploitation taking the lead in shaping culture. He argued that capitalism created the concept of a "hip" critique of consumer culture to promote consumerism in the 1960s.[100] Savage argued for a more complicated narrative that shows how young people had agency in that process. He said that many who embraced the new commercial culture because it marked them as modern and cutting edge. Zelda Fitzgerald said that flappers were "merely applying business methods to being young."[101] Young people in the 1920s set the tone for youthful engagement with mass culture for the rest of the century. There were tensions between the production of mass culture, which many found inherently pleasurable, and the consumption of that commercially for-profit culture. Young people embraced mass culture in part because it was a rebellion against their parents and a society increasingly concerned with their morality.

Savage argued that the struggle over youth culture was weaponized in the 1930s. Politics became "a new mass religion" during the instability of that decade. He says that "politics had a mystical quality in the early 1930s," with youth particularly prone to black-and-white thinking about such things.[102] Fascists believed that youth were "agents of change" who spoke to a desire to belong and forge a meaningful life. They harnessed that belief to create a youth vanguard to carry out acts of violence to secure fascist control over European governments.[103] Fascist and left-wing groups clashed in the streets during the 1930s, led by their youth wings.[104] In the United States, consumerism came to be seen as an antidote to the extremes on the left- and right-dominating politics in Europe. Savage argued that "mass consumption offered another kind of social inclusion."[105] According to Claud Cockburn, "it could be represented as a kind of democratization of economic life."[106] This was a sentiment shared with some in Great Britain as well. The dancehall attracted many British youths who rejected the political extremes. As such, "a separate youth culture had become part of everyday life in Britain."[107] The invention of new cultural traditions during the first two decades of the consumer economy shaped how young people saw themselves and their relationship to the adult world for the rest of the twentieth century and into the next century.[108] These new traditions fractured into subcultures and sometimes into countercultures that challenged the mainstream.

By the late 1930s, music became a key defining feature of youth culture in the United States and Europe. According to Savage, "swing opened a new chapter in the history of youth and mass communication."[109] Savage argued that the subgenre of jazz known as swing encouraged active participation via dancing. It also created "a whole adolescent world, with its own slang, magazines, fashions, and heroes. This was generated by the fans themselves."[110] In other words, a set of institutions and traditions grew up around an interest in a particular form of music, like many later youth-oriented subcultures. Savage argued that participants created this subculture.[111] The swing subculture was globalized. Even in Germany during the early years of the Nazi era, some allowances were made for the subculture, which eroded by the late 1930s. The Nazi regime positioned itself as modern government, actively touting German high technology and consumerism. Jazz was a key cultural artifact of modernity. Hardcore swing fans figured out ways to fly under the radar for a bit longer as the regime worked to bring youth to heel.[112] But as we saw already, concerns about youth and mass culture were not unique to the fascists, even if they took it to an extreme with regard to indoctrinating youth.

The 1940s saw a new phenomenon emerge out of the public education system: youth culture cliques. Ten million young people between the ages of fourteen and seventeen were in high school by 1940.[113] Cliques were self-selecting groups that codified group loyalties and grew out of the length of time that young people were thrown together—seven hours a day for much of the year. In many cases, the students also lived in the same neighborhoods. The media played a role here as they began to "broadcast back" these cliques. For example, *Life* magazine had a profile of "sub-debs" (a subset of debutantes) in January 1941. The growing economic power of young people reinforced the rise of high school cliques, as producers of goods rushed to cater to this demographic, while class-based divisions remained.[114] Cliques in some cases became subcultures when they were centered on music and dress. Swing was one such case. A distinct subculture grew up around the music and the mode of dress. Young people across the United States and Western Europe embraced swing and created a translocal subculture during the war years. In Nazi-occupied Europe, zazous in France and swing youth in Germany ran a major risk for their nonconformity.[115] In the United States, racial tensions contributed to some high-profile outbursts against fashionable swing kids, illustrating the problems that accompanied youth culture. In 1943, a group of white servicemen in Los Angeles carried out six days of racist attacks on Mexican American youths wearing zoot suits, the uniform of choice among male swing fans.[116] Given the roots of swing culture, white youth embracing it were sometimes seen as embracing Black culture. US youth culture became even more influential in the postwar period in Europe. Savage said that American GIs arriving in Britain during the war represented a turning point in attitudes toward Americans and their youth culture, with American music making "the most dramatic impact."[117] Jitterbug dancing went mainstream among British youth during the war years. Glenn Miller, an air force major, performed live for about a quarter of a million British fans and even more via radio broadcasts.[118] In the following years, British and American popular culture that appealed to young people was traded back and forth.

Slowly, the term "teen" started to appear in the general cultural lexicon. In February 1941, *Parents* magazine published an article called "Tricks for Teens." Around the same time, there was a general proliferation of magazines aimed at this demographic. In some cases, the magazines promoted music-based youth cultures, such as *Calling All Girls*, which embraced swing culture.[119] In 1944, *Seventeen* began publication and sought to directly harness the spending power of American teens, estimated to be around $750 million.[120] If the culture industries celebrated this powerful youth demographic, a new round of moral panics also marked the rise of the teenager. Magazines magnified a fear of delinquent behavior among young women during the war years. In some cases, young troublemakers were treated sympathetically, more as victims than as perpetrators.[121] One solution to the problem of wayward youth was social clubs known as "teen canteens." It was argued that youth centers (originally proposed in 1944 by Ruth Clifton, editor of her high school paper) would reduce juvenile delinquency and channel youthful energies in positive directions. The idea was even discussed in Congress as a solution to juvenile delinquency.[122]

During first half of the 1940s, the concept of the teenager became fully cemented in North American and European culture. This new demographic reality was shaped by the rise of compulsory high school, which created a peer culture and the attempt to cater to that demographic by the culture industries. Savage says that "during 1944, the words 'teenage' and 'teenager' become the accepted way to describe this new definition of youth as a discrete, mass market. . . . Consumerism offered the perfect counterbalance to riot and rebellion: it was the American way of harmlessly diverting youth's disruptive energies."[123] A year later, the *New York Times Magazine* published "A Teen-age Bill of Rights" that advocated for greater social autonomy for this new demographic, which coincided with postwar rights movements already beginning to make demands. The new teen culture often explicitly positioned itself on the progressive side of the social issues that roiled the United States and the world, such as when Frank Sinatra, popular among teens at the time, made a short film advocating for racial tolerance. *Seventeen* magazine published a story by Anne Clarke about anti-Semitism that same year.[124] The year 1945 became "year zero" in many ways, according to Savage. It saw the end of one of the most destructive wars in history, the use of the most destructive weapon in history, and the emergence of the teenager.[125] All three reshaped the world in their own ways during the so-called American century.

Popular Music and Youth Subcultures in the Cold War

The violence of two world wars coupled with the failures of the capitalist economy during the Great Depression led many to rethink the world they had been living in. Youth culture, now a recognized social and economic domain, contributed to this discussion. It was an era of economic expansion and prosperity, especially in the United States. Even the existential threat of nuclear annihilation posed by the Cold War could not diminish the good times at home, which America sought to export. While the Americans and Soviets might have been about even on a number of fronts, it became clear over a few decades that US popular culture had an edge on the global stage. Probably more than anything, popular music like jazz and rock became one of the most potent weapons of the Cold War.[126] That same culture was a problem on all sides of the Cold War struggle, and it was dealt with in different ways. Music became an increasingly important signifier of allegiance to a particular youth culture. This informed how punk evolved. This section deals with some of the youth subcultures that developed in Western Europe and the United States and how the Cold War became a means of promoting American values through popular culture. Reactions in both the capitalist and socialist countries are also addressed.

In the years after World War II and the early years of the Cold War, a series of youth subcultures emerged in the United States and Great Britain that would influence punk and postpunk subcultures. Beginning with swing, some young people began to hammer out a distinct cultural identity that opposed aspects of more mainstream culture and music. Not all youth cultures were built around the consumption of music. Fashion, sports, academic achievement (or lack of it), art, drug use, science-fiction/fantasy literature, comics, various kinds of gaming (like role-playing games), and later video gaming all became centers for building subcultural identities during the second half of the twentieth century. But many of these subcultures focused on the production and consumption of music. These subcultures globalized in part due to the US government's promotion of its culture during the Cold War. As the American culture industries commercialized youth entertainment and leisure, young people pushed back by seeking to create their own, more democratic cultural spaces. Youth were consuming the goods offered by commercial culture but also looking to make them more responsive and truthful to their lived realities.

In Britain, the 1950s were a rich landscape of overlapping and competing youth subcultures in the austere postwar years. The government of Prime Minister Clement Attlee ushered in a set of radical policies that transformed British life. In addition to greater government regulation and nationalization of industry, they crafted a "cradle to grave" welfare state that continues to shape the lives of British citizens.[127] This great leveling materially improved the lives of the working classes. At the same time, a wave of immigration was changing the cultural and racial landscape. In 1948, the Attlee government passed the British Nationality Act, granting citizenship rights to what had previously been Commonwealth subjects in the British colonies.[128] This new status prompted a wave of immigration from the colonies, and the immigrants brought their culture with them. This mix of a new affluence for the working classes and new working-class people bringing their culture with them indelibly shaped youth culture. Young people across classes had more time, money, and freedom in the postwar world, even as rationing continued for several years.

In both the United States and the United Kingdom, race, culture, and youth collided to be a new and powerful cultural and economic force in society. In 1957, novelist, cultural critic, and essayist Norman Mailer published a controversial essay, "The White Negro." Mailer drew on a number of critical and psychological concepts, but jazz and white youth were at the core his argument. Young people dubbed "hipsters" found themselves at odds with modern society thanks in part to the brutality and violence of World War II. Since the end of that conflict, discussions about concentration camps and atomic bombs called the humanity of the modern world into question. Rather than accept reality and conform, Mailer argued that this "American existentialist" instead "accept[ed] the terms of death." For the hipster, this meant dropping out of polite (white) society and embracing a more "rootless" existence at the fringes of society.[129] Mailer conceptualized hipsters as adventurers for their embrace of African American culture like jazz. He noted how they sought out thrills in cities with large Black populations, in essence becoming a "white negro."[130] The rest of the essay explores the psychic impulses that were driving some to embrace the hip culture of the Black community, who Mailer sees as the ultimate outsider because of white supremacy. For our purposes here, the focus on jazz and rebellion speaks volumes about how the coming generations of young people engaged with commercial culture to act out rebellion against a society seen as stifling and conformist. From jazz to rock to hip-hop, rebellion could be expressed through the type of music consumed, especially if that music managed to challenge norms—in this case, the racial divide that was fast becoming the center of political discussions in the United States at the time.

The Beats were an important segment of this population in Mailer's essay. A cohort of artists and writers challenging mainstream culture in the 1950s and 1960s, they had a major effect on the development of the American countercultures in the 1960s and 1970s. In addition to a fascination with the culture of Black America, Raj Chandarlapaty argued that the Beats also explored global cultures in search of enlightenment. Some accused Beat figures like William S. Burroughs, Jack Kerouac, and Paul Bowles of perpetuating Western imperialism, Chandarlapaty countered that instead they were opposing the American imperialist racist culture by "exposing the lack of knowledge and functionality of Americans and their cross-cultural understanding of the outside world." They sought to engage with and demystify non-Western culture for an American audience to challenge the racism of American culture.[131] The work produced by the Beats, in this case Burroughs and Bowles, "manifested opposition to three major (and universally active) ideologies during the 1950s and 1960s—*colonialism, orientalism, and postcolonialism.*"[132] The Beats were more than just a youth subculture. They were a counterculture that opposed key aspects of American and Western culture. They were primarily a literary movement, although their work intersected with music. Beats were known for their love of jazz.

Amiri Baraka began his writing career as a Beat before shifting to a more radical Black nationalist stance. His first major work, *Blues People*, explored the complicated relationship with modern popular music and the history of the people who originated that music—African Americans. Although Baraka eventually broke away from his association with the Beat movement to focus primarily on Black nationalism and the Black arts, he made clear that his interest in Black nationalism began with his love of jazz. He said, "Oh yeh, we was hip to Bird and Diz and Monk, you dig. Albeit in a Dave Brubeck, Paul Desmond, Gerry Mulligan, Stan Getz period right then. Thanks to Miles' [Davis] 'Birth of the Cool,' which we swore was the big number."[133] His English professor at Howard University, poet Sterling Brown, encouraged Baraka to explore the deeper history of the music pro- duced by African Americans and how it was a core aspect of the history of Black America.[134] *Blues People* showed how commercial cultures like jazz and blues can be more than just a leisure product for sale. The story of Black music in America tells us of the central importance of culture in the lives of human beings. Baraka's history of Black music reminds us how even commercialized culture can transcend that commercialization to perform a vital role in social and political life, a sentiment echoed by Mailer in his essay. The hipster embraced jazz because it reflected the struggle expressed through the music of the Black community. In the coming years, the hippie subculture would embrace various genres of Americana in addition to rock music because of that sense of "authenticity" and realness of the music. Although the Beats were not all young people, their influence on the hippies brought a critique of mainstream culture and an embrace of popular culture.

The United States was not the only place where youth cultures were evolving and making connections with popular culture. One of the first major postwar youth cultures were the Teddy Boys, sometimes known as Teds, in Great Britain. Their main style influence was the fashions of the Edwardian period from the first decade of the twentieth century. They adopted Edwardian clothing as a cost-saving measure. Cheap suits with waistcoats that were similar to zoot suits popular in the 1930s and 1940s in the United States could be had for a song in secondhand shops. They were dressed up with colorful accessories, like brightly colored socks and "brothel creepers," shoes with thick crepe soles. The big difference between zoot-suited Americans and the Teddy Boys was the type of pants, with "drainpipe" trousers preferred by the Teds. Young working-class men, especially those in gangs, snapped them up when more well-to-do young men ignored them, with the style spreading across Britain by 1952. The Teds listened to a variety of music imported from North America, from big band swing to early rock. Associated with gangs from working-class neighborhoods, the subculture caused a moral panic in Britain in the 1950s, especially after a high-profile "rock-n-roll riot" in a cinema showing the film *Blackboard Jungle*. The crowd of young people danced in the aisles to Bill Haley's "Rock Around the Clock" and spilled out into the street.

The Tory Party (the conservative party in Britain) made youth rebellion a campaign issue, associating Teds culture with juvenile delinquency and violence. Among other measures, the government passed legislation for mandatory military service for young men. The tabloids had a field day after a 1958 race riot in Notting Hill. The state backlash meant that the subculture flamed out by the late 1950s. In his brief overview of this subculture, Mitch Mitchell argued they were the first major "youth cult" in Britain.[135] A pattern was beginning to emerge that played out across the rest of the century. A new youth subculture would emerge, embracing fashion and music; some violence would occur involving members of said subculture; the state and media would respond to the events; and in some cases, the subculture would dissolve or evolve. The collapse of these subcultures seems more likely if there was not much to be had outside of identity formation via consumption. As we will see, other subcultures carved out more proactive means of creating and cementing a shared cultural identity.

There were many youth subcultures that became influential, such as the mods and rockers, but the skinhead subculture had a direct influence on punk. It emerged out of the interplay between white English and Jamaican working-class cultures. Dick Hebdige argued that the immigrants and children of immigrants from the Caribbean replicated their culture in their new communities, such as in working-class neighborhoods of south London. The "stingy-brim" (pork pie) hats, boots and braces, short-cropped hair, and short jeans popular among Jamaican rude boys were eventually replicated by their white counterparts in London. They became known as "hard mods," a spin off of the earlier mod subculture.[136] While the mods embraced jazz and rock, these hard mods contributed a love of Jamaican music and culture. Hebdige argued that "the music was transmitted through an underground network of shebeens (house parties), black clubs, and the record shops of

Brixton and Peckham, and Ladbroke Grove, which catered almost exclusively to a West Indian clientele. Almost but not quite."[137] Consuming particular music was becoming a critical way to enact and enhance subcultural ties. In the mid-1960s, some hard mods embraced ska after hearing music by Prince Buster. Hebdige said "that liaison between black and white rude boy cultures which was to last until the end of the decade and was to provoke such a puzzled reaction from the commentators of youth culture had begun in earnest." Ska filled a need that pop could not.[138] Earlier subcultures like the Teds embraced rock music, but music proved more central to the hard mod/skinhead identity. Violence became a defining feature of how the media understood the subculture. "By 1967, the skinhead had emerged from this larval stage and was immediately consigned by the press to the violent menace category which the mainstream pop culture of the time appeared increasingly reluctant to occupy."[139] Anti-Black racism that marks the current globalized iterations of "skinhead" culture was not an immediate defining feature of these early skins, although violence against Southeast Asian immigrants was already becoming common, Hebdige argued. They embraced West Indian culture and style, including ska. In a callback to Mailer, Hebdige called them "aspiring 'white negroes.'" This was true until more explicitly Black nationalist reggae gained popularity among young West Indian immigrants. The embrace of Jamaican music by skins "was all a little artificial—just a bit too contrived to be convincing. . . . And when he found himself unable to follow the thick dialect and densely packed Biblical allusions which mark the later reggae he must have felt even more hopelessly alienated."[140] The shift to reggae among West Indian communities in London did not have the same embrace by the white rude boy counterparts and this split the majority white skinheads off for good. Some skinheads later embraced the hardcore scene of the 1980s that bore similarities to skinhead style and temperament. The punk rock subgenre of Oi! illustrates the overlap between punk and skinhead subcultures over the years.[141]

Of all the youth subcultures we should consider, few have had the ongoing impact of the hippies, who many use as the template for youth countercultures. There are several key developments that this very large and influential group brought to the table. Hippies went global early on. This was not the first youth culture to spread from the United States to the rest of the world, but it might be the largest. It was built on rock music. It was already associated with younger consumers and globalized early. The Teds embraced rock as their soundtrack of choice. In the Soviet Union, the Stilyagi subculture challenged the government's insistence on politicization of youth culture. Instead, many maintained a deeply apolitical worldview that turned on consumerism, with a deep love of American culture and goods. Some participated in an underground trading network for albums recorded onto old X-rays, especially jazz and some rock music.[142] In a divided Germany, American youth culture and how each state responded to it was part of a larger struggle over the "(re)construction of German identities in two states."[143] In these cases, the local situation was paramount in shaping the contours of these subcultures, even if the expression was often through the consumption of American culture.

The divergence between hippies and previous youth subcultures was that hippies explicitly positioned themselves as a counterculture rather than just a subculture. The realities of the suburban life in the American (mostly white) middle class proved too conformist and inauthentic to some of the Baby Boom generation. The 1950s and 1960s were a tumultuous period in US history. Boomers grew up with violence aimed at the suppression of the civil rights movement, which included many Boomers as participants, the Johnson era expansion of the Vietnam War, and a real fear of nuclear annihilation. By the mid- to late 1960s, the cultural criticism from the Beats made a good deal of sense to many young people in America. They felt a disconnect from what the United States claimed to be and what it was actually doing on the world's stage and at home. This politicized some, who cohered around the New Left, such as groups like the Students for a Democratic Society.[144] Other young people began to express dissatisfaction with the abundant society and decided to drop out of it. Taking drugs became increasingly popular among some as a means to expand the mind. Some first learned about the power of psychedelics via the infamous Project MKUltra, a CIA program that tested the use of LSD as a mind-control drug. Novelist Ken Kesey hosted "acid tests," parties where he turned others onto the drug set against a backdrop of trippy music and light shows. His "Merry Pranksters" traveled around sharing their adventures in 1964, which was described and popularized by Tom Wolfe.[145] Works like these attracted alienated young people to cities like San Francisco to "turn on, tune in, and drop out" of mainstream society. This phrase, uttered by Timothy Leary at a speech he gave at the Human Be-In in 1967, became the mantra of many hippies.[146] Hippies also created counterinstitutions. Many set up secondhand shops to support themselves and serve their communities. In the 1960s, secondhand shops along King's Road and the World's End in London provided a living and a gathering place to see and be seen for the "swinging London" scene.[147] The counterculture also built an "alternative media" that would influence later subcultures. John McMillian described the rise of the underground press in the 1960s and the role it played in the counterculture.[148] Squats or shared housing in empty or abandoned buildings also took off during the 1960s. Communal living offered an alternative to the traditional family structures or space for artists to explore their mediums, often for cheap or free.[149]

In the late 1960s, the counterculture cropped up in cities around the world. The year 1968 was a hinge point. Inspired by Americans protesting the Vietnam War, students in Mexico used the 1968 Olympics (in Mexico City) to amplify their call for greater civil liberties. It culminated in the Tlatelolco massacre, where hundreds were killed when the police and soldiers shot indiscriminately into a crowd of protesting students.[150] In the aftermath (and after a scandal caused by the "Mexican Woodstock," Festival Rock y Ruedas de Avándaro in 1971), rock music associated with the counterculture and youth protests were largely banned across Mexico until the 1980s, with foreign acts prohibited as late as 1989.[151] In Paris, students, radicals, and workers came together to grind the city to a halt for nearly a month in 1968.[152] In Vietnam, at the height of US involvement, a group of young Vietnamese formed the CBC Band. Playing for American GIs and some young Vietnamese, they staked their claim to inclusion in the growing global counterculture defined in part by a love of rock music.[153] West German youths rebelled against "both conservatism and Cold War liberalism" in the 1960s, despite a decade-long attempt to "depoliticize" youth culture imported from the United States.[154]

Music became a central means of spreading countercultural values around the world. Beginning in the 1960s, this included the "San Francisco sound" associated with the hippie counterculture. In addition to rock music that Baby Boomers had been consuming since childhood, artists started to explore new genres of music and combine it with rock. Members of the Merry Pranksters became the Grateful Dead, a key band associated with the hippie counterculture. The Dead (like other bands of the era) incorporated older genres of music, such as folk, country, bluegrass, and blues into their music.[155] In New York City, when Hilly Kristal set up a nightclub for bands to play, he optimistically named the club CBGB, for country, bluegrass, and blues, in the hopes of attracting those kinds of bands. CBGB ended up playing host to the first-wave punk bands in the city instead.[156] Artists like Bob Dylan were seen as bringing a new authenticity to rock music.[157] Like with punk, music was an organizing feature of the hippie subculture. Unlike punk, many of the bands associated with hippies were on major labels.

During the 1960s, many of the independent labels that were founded to cater to the rock boom of the 1950s and 1960s were bought out by larger labels. Atlantic, founded in 1947, became a division of Warner Bros.-Seven Arts in 1967.[158]

The Beatles had been an international sensation since the early 1960s, with fans around the world no matter how repressive their governments. They sought to imitate their heroes through clothing and music. One such case was The Plastic People of the Universe, a Czechoslovakian band that formed in 1968 during the Prague Spring and the Soviet backlash. They were part of a wave of young people in communist countries embracing the counterculture.[159] American visitors were part of driving the counterculture in the communist East. In 1965, Beat poet Allen Ginsberg made a high-profile tour of the communist country, eventually being expelled by the authorities. But his advocacy of countercultural thinking made a mark. Soon, according to Joseph Yanosik, young Czechoslovakians formed underground scenes and clubs to accommodate the numerous new rock bands that appeared. In these years, the post-Stalinist thaw meant a bit more freedom. The hardliner Antonín Novotný was soon replaced in the party leadership by the proponent of "socialism with a human face," Alexander Dubček, kicking off the Prague Spring in 1968. By August, the tanks were rolling in to roll back Dubček's ambitious reforms. The normalization instituted by Moscow included an end to the more rebellious youth culture that had managed to flower. Many of the bands capitulated, except the newly formed Plastic People of the Universe, resulting in their license to play professionally being pulled by the government. The band continued to play when they could for years, often risking imprisonment. By the fall of communism, members still in prison were released and began legally playing concerts with the Czech Philharmonic in 1989. Václav Havel—who had spent years in prison for his political opposition—was soon elected Czech president. A stalwart of the Czech counterculture, Havel formed relationships with rock stars from the West, such as Lou Reed, and told them the story of The Plastic People of the Universe. Havel became the first postcommunist president of Czechoslovakia and the first president of the Czech Republic after the former nation's dissolution.[160]

The cultural Cold War was a major cause of the globalization of youth counterculture. It allowed those rebelling against their local version of the establishment to have a shared cultural connection. The American propaganda machine helped make that possible. In addition to the jazz tours, US culture was promoted via shortwave radio officially and unofficially affiliated with the US government. One of the most popular programs on Voice of America was *The Jazz Hour*, hosted by Willis Conover Jr., a jazz musician and DJ. Conover's program ran from 1955 until 2003, reaching up to 100 million people globally. When the program was originally suggested, Congress was skeptical and some Congressmen actively opposed this "too commercial" music representing the best of America to the world. But pop culture proved to be one of the best ways to reach people behind the Iron Curtain. Conover became a global superstar.[161] The musical landscape allowed young people around the world to create a shared community built around popular music, providing a template for later subcultures like punk.

Rock music eventually made it onto international airwaves, generally via the unofficial shortwave radio broadcasts supported in part by the CIA. The DJs for these stations were from the target countries, broadcasting in their own languages to their own people. In the late 1960s, younger people with a taste for American and British rock took to the airwaves and played rock music. Many young people behind the Iron Curtain also listened Armed Forces radio, which by the late 1960s played the music of the average American soldier such as those in Vietnam.[162] Rock music of the 1960s provided a soundtrack for rebellion, even as the music was part of institutions and systems that many young people sought to bring down or change. This cemented the concept of youth rebellion against a sometimes amorphous concept of mainstream culture into the public consciousness. It shaped how young people in the next several generations would think about youth rebellion. We will see how punks were deeply influenced by this way of thinking. They sought to make their cultural consumption a meaningful way to state their opposition to the inauthentic commercialism of popular culture and political and social institutions they found oppressive and to build meaningful social communities that were local and democratic but global in their reach. In the next chapter, I explore the origins of punk as a genre of music and its early relationship to the mainstream music industry.

Chapter 2

From Proto-Punk to First-Wave Punk

1970 to 1980

Scene: Atlanta, Georgia, Great Southeast Music Hall, January 5, 1978

The hall was cheek to jowl, anticipation high. You wondered who had heard the Sex Pistols already and who was just here to rubberneck. A reporter from NBC was there to sell ads to shocked middle America. You look for familiar faces, craning your neck around to better identify friends in the crowd. You wave at the guy who recently opened up that record shop in Little Five Points. You pass a group of kids decked out in leather, including Chris Woods in his Coke-bottle glasses. You see promoter Alex Cooley nursing a beer at a table in the corner through the crowd. Your friend Sally waves you down from near the stage, so you make your way to her. She's managed to secure some "Never Mind the Bullocks" shirts, and she hands one to you, chiding that "you always say I never get you nothing." The crowd is loud, rowdy, mostly male, so you're happy to be with a girlfriend.

The lights go down. The band comes out. They are not nearly as scary as the media had been making out. They rock, for sure. And Johnny Rotten kept blowing his nose. They went through their repertoire in less than an hour and then they were done. You knew enough about music to know how much the bass player, Sid Vicious, really sucked. But the rest of the band was okay, and Rotten was entertaining to watch. He came over to where you and Sally stood with your friends, kneeling down to sing at you at least once during the show.

As the eclectic crowd filed out, some giving their two cents to the NBC guy, you heard some people declare that the show was just okay. Some expressed disappointment. Still, others said it was all they expected, and the Sex Pistols were the real deal. But everyone walked away with a similar thought in their head—why not me, too?

The Troggs	The Fugs	? and the Mysterians	The Velvet Underground
MC5	Death	The Stooges	Suzi Quatro
The Runaways	Suicide	Television	David Bowie
The Modern Lovers	Dr. Feelgood	Patti Smith	New York Dolls
Jayne County	Ramones	Blondie	Talking Heads
Sex Pistols	The Damned	The Clash	Neon Leon
The Senders	The Screamers	Weirdos	

When punk emerged in the public imagination the 1970s, it arrived globalized into a pessimistic world. The 1960s began in hope and ended in despair. The 1970s were darker, more violent, and more uncertain. There was a growing sense of mistrust in the institutions built up in the United States and elsewhere. In the United States specifically, the scandal around Watergate became a breaking point on the left and right after years of unrest. The economy was struck by a new phenomenon known as "stagflation," which was stagnating economic growth (high unemployment and little growth in wages) coupled with high inflation. The 1970s also saw a wave of high-profile terrorist attacks and plane hijackings. The energy of civil rights and the youth rebellion that had marked the 1960s as a period of hope curdled into cynicism. Many young people abandoned the counterculture, and some activists turned to acts of violence to continue their cause. It also became increasingly clear that law enforcement in the United States had illegally surveilled the protest movements of the 1960s. In one of the few positive spots, Cold War tensions diminished during the Nixon administration in the Global North. Detente eased tensions with the Eastern Bloc, and his administration began realignment with China. The war in Vietnam finally ground to a halt. But the United States and the Soviet Union exacerbated devastating conflicts in other parts of the Global South, like Latin America and Africa. This set up new hostilities between the two countries that would lead to a second arms race and greater tensions in the 1980s until the collapse of the Eastern Bloc in 1990.

Against this backdrop, culture industries went through some changes. In Hollywood, the restrictive Hays Code ended in the late 1960s, and the center of gravity shifted away from the studios to independent talent. In the recording industry, the independent labels that had put rock music on the map were being bought out by major labels. This consolidation in the music industry of the late 1960s and early 1970s would prove stifling to many artists and fans, as the rock stars seemed out of reach and inauthentic. New genres of music flourished during the 1970s, including metal, disco, hip-hop, and of course punk. Punk and hip-hop had profound impact on the recording industry and how consumers thought about their relationship to music. Meanwhile, American and British major record labels came to dominate the global market for popular music.

Despite these realities, some of the rebellious spirit of the sixties counterculture persevered into the 1970s. Though we are accustomed to thinking of punk being a break with the previous counterculture, in reality, it carried on the community building that marked the 1960s counterculture. Stylistically, punk music was very different from the San Francisco sound. The bricolage nature of punk fashion and art brought in a new aesthetic. Punks leaned into the concept of democratically created culture and spaces, eventually pushing for more democratic and less commercially oriented cultural production. The differences and disconnects between the subcultures matter, but the roots of punk emerged out of both respect for and dissatisfaction with the counterculture of the earlier period. Many early punks grew up with the hippie counterculture as part of their worldview. Punk rock as a concept first emerged out of discussions among rock critics in magazines. Once a genre began to cohere around the name "punk," a set of cultural practices emerged locally that were shared transnationally. At first, punk was much more of a subculture than a counterculture. "Punk" came to describe a set of cultural practices that looked more alike across vast distances reinforced by a shared taste in music and style. In this chapter, I look at the intersection of art and popular music, the rise of punk in the discourses of rock critics, the diversity of bands that influenced later punks, and how people began to deploy the term "punk" to describe their cultural practices and a genre of music.

Art and Music Collide

In the previous chapter, I discussed how the rise of the modern consumer economy brought about important questions with regard to the production of culture. Walter Benjamin's insights into the possibilities afforded art by the process of mass production influenced how artists later in the century thought about the intersection of art and popular culture. Pop art emerged halfway through the century, remixing and recontextualizing mass culture into an artistic setting. Artists began to explore fields of cultural production outside of canvas and sculpture. Rock critic Greil Marcus made a direct connection between the modernist avant-garde and the punk movement of the 1970s and 1980s. He drew a direct line between the Dadaists, the Situationists, and punk rock—or at least the British variant represented by the Sex Pistols.[1] Attitudes regularly expressed by the Situationists mirror the punk attitude, according to Marcus, "a voice that denied all social facts, and in that denial affirmed that everything was possible."[2] He drew other similarities as well. "The dada aesthetic went into the books as 'anti-art'; punk was 'anti-rock'."[3] The concept of disruption applied equally to the Letterists/Situationists in the 1950s and 1960s and punks in the 1970s. Those who had gone before were to stand aside for the new and novel, as seen in Isidore Isou's disruption of Dadaist Tristan Tzara's play in 1946.[4]

Andy Warhol looms large in this cultural realignment as a pioneering figure in the pop art movement. In addition to turning to mass media for inspiration, Warhol explored several platforms for creative expressions. His interest in exploring the limits of incorporating elements of popular culture into high art aligns with the concept of *Kunstwollen*. According to Jed Perl in his study of art in New York City, "Pop art could be seen as some kind of ultimate fulfillment of that decades-old idea that a work of art defined an era's will to form. Like it or not, *Kunstwollen* had become a cartoon."[5] Hence, Warhol was interested in playing with various forms of mass media and constantly recontextualizing mass culture into paintings and sculptures. He explored other mediums, such as filmmaking. He used silk-screening to mass produce his paintings. Warhol was also interested in live performances and popular music. According to John Walker, Warhol employed the band The Velvet Underground in his "Exploding Plastic Inevitable" exhibitions as "part of this expansion program," with a goal of " 'expanding sideways,' to encompass more and more art forms and media."[6] The band's relationship with Warhol shows how the art world was increasingly crossing over into the pop world, with performances becoming a location for exploring that intersection. The Velvet Underground went on to influence a new wave of artists in the 1970s and 1980s, especially in punk scenes.[7]

This connection between postmodern art and punk emerged in the UK punk scene thanks to several individuals. First was the controversial manager of the Sex Pistols, Malcolm McLaren. He spent several years in art school before opening a clothing shop that catered to the Teddy Boy revival scene and then to punks. Often dismissed as little more than an exploitative Svengali, he was interested in the cultural politics of disruption.

McLaren embraced the Situationists ethos in the 1960s. For a while he worked with King Mob, a British Situationist group.[8] In one escapade in December 1968, members of King Mob disrupted the toy department of a Selfridges department store. One member dressed as Santa Claus and they handed out toys. It was an attempt to rail against the commercialization of the holiday, as they exhorted onlookers to "smash the great deception."[9] McLaren's foray into business and fashion was likewise driven by an interest in shock and disruption influenced by the London countercultural scene. Despite an interest in countercultural ideals, he rejected the colorful psychedelic fashions of the hippies. McLaren took over a shop called Paradise Garage located on King's Road in London. He stocked items from the revival of 1950s rock fashions, but he soon attracted a problematic set of Teddy Boys. These young men were constantly fighting and alienating other customers.[10] His real goal was to build a scene around the store rather than reach any kind of real commercial success.[11] By 1971, he and his business partner and friend Patrick Casey (who boarded with McLaren and his partner, Vivienne Westwood) renamed the store Let It Rock and rolled out the red carpet for the members of the Teds revival. Westwood, who was proficient with a sewing machine, contributed women's fashions to their wares.[12] Eventually bored with of the often violent and boorish Teds crowd, McLaren and Westwood began to experiment with even more outlandish fashions. Westwood once incorporated chicken bones as decorative accents on shirts.[13] This drive to shock and titillate was heightened by a fateful trip to hawk their wares in New York City. There, they met and mingled with the New York Dolls and met Patti Smith, among others.[14] Another interconnection between the art world and the rise of punk came from Genesis P-Orridge, Cosey Fanni Tutti, Peter Christopherson, and Chris Carter of the industrial band Throbbing Gristle. In the mid-1970s, P-Orridge coined the phrase "industrial music" to describe the soundscaping the band was doing. Before that P-Orridge and Tutti, who met in 1969, were known for their challenging artistic endeavors.[15] P-Orridge was a college drop-out who had worked with an artist collective known as the Transmedia Explorations, a spin-off of an earlier group known as Exploding Galaxy. They founded COUM Transmissions, where with Tutti, they explored the boundaries of life and art with a strong emphasis on "rejection of conventions."[16] The COUM project incorporated music but only managed a few performances in 1969 and 1970 at Hull University.[17] Critically, a key element of these performances was direct interaction with the audience, such as with one performance where they staged a massive interactive performance piece that included costumes and music.[18] Their most high-profile success was with their band Throbbing Gristle, which used the growing popularity of punk to find a place for their challenging form of music making. Industrial music came to be influential as a genre in its own right, but it was shaped by the embrace of independent music production of the punk scene. They were also influenced by the art world. They named their label Industrial Records, but they almost named it Factory Records after Warhol's Factory.[19]

The members of Throbbing Gristle were part of a larger performance art movement that swept Europe in the 1960s and 1970s. P-Orridge considered their work more radical than groups such as Fluxus. They described sending a pint of live maggots to a Canadian exhibition, while other works were "Fluxus-type things."[20] But Fluxus was foundational to postmodern art and performance art. Fluxus operated (and continues to operate) in a variety of spaces. It brought together artists, poets, and composers and centered artistic processes over outcome. Music proved very important to this movement thanks to the influence of figures like Marcel Duchamp and avant-garde composer John Cage. The immediacy of performance and experience set the guiding principles for the movement, as did "flipping off" the art establishment.[21] The performance art movement was expanding in Europe and North America by the late 1960s and early 1970s. In some cases, this form of art spilled out into the streets, anticipating how punk would not only create punk-centric spaces but also fill public spaces. Groups like the Diggers in California in the 1960s used street theater for social and political commentary. The group engaged in direct action and distributed food, but were most well known for their street theater, with "the streets and parks of Haight-Ashbury, and later the whole city of San Francisco" as their stage.[22] Tomata du Plenty of the LA punk band the Screamers got his start in music and performance after an encounter with the San Francisco theater and drag group the Cockettes. Back in Seattle, he formed Ze Whiz Kidz before moving to Los Angeles and forming the Screamers.[23] Punk's style and interaction with the larger, non-punk public were deeply influenced by the rise of performance art.

Critical Origins of a Genre

The art world contributed a set of practices that punks embraced. Music criticism helped develop the terminology around punk as a musical genre. The origins of the term remain up for debate. J. P. Robinson argued that the term as applied to music goes back to the nineteenth century. He pointed to a citation in the *San Francisco Call*, where the term "punk music" described a poorly performed song at a B'nai B'rith meeting hall. Disconnected from music, the term goes back at least to Shakespeare.[24] Perhaps the rock critics of the 1970s who tried to define a new genre and took notice of this discourse and it influenced their definition of low-fi, amateurish, and raw rock music. Rock critic Dave Marsh generally gets the credit for coining the term "punk rock" in his review of ? and the Mysterians in *Creem* magazine in May 1971.[25] In his biography of Lester Bangs, Jim DeRogatis confirmed the narrative of Marsh first using the term. Bangs's role in defining punk and heavy metal was more behind the scenes. But DeRogatis argued that punk as applied to "a rock 'n' roll aesthetic" came from Nick Tosches in *Fusion* magazine in reference to the Fugs.[26]

The term was in general usage among the writers of *Creem* and *Rolling Stone*. "Punk" eventually came to describe a particular attitude and sound. Bangs first used the word to dismiss the MC5 in *Rolling Stone* during the 1970s.[27] This changed with his review of the Troggs, called "James Taylor Marked for Death." He did not focus on a recent release, but instead explained the band's entire catalog, comparing them to Iggy Pop and calling them "Trogg-Punk."[28] Greg Shaw, founder of the zine *Who Put the Bomp!*, also used "punk" to describe bands such as the Standells. He called their producer a "punk pioneer." He considered Southern California garage rock bands to be the original punk sound.[29] Other critics picked up on the theme and ran with it in the coming years, such as *New York Times* critic John Rockwell, who began to use the term by 1974, the same year Shaw was writing about the Standells as punk pioneers.[30] By 1977, *Rolling Stone* had a cover story on punk. William Safire, a former staffer from the disgraced Nixon administration, pontificated about punk in the *New York Times*, giving readers a preview of the "punk panic" that became mainstream in the 1980s.[31] So it seems the earliest use of punk rock as a genre of music emerged from the imaginations of rock critics eager to jump start a new revolution in popular music. Shaw sought to put fans at the center of shaping popular music again, rather than the industry dictating to fans what they should like. Shaw was also heavily influenced by sci-fi fanzines he read in his youth.[32] He believed that professional critics should not dominate how we understand music, and fans should be in the drivers seat. Sci-fi fandom had a well-established reputation for being proactive in their community through fanzines and conventions by this time. Shaw had the same focus with music, starting his own magazine, *Bomp!* (shortened from *Who Put the Bomp!*).[33] People who identified as punk embraced a proactive fanbase advocated by Shaw. These critics offered a language to describe a new take on an older musical style that they hoped would revitalize rock while influencing cultural practices around popular music, such as the production of fan-centered media.

Proto-Punk: Early Musical Influences on Punk

Influence is a funny thing. Sometimes it is easy to chart; other times, it is not so clear. Plenty of musicians who began their careers in the late 1960s and 1970s remember the impact of the Beatles on their understanding of rock music. When Iggy Pop gave the John Peel Lecture for the BBC in 2014, he began his talk on capitalism and music by noting how as a kid he had impatiently waited to hear the Beatles and the Kinks when listening to the radio.[34] Other influences are harder to track, such as the general musical zeitgeist of one's childhood. The late 1960s saw an explosion of harder rock music, such as Led Zeppelin and Black Sabbath. The music of the late 1960s also included more off-the-wall artists like Frank Zappa and the Residents.[35] Even if we cannot pinpoint a direct influence, the zeitgeist can shape ones approach to music. A variety of bands directly or indirectly influenced the earliest punk scenes that sprang up in cities like New York, LA, London, Berlin, and Ljubljana (among others). In addition to some of the bands rock critics labeled punk, other bands arrived on the scene that did not fit into the sound of times. Some were playing music that was too fast or loud for many contemporary audiences. Others were experimenting with new sounds, instrumentation (especially electronics), or stage persona. Many of these bands inspired punk bands later in the 1970s.

The Velvet Underground was founded in 1964 by Lou Reed and John Cale. They met when the two were working as songwriters at Pickwick Records.[36] They shared an apartment in New York and a taste in the weirder music of the day, such as Zappa. According to Reed biographer Mick Wall, they believed they were working on the next big thing in music. They formed the Velvet Underground, which performed as part of Warhol's "Exploding Plastic Inevitable." The band found themselves out of sync with the peace and love generation. Some considered them "a sick joke" due to the subject matter of their music, such as heroin ("Heroin" and "I'm Waiting for My Man"), S&M ("Venus in Furs"), and outsider individuals like Candy Darling ("Candy Says").[37] Such odd subject matter coupled with the unusual sound turned off many. But the band represented a subset of the counterculture seeking more confrontational performances. They had more in common with the Doors than with the Beatles. Members of the "Exploding Plastic Inevitable" such as Nico and Ronnie Cutrone had encounters with Jim Morrison in the 1960s.[38] The Doors shaped proto-punk and early punk. Iggy Pop was skeptical of the band because the Doors' approach to music "was so different from the Detroit rock approach." But after seeing them live, he was inspired by the antagonistic relationship that Morrison imposed on the audience.[39]

Detroit incubated some of the earliest direct influences on punk rock. In the 1960s and 1970s, the once prominent and wealthy city saw a sharp decline thanks to white flight and deindustrialization. Although not the only major US city to experience urban blight, Detroit became the stand-in for the fears haunting the fevered imagination of white, middle-class, suburban America. It also represented the phenomenon of cities struggling during this era. According to historian Thomas Sugrue, "Detroit's journey from urban heyday to urban crisis has been mirrored in other cities across the nation."[40] He argued that the origins were in "two of the most important, interrelated, and unresolved problems in American history: that capitalism generates economic inequality and that African Americans have disproportionately borne the impact of that inequality."[41] Despite the very real problems caused by the urban crisis of the 1970s, the hollowing out of US cities opened up opportunities for some. Sarah Schulman said of New York City during that era, "We loved Avenue A because we could be gay there, live cheaply, learn from our neighbors, make art—all with some level of freedom."[42] This was not just an American phenomenon. In a 2015 documentary, musician and producer Mark Reeder narrated the explosion of creativity in his adopted city of West Berlin, an outpost of the capitalist West deep inside communist East Germany. Berlin had been generally left out of the West German "economic miracle" of the Cold War. As such, a certain kind of freedom existed for those looking to create something new. Musicians like Nick Cave and David Bowie spent time in Berlin in the 1970s and 1980s, finding freedom to create and endless inspiration from the city's unusual situation.[43] Historian George Katsiaficas noted that during the economic downturn of the late 1970s and early 1980s, "West Berlin was particularly hard hit, not only as a result of the international economic downturn, but also by a series of financial scandals as well. The magazine *Der Spiegel* put it succinctly: 'The City is being made poorer because financial capital is plundering the government's bank account.' "[44] But that meant that "hundreds of abandoned buildings along the wall were an invitation to squatters, and beginning in the late 1970s, organized groups of 50 or more people successfully seized many buildings."[45] Since the city was officially governed by the Allied Coalition, not from Bonn (the capital of West Germany), it attracted young West Germans avoiding their mandatory military service.[46] Katsiaficas said that by the late 1970s and early 1980s, punks were a major part of the thriving West Berlin youth culture.[47] The rise of the urban crisis in cities in the capitalist West gave space for creativity, even as it lowered the quality of life for many who lived there. We should take care not to glamorize the impact of deindustrialization, given the negative consequences for many. But opportunity did exist in these places.

Bands from the 1960s took advantage of these spaces in cities, including some groups that directly influenced punk. Detroit contributed some of the most important bands that shaped punk. The MC5 hailed from Lincoln Park in metro Detroit. Guitarists Wayne Kramer and Fred Smith with vocalist Rob Tyner turned their love of R&B and garage rock into a new band while in high school. Rather than just play what everyone else was playing, they began to experiment with feedback and distortion, much like their contemporaries the Velvet Underground. They added bassist Michael Davis and drummer Dennis Thompson in 1966. John Sinclair (an activist from Detroit) became their manager. They were signed by Elektra Records after their appearance at the Chicago Festival of Life, staged by the Yippies (Youth International Party). This event ended in a notorious riot in front of the Democratic National Convention in 1968. Despite using "motherfucker" in the title of one of their songs, MC5's album charted in the top thirty. But by 1972, the MC5 were done, though they reformed with various artists later.[48] They made an impression on burgeoning punk bands. MC5 combined hard rock with a social and political stance, in part driven by Sinclair's interest in radical politics. The band was aligned with the White Panther Party, a white support group for the Black Panthers. Their harder music attracted an audience who saw the West Coast psychedelic music of the 1960s as boring. MC5 covered artists like Sun Ra and drew influence from free jazz greats like John Coltrane. They also layered on the loud distortion.[49] MC5 also highlighted another critical piece of the proto-punk puzzle, squaring operating in the mainstream music industry with a countercultural drive toward authenticity. The pressures of threading that needle contributed to the ultimate break-up of the band, Clinton Heylin argued. The band wanted commercial success but sought integrity that came along with staying true to their original vision.[50] Punks also struggled with how to produce their music and maintain integrity. This tension eventually drove a new wave of independent, artist-run labels.

MC5 were not the only Detroit band that influenced punk. The Stooges began as an opening act for MC5 and then blew right past them. According to Heylin, "As the MC5's power began to fade, the Stooges, whenever they played at Detroit's Grande Ballroom, were cranking up the volts."[51] Iggy Pop almost singlehandedly shaped the confrontational style that many punks adopted. John Sinclair said of his performance style: "he might do anything" on stage.[52] He once walked out *onto* the crowd at a gig in Cincinnati. In another show, he cut himself with the tips of broken drumsticks.[53] Pulling the audience into the performance was central to the Stooges' live shows. It also covered for their lack of musical mastery. Guitarist Ron Asheton described a typical show from around the time Danny Fields signed them to Elektra Records. They said they "jammed one riff and built into an energy freak-out, until finally we'd broken a guitar or one of my hands were be [sic] twice as big as the other and my guitar would be covered in blood."[54] Meanwhile, Pop "gyrated around the stage and usually made a crazy fool of himself to everybody's pleasure" said bassist Michael Davis.[55] Others eventually adopted the confrontational style of the Stooges, including the Sex Pistols and the Germs. The social disruption of the early Stooges shows, which rested on a certain level of audience participation, came to be an important focal point of punk by the 1980s. The goal was to make the "spectacle" of the rock concert a democratic and participatory activity rather than a passive one-way encounter.

If the music scenes in New York City and Detroit contributed the musical bedrock of punk, other cities offered bands that built on that foundation and contributed other elements, such as the gender-bending style from glam rock. Journalist Richard Cromelin said that glam provided "an alternative to your more proper and corporate kind of music. It was renegade, it was dangerous, it was fun, exciting, glamorous. A lot of things that the mainstream had stopped being."[56] Glam got its start in the British music scene when figures like David Bowie, Bryan Ferry, and Marc Bolan married psychedelic rock with feminine clothing.[57] In 1978, music critic Ken Barnes declared that Marc Bolan of T. Rex originated the genre.[58] David Bowie's album *Ziggy Stardust* put the genre on the international map. Bowie embraced the label, citing Marc Bolan and Alice Cooper as influences.[59] Other British bands such as Slade, Mott the Hoople, and Roxy Music followed in their footsteps.[60] Glam influenced the New York Dolls, a band managed by Malcolm McLaren for a short time in the mid-1970s.[61] A second-wave glam artist that hailed from Detroit, bassist Suzi Quatro, made it big in the United Kingdom. She moved there in 1971, leaving behind her first band formed in 1964, the Pleasure Seekers.[62]

In Los Angeles, a glam rock club became an early location for proto-punks to gather. Rodney Bingenheimer opened the English Disco on the Sunset Strip in 1972 to cater to the glam moment.[63] The club garnered attention outside of the growing local glitter scene. Sylvain Sylvain of the New York Dolls remembered reading about groupies that frequented the club. The club got coverage in *Newsweek* ("twice in one month" according to co-owner Barry Barnholtz) and once the center spread of *People*. The attention came before the fixation on New York's infamous Studio 54, said Barnholtz. The club was not a live performance venue, with the exception of the occasional performances by the campy Zolar X.[64] Plenty of young people congregated at the club hoping to meet with their favorite glam rock stars. Kid Congo Powers, later of the Gun Club, the Cramps, and now the Pink Monkey Birds, started hanging out in Bingenheimer's club as a young teen. He said of that time, "I was one of those young glitter kids scurrying around like that."[65] Others found community and inspiration at the English Disco and formed their own bands in LA. The Berlin Brats formed that year, which Bingenheimer called "the first real L.A. homegrown rock band," while Robert Lopez, who was in the Zeros, cited them as the first bridge between glam and punk.[66]

The Runaways built a bridge between proto-punk, glam/glitter, and punk. They also inspired women to make space in punk. Their influences came from proto-punk and glam. Joan Jett, guitarist, was influenced to form a band by her love of bassist Suzi Quatro. Jett said that Quatro offered a different position for women in rock at the time. As a result, she saw a different way of interacting with rock music. Jett began hanging out in downtown Los Angeles in the early 1970s. She eventually looked for others to put a band together.[67] Bingenheimer first encountered a young Jett at the English Disco. She later said she reminded him of Quatro, while Toby Mamis (manager for Alice Cooper, Blondie, and the Runaways) remembers Jett showing up at the hotel where Quatro stayed when playing the Roxy in LA in 1974. Even then, Jett hoped to be a rock star, not just chase them. Jett met Kari Krome and then Kim Fowley, a record producer who became their manager. Krome was already writing songs prior to the band getting together.[68] Krome did not end up in the band's line-up, pushed out by Fowley except for songwriting duties. Fowley brought the other members into the band, such as drummer Sandy West.[69] Lita Ford, Jackie Fox, and Cherie Currie came in later, rounding out the line-up.[70] The band signed with Mercury Records, a major label, in 1976, going on tour as a supporting act for several bands that year.[71] More of a rock band than a punk rock band, the Runaways had a major impact on the sound of punk. They opened the possibility to younger women that they could be more than just groupies or ornaments in a band, but rock stars in their own right. But women faced an uphill battle to be taken seriously by many in the music industry. Many in the mainstream industry saw them as a novelty act. Even Fowley, who claimed to be a driving force in bringing the band together, later dismissed them as squabbling teen girls, rather than serious musicians. He said, "They were girls, they weren't women, they were actually as we advertised them to be."[72] Jett discussed the uphill struggle to be seen as serious act when they began recording and touring. She and some of the other members eventually managed to carve out careers in the industry. For her part, Jett found a trusted partner in Kenny Laguna, a songwriter and producer who encouraged her to form an independent label, Blackheart Records, in 1980.[73] This might have been made possible by the founding of punk labels around this time.

Although glam/glitter in the United States was primarily a West Coast phenomenon, the New York Dolls were a by-product of the musical genre. The Dolls came together in New York City in the late 1960s and were signed by Mercury Records in 1971.[74] The Dolls took inspiration from R&B and the blues. Johnny Thunders's biographer Nina Antonia called the band's style "unruly blues cacophony."[75] The band adopted a highly androgynous look reminiscent of Bowie or Bolan, but they played a much heavier music, more akin to the sound out of Detroit—the image was more contentious than the music. They attracted the attention of Malcolm McLaren when he and Vivienne Westwood were in New York in 1973 to make connections for their London shop.[76] McLaren later returned to New York for a long-term stay in 1975. He spent a tumultuous stint as the band's manager when they'd hit a low point. He injected some political theater into the band's image, having them dress in red, with lead singer David Johansen waving around Mao's *Little Red Book*. Finally, he booked the band on a tour of the US South, which ended up with the band going their separate ways.[77] They brought a disruptive style influenced by fashion and art, with a heavier musical sound that was much less polished, and a challenging take of gender—all elements of later punk scenes. Much like other proto-punk bands, they signed on to a major label for an unsuccessful stint before imploding.

McLaren took great inspiration from his time managing the Dolls, which influenced how he managed the Sex Pistols a year or so later. By the time the Dolls arrived on the scene, punk was starting to move out of the realm of theory and into the streets.

In recent years, there has been some revisionism with regard to the history of punk. Historical revisionism occurs when new facts or new ways of thinking can help us create a more accurate understanding of the past. Some seek to insert artists from this period into the narrative of punk rock origins. This is true of another band from Detroit, Death. Listening to tracks like "Politicians in My Eyes," they easily strike all the right chords for inclusion into the proto-punk pantheon. As an all-Black rock band, they upend the whitewashed narrative of rock and punk. But the full story of the band shows how successfully the mainstream music industry was in racially segregating musical genres well into the 1970s if not longer. Rock (and punk) was firmly a "white" genre despite its origins in Black music. In the documentary on the band released in 2012, *A Band Called Death*, we find little evidence of them directly influencing early punk. For one, they received little airplay at the time. The band consisted of three brothers: Bobby, Dannis, and David Hackney. David, the guitarist and heart of the band, passed away in 2000. In the documentary, the surviving members laid out their interactions with the music industry as Death. David steadfastly refused to abandon the name, as he saw it as integral to the concept he wished to convey to the world. But the documentary implied that no major label would touch them because of the name. The closest they came was with Columbia Records. President of the label Clive Davis tried to persuade them to change the "unmarketable" name. David refused to compromise his vision. They ended up in possession of their master recordings, which Davis paid for, and pressed five hundred singles of "Politicians in My Eyes" with "Keep on Knocking" on their own label, Tryangle Records. The band sent some out to radio stations, but the track received only sporadic airplay because of (it is implied) the band's name. The trio settled in Burlington, Vermont, in 1977, but David eventually moved back to Detroit, where he made at least one recording under the name Rough Francis (not to be confused with the band formed by the sons of Bobby Hackney in 2008 as a tribute to their late uncle). In 2008, the band finally found a ready audience when the magazine *Chunklet* began circulating an MP3 of their single. The new Rough Francis covered songs from their album once they figured out their familial connection to the recordings. The masters were found and an album pressed by Drag City in 2011, with a new album released in 2015.[78] The story of the band and their path to finding an audience was bittersweet because of David Hackney's death. He was absolutely the uncompromising driving force of the band. But just how much industry racism played a role in burying this group is unclear. We do know that the racial divisions created by the early recording industry continued well into the second half of the twentieth century and continue to shape the industry today. Unfortunately, there seems to be little direct evidence for the band being an influence on the earliest punk scenes, even as we cannot rule out people stumbling across them from the meager radio play they did receive from their first single.

The band still matters in the history of punk. They illustrate how more musicians were showing an interest in harder music. Their sound very much evokes hardcore punk rock, especially their single "Politicians in My Eyes." David Hackney's unwillingness to compromise illustrates the changing relationship between the music industry and artists that happened in the 1970s. By the end of the decade, many artists who embraced punk rejected compromising their music for sales and demanded more autonomy. The band's rediscovery did influenced a new wave of Black punk rock, typified by the Afropunk Festival founded in 2005. Rough Francis were part of the rise of Afro-punk in the modern period, and they were directly influenced by Death.[79] Race and racism does play an important role in how the history of popular music has been written. Often the origins and connections from Black musical forms are elided to such a degree that they distort the historical record. As such, race is discussed again later in the book.

First-Wave Punk Scenes

New York City is the most logical place to start, as punk first emerged there and influenced scenes in other cities. The bands cited above as major influences have become commonly accepted as such by most who write about punk. Legs McNeil, the cofounder of *Punk* magazine, began *Please Kill Me*, his oral history of the New York punk scene, with the Velvet Underground. The band might have been out of step with the 1960s counterculture, but many punks found their transgressions inspirational.[80] McNeil included MC5 and the Stooges in Detroit, as he saw those bands as critical to how punk sounded and was enacted. The title of the third chapter, "The Music We've Been Waiting to Hear," hammered home that message to the reader.[81] The connections between these bands and the first wave of punk were direct, not just theoretical. One particular show in New York in 1969 included the Stooges and MC5. Alan Vega of the band Suicide compared the Stooges performance to the theatrical style of Alice Cooper, saying that "it [the Stooges' performance] wasn't theatrical, it was theater . . . with Iggy this was not acting." He concluded with "Do you know what I'm saying, man? It changed my life because it made me realize that everything I was doing was bullshit."[82] Poet and musician Jim Carroll saw the Stooges with Patti Smith. He recalled being ready to fight if Iggy Pop ran into the crowd at them. But he said, "Patti was into anything like that, man. Raw energy in any form just lit her up."[83] Leee Childers, later the manager for the Heartbreakers, described the physical interactions between the audience and Pop. He said that at one show, Pop dragged Warhol superstar Geri Miller across the floor by her face. He argued that "Iggy was the first time I ever saw what was to become my rock & roll."[84] Dee Dee Ramone saw the Stooges at a club in 1971. He remembered how late the band went on due to Pop being unable to shoot up. When the band finally did appear, Pop vomited after telling the audience that they made him sick. Pop later quipped of that night, "It was very professional. I didn't hit anybody."[85] Disruptive performances like this, with direct interaction between the crowd and band, became a central aspects of punk culture. Many who saw the Stooges went on to create bands of their own and were part of the first-wave New York punk scene.

Other New York bands were inspired by the Velvet Underground, MC5, and the Stooges. Two critical bands bridged the gap between the proto-punk scene and the punk scene proper. The members of Suicide, Alan Vega and Martin Rev, met in 1969. Vega was living in an artist workshop while supporting himself by working as a janitor. Meanwhile, Rev performed in an avant-garde jazz band. After the jazz band ended, Rev and Vega decided to start their own band, inspired by an Iggy Pop performance Vega attended. The pair began performing in artist spaces in 1970. In one ad at the Project by Living Artists, they advertised it as "punk music by Suicide." This might be the first use of the word "punk" by a band to advertise their shows.[86] A key influence was Rev's soon-to-be wife, Mary (or Mari). She was a member of the Living Theater, a New York performance art group that Steve Lee Beeber said "erased the boundary between audience and performer in an effort to do away with the fourth wall."[87] This was similar to "Vega's later approach to rock 'n' roll."[88] After experimenting together with found sounds and tape loops, they worked with Mari to "blend high and low culture" into a new sound.[89] The band name came from their sense that "the country was killing itself."[90] Their sound reflected that growing sense of unease and distrust of the 1970s. According to Ian Port, "Vega wanted to bring to bring the hostility of the streets into the club, to turn violence he saw everywhere in postindustrial New York back on his audience."[91] One can't help but think of the infamous cover of the *New York Daily News* on October 30, 1975, with the headline "Ford to City: Drop Dead" after the federal government refused to intervene as the city struggled with bankruptcy.[92] Many felt that the city was a wasteland beyond saving, even as people found space for cultural production. Suicide sought to reflect the post-1960s reality back to their audiences in the form of music. Although Beeber dated the band's earliest performance as 1972, the website *From the Archives* listed at least a dozen or more shows in the two years prior. By 1972, the band was playing alongside the New York Dolls and the Massachusetts-based Modern Lovers at the Mercer Arts Center.[93] Suicide played shows in the New York scene for years until they released an album, *Suicide*, in 1977. Here we see again punk emerged in part out of the rise of changes in the art world and an embrace of what most considered disposable, mass-produced culture.

The New York Dolls were the second band that bridged the gap between the proto-punk bands and punk rock. They took major influence from the proto-punk bands. In Antonia's biography of the band Gail Higgins Smith described MC5 as Johnny Thunders's heroes.[94] The band coalesced in 1972.[95] In addition to proto-punk bands, the group embraced R&B and the blues, influenced by the Rolling Stones.[96] The band did an extended residency in 1972 at the Mercer Arts Center, managing to stir up protests from people opposed to gay rights due to their gender-bending style. Others, like Jayne County, received similar treatment when she incorporated elements of drag into rock performance. The band wore makeup and heels, which caused problems at least once. Once the original drummer, Billy Murcia, turned over a table after being accused of being gay.[97] The band was courted by David Bowie, who sought to burnish his underground credentials in the United States. He attended two shows in a row and afterward quizzed the group on their style.[98] The Dolls were underground faves, but they initially lacked attention from labels. Paul Nelson got a job doing A&R at Mercury Records and began to court the band, but no contract was secured until 1973. The band toured the United Kingdom as the opening act for the Faces.[99] Steve Jones, later guitarist for the Sex Pistols, saw the Dolls and was impressed by their sloppy musical style.[100] Their influence in the New York scene grew. Fans and other bands started copying their style, including Debbie Harry. Her first band, the Stilettoes were inspired by the Dolls. They also influenced other rock genres. The Dolls' second drummer, Jerry Nolan, taught Peter Criss of KISS to play.[101]

Suicide and the New York Dolls held sway over a new wave of bands in New York City, who collectively created a new scene. Richard Hell started the band Television because of the Dolls. He said, "Me and Tom Verlaine went together to see the New York Dolls at the Mercer Arts center—and the Dolls had a lot to do with me wanting to do a band. . . . After seeing the Dolls, I kept pressing Tom to get together a band instead of just this acoustic guitar hootenanny stuff. An electric band."[102] After putting out a call for auditions in *Creem* magazine, Chris Stein (later of Blondie) and Dee Dee Ramone showed up. "This was before we'd ever met either one of them," Hell noted.[103] According to Dee Dee, "I was kicked outta there because I couldn't play good."[104] Their approach to gaining attention was shaped by the Dolls. They decided on a residency, too. Hell said, "they [the Dolls] would play the same night every week at the Mercer Arts Center . . . and I thought that was perfect, because people could depend on that. They didn't have to read the paper in order to follow you."[105] So the goal became to find a location where they could have a regular, dependable gig each week. After scouting some clubs, Hell and Verlaine stumbled on CBGB. Terry Ork, manager of Television, managed to convince a skeptical Hilly Kristal to give the band a run of nights, which ended up being three Sundays in a row.[106] Patti Smith heard about the shows, and her newly formed band asked to perform there as well. As word spread, more people showed up to see them play, with both bands playing there for six weekends straight. Terry Ork said, "I consider that the official beginning of the scene."[107]

Although there were other clubs that gave space to punk bands, two places play a major role in the evolution of punk. Many associate the rise of punk with CBGB, a hole-in-the-wall club in Manhattan. Hilly Kristal opened the club in 1973 hoping to attract the sort of music he named the club for: country, bluegrass, and blues. Instead, the bar became a hangout for Hell's Angels. The burgeoning punk scene in New York benefited from Kristal's insistence that the bands at least play original music as much as it did from him taking a chance on new artists.[108] In the late 1960s, there was Max's Kansas City. During that time, it served as a hangout for many New York artists, intellectuals, and writers—most famously Andy Warhol and the crowd that regularly gathered at the Factory.[109] In her memoir, Patti Smith called Max's "the place to go" in 1969, when she and Robert Mapplethorpe first spent time there. What drew them there was the connection to Andy Warhol, as Mapplethorpe was an aspiring visual artist and hoped to get to know the legendary pop artist.[110] Debbie Harry of Blondie worked there as a waitress for a time.[111] The version of Max's that was run by Mickey

Ruskin functioned as a gathering place and restaurant, rather than a live music venue. Ruskin closed the club in 1974, but it was soon reopened by Tommy Dean Mills. The growth of the various music scenes in mid-1970s New York inspired Mills to reopen it as a music venue. He hired Peter Crowley as a booker, who had worked at both CBGB and Mother's, a gay club giving new bands a chance to play.[112] Both provided spaces for the growth of a local scene that expanded and influenced other punk scenes.

This brings up another important element of punk culture and community: its dependence on location or place. Sociologist Jeffrey Debies-Carl argued that place, as much as sound and style, plays a critical role in understanding punk as a phenomenon.[113] In these first-wave scenes, punks sought locations that were willing to let them play and often made it their own, such was the case for CBGB and Max's. As such, these locations are linked in the public imagination with the rise of punk rock in New York City. This became a key moment for the punk scene to grow—the ability to have a regular location in which to nurture a scene. It allowed people to build social networks and a shared cultural framework. Night life was expanding during the 1970s in New York City, and clubs like Max's and CBGB ended up benefiting from the rise of punk scenes. Both are fondly remembered because of their association with punk rock (probably more CBGB than Max's). Pioneering punk bands forged a strong connection between finding or creating spaces and building a viable scene. In these New York dive clubs, the connection in punk between people and place began in earnest.

In his memoir, *Punk Avenue*, Phil Marcade of the Senders reminisced about his time in the New York scene. He moved to New York City in 1974. He was introduced to the underground music scene when he attended a party where the Ramones made their debut. He described them as "anti-hippie" and in equal measures "fabulous and hilarious."[114] Max's Kansas City became one of the epicenters of this growing scene, Marcade recalled. Television and Patti Smith regularly performed there, bands that Marcade called "direct descendants of the Velvet Underground."[115] He said that a definition of punk was being worked out on the fly. Rather than a particular sound or shared musical idiom, "none of them were in quite the same style as any of the others and no one really knew who was punk, but in general it meant, " 'not too good and proud of it' or something like that."[116] Nor did all the bands he encountered there become famous. The first band he saw at the club was Neon Leon (Leo Matthews).[117] Although not well known today, Leon was an established member of the scene. The zine *Roctober* tracked him down for an interview in 2005. He recounted his band opening for the New York Dolls in 1973 or 1974. They went to London at the invitation by the Rolling Stones and found an audience in Europe, especially Scandinavia.[118] The CBGB bands had similar diversity of sound. Marcade praised Mink DeVille, which he called a "retro" band. They played soul and R&B alongside bands like the Dead Boys, known for their more aggressive rock style.[119]

Marcade and others were galvanized by the rise of proto-punk. First-wave punks like Patti Smith, Ramones, and Blondie benefited from spaces carved out by bands like Suicide, the New York Dolls, and Television. Patti Smith became the first real breakout star of the fledgling New York punk scene that started out in these clubs. Smith came to New York to break into the arts, influenced in equal measures by rock music and poetry. She began to blend spoken word poetry with music while on a trip to Paris in 1969. Back in New York, she lived with Robert Mapplethorpe at the Chelsea Hotel and worked in the theater alongside playwright Sam Shepard. By the early 1970s, Smith was opening for the New York Dolls at the Mercer Arts Center and writing songs for Blue Oyster Cult, in addition to writing music reviews for magazines. Her work with guitarist Lenny Kaye resulted in the Patti Smith Group playing at Max's and CBGB and traveling to LA to perform in clubs there. Eventually the band caught the attention of Clive Davis and his label, Arista, another major label for which they released several successful albums. Her biggest hit was "Because the Night," cowritten with Bruce Springsteen. She retired in 1980 (she has since reemerged to make more art), marrying Fred Smith from MC5 and settling in Detroit to raise a family.[120] Smith's commercial success helped put the New York scene on the map while influencing musicians outside of New York. Michael Stipe of R.E.M. cites her album *Horses* as decisive on his decision to start a band.[121] Other bands playing at these clubs began to garner attention. Two directions emerged for the punk bands in New York City—mainstream success by signing with an established label or putting out independent recordings. An artist-run punk label popular among second-wave punks had not really developed as a strategy yet. Blondie produced a demo with Alan Betrock in 1975 and signed to the independent label Private Stock, started by Larry Uttal in 1974. Blondie's debut album was released in 1976. Later, the band moved to Chrysalis Records, a British label.[122] Ramones, the Talking Heads, and Blondie, much like Patti Smith, eventually all found mainstream success after drawing in crowds at the New York clubs and getting some positive critical attention. Ramones formed in 1974 and played their first show in

1974 at the party attended by Marcade. That year, Ramones made a splash at CBGB, where Marc Bell (later Marky Ramone) first saw them play.[123] Marty Thau worked with the band to produce a demo and later recorded Blondie's single "X Offender." Thau set up an independent label, Red Star, to put out other bands on the punk scene. He signed the Fleshtones, the Real Kids, and Richard Hell and the Voidoids.[124] Danny Fields was another early champion of Ramones. He said of the first time he saw them play, "The first thing I remember was that whole first 11-minute set. They sang 'I don't want to go down to the basement.' I thought 'This is the most brilliant thing I've ever seen in my life.'"[125] He acted as the band's de facto manager and championed the band to labels, shopping around their first demo. Fields was friendly with Seymour and Linda Stein. He convinced Linda to get her husband to come see the band play. He eventually did so in the fall of 1976, which led to a deal with his label, Sire Records.[126] The Talking Heads became their label mates. David Byrne and Chris Frantz first met at the Rhode Island School of Design. They moved to New York with Frantz's girlfriend, Tina Weymouth, and the three formed a band. They played shows at CBGB and Max's by 1975. Sire signed the band to a contract in 1977 and released *Talking Heads: 77* that same year.[127] Sire signed other bands from the New York City punk scene, including the Undertones and the Dead Boys. Controversially, the label actively eschewed calling these bands "punk" and insisted on the term "new wave."[128] By the time the bands were putting out records, the Sex Pistols made a splash in the United Kingdom. Many in the music industry had started to see punk as toxic on both sides of the Atlantic because of the controversy around the Sex Pistols.

New York City hosted the first punk scene. But it was most certainly not operating in a vacuum. London was not far behind. These scenes were intertwined from the start. People created direct connections between what was happening in New York and London. McLaren and Westwood spent time in New York, and bands from New York toured the United Kingdom. By the time the Heartbreakers toured with the Sex Pistols in 1976, there had been several examples of New York bands playing in the United Kingdom, including Patti Smith in 1976.[129] Phil Marcade spent much of the 1970s traveling around the United States and Western Europe. His travels allowed him to have a front row seat to some of the artists who influenced punk. While living in Boston in 1974, he met and befriended the New York Dolls.[130] Not long after, on a visit home to France, he discovered British pub rock band Dr. Feelgood, who he described as "a true revelation. Short hair, tight black suits, thin wrinkled ties. Dr. Feelgood played a sped-up old American rhythm and blues."[131] He concluded that "they blew away every other group of the time."[132] He argued that Dr. Feelgood and other pub rock acts were "were opening the doors for a whole generation of punk rockers."[133] Influences on punk came from Europe, not just the United States. There was enough overlap between the pub rock sound and the punk ethos that Malcolm McLaren attempted to get Mike Spenser of the pub rock band the Count Bishops to be the singer for the Sex Pistols.[134]

Others associated with the New York scene also spent time in Europe. Neon Leon was already discussed. Jayne County, originally from Dallas, Georgia, made her name in New York City. She contributed several tracks for a New York–based compilation, *Max's Kansas City: New York New Wave*, with her band the Back Street Boys that also included Suicide and Pere Ubu.[135] She appeared in *The Blank Generation*, a 1976 film about the punk scene.[136] County was living in London when she appeared in Don Letts's *The Punk Rock Movie* and in Derek Jarman's punk-inspired apocalyptic film *Jubilee*, both released in 1978.[137] She spent time in Berlin and officially began transitioning, making her possibly the first rock musician to come out as trans.[138]

Early on, the New York scene was part of a transatlantic cultural exchange that was part of the broader cultural Cold War. The promotion of culture became one of the most effective weapons in America's Cold War arsenal, but it opened up unofficial spaces for cultural sharing.[139] Loving American pop culture was not necessarily procapitalist. Tim Mohr argued that love of Western pop culture did not necessarily correspond with anti-communist sentiment or a desire to embrace capitalism. But communist states did not embrace punk as aligning with their values. East German punks certainly saw punk rock as making political statements. One young man known as Speiche was told the British punk bands on his mix tape were "protest music," not just ordinary rock. Soon Speiche was subject to arrest. He was beaten and had his mohawk forcibly shorn after police dragged him off a tram for spraying graffiti.[140] But the goal for some of the punks there was not entirely scrapping the socialist system in East Germany, but reform. Singer Pankow of the band Planlos was subjected to regular interrogation by both the police and the notorious Stasi (the East German state security service) during the 1980s for his musical and political activities. A committed anarchist following in the footsteps of figures celebrated by the regime like Rosa Luxemburg, he made clear in his interrogations that his goal was not to reunite the two German states or to do away with a socialist state, but democratic reform. Mohr quoted Pankow as saying that "it's a great country, but we need to improve somethings."[141] Mohr said that the punk scene in general was "stubbornly egalitarian, not hierarchical," which upset the control the party was attempting to assert over East German youths.[142] By the early 1980s, young people there were discovering punk.

In the West, the spread of first-wave punk often depended on the movement of individual people. But much of this was still being mediated via the mainstream music industry to some degree. When Ramones undertook their first major international tour, it was backed by their label, Sire Records. Danny Field said the Linda Stein was crucial for organizing their European tour. He said, "she's got some connections in London."[143] An audience already existed for the band in London. John Giddings, the booking agent for the band, said, "there was a strong scene in London and everyone was talking about the Ramones. They were the gods from America. They already started it. The Pistols were quite good, but none of them could play like the Ramones could play."[144] But radio airplay was also central to sharing the early punk bands from New York with a listening audience in Britain. DJ John Peel introduced an entire generation of young Britons to punk rock in 1976. In his biography of the famed DJ, Mick Wall said that "it was John's fault that I also bought Patti Smith's *Horses* album that year, followed by the first Ramones album, the later the first Damned, Clash, Jam and Pistols singles."[145]

Other kinds of mass media shaped the British punk scene. Mick Jones of the Clash was influenced by novelist J. G. Ballard, films like *A Clockwork Orange*, and the proto-punk band like MC5, the Stooges, and the Flamin' Groovies. He discovered the bands through *Creem* magazine, which he received from packages sent by his mother from the United States. He and a classmate sought out these albums at specialty record stalls that focused on imports.[146] As such, there were multiple ways that New York punk exerted influence on British punk. But other culture did as well.

This included the Sex Pistols. I examine their story in some depth here because they foreshadowed the deeply contentious relationship punk rock would have with mainstream culture throughout the 1980s. The Sex Pistols and the controversy that surrounded them were part of the process of making the second-wave punks into an underground, countercultural phenomenon. They also illustrate how important live shows were to creating punk culture, although sound recordings also matter. Their story highlights the Situationist influence because of McLaren. He was also an important connection between these two major punk scenes. Based on his experiences in New York, McLaren decided to create a punk band that would disrupt the British establishment through music. He recruited some of the regulars of his shop on King's Road, SEX (soon renamed Seditionaries), to form a band that he would manage. Glen Matlock first appeared in the shop looking for shoes in 1973.[147] Paul Cook and Steve Jones began hanging around as early as 1974.[148] John Lydon did not frequent the store until 1975, along with Simon Ritchie (Sid Vicious).[149] But Lydon did not join the band until later in the year, and then to much controversy in the band itself.[150] Like it or not (and many do not), the Sex Pistols became the most consequential punk band of this era, even if were not the first, most original, or best of the first-wave punk bands.

The trajectory of the band came from the interplay between the members and their manager. Initially McLaren had little interest in getting involved in music, preferring to try and disrupt the fashion world with his shop. Matlock argued that the turning point for McLaren came in 1975 when he convinced him and Bernie Rhodes (later manager for the Clash) to see a Scottish band, the Sensational Alex Harvey Band, at the Hammersmith Odeon club. Matlock said of the show, "it was absolutely packed with kids going mad; that's when the penny dropped with Malcolm."[151] After the seeing the reaction, Matlock argued that McLaren began to get more deeply involved in the Sex Pistols. Matlock along with Cook, Jones, and their friend Wally Nightingale had already been practicing as a band. McClaren began trying to make them into a funhouse mirror version of the popular disco act the Bay City Rollers. According to Gorman, McLaren did not want to go for "just another rock band," but he did not want to abandon the idea of mass appeal either. He believed that a band that was just as constructed as the Rollers but was a "street alternative" could be wildly popular.[152] In doing this, McLaren viewed himself as carrying on the spirit of the 1960s counterculture, which sought to change things for the better but had failed, in his estimation. McLaren wanted to disrupt the "major entertainment combines" from within with a band like the Sex Pistols.[153] McLaren was good at theory, but not so much on the nuts and bolts of building and managing a band. Clash biographer Marcus Gray argued that Rhodes was far more important in encouraging the band to practice. McLaren and Rhodes had a fascination with Situationist theory and cultural disruption, but Matlock said that Rhodes was the one encouraging the band to do their due diligence early on.[154]The Situationist machinations of McLaren often dominate discussions about the Sex Pistols. But McLaren does not deserves all the credit or blame for the success or failure of the Sex Pistols.

The individual band members put in the work to ensure their success. They did not necessarily share McLaren's radical vision of culture jamming.[155] The members brought along their own experiences, goals, and tastes in music to the project. Steve Jones was the one who wanted to form a band in the first place. He brought McLaren on board to manage the group. Savage said that Jones "chose McLaren, not vice versa . . . It was Jones persistence, and ultimately, his presence, which convinced this restless yet ambitious shop owner to commit himself to the group that would become the Sex Pistols." Jones's background also played a role in his interest in music. He described himself as a one-time skinhead who indulged in trouble-making to deal with coming from a broken home.[156] Jones's and Paul Cook's tastes in music shaped the band's musical direction. In addition to Rod Stewart's early band the Faces, they enjoyed glam artists like David Bowie (whose PA they stole in July 1973) and Roxy Music. Savage said they also enjoyed the "lad's rock" bands such as Mott the Hoople and the New York Dolls. Savage quoted Cook on the Dolls, saying that, "they were so funny on the Old Grey Whistle Test [a British music program on the BBC] . . . they were so anti-everything, lurching about, falling into each other on their platform boots."[157] Glen Matlock, who came from the London suburbs, contributed an interest in the Kinks and the Rolling Stones.[158] John Lydon's musical tastes included Iggy Pop and reggae.[159] Lydon also introduced the band to more avant-garde music like Captain Beefheart.[160]

Live shows became critical for garnering wider attention for the band. Here, too, the Sex Pistols played key roles in getting live shows. Matlock organized their first public gig in late 1975, opening for a pub rock band called Bazooka Joe at Central Saint Martin's in London. The band arrived with just a guitar and bass and borrowed the rest of the necessary gear from the headliners. They played some covers and smashed up that gear. Bazooka Joe's frontman Danny Kleinman recalled that he "wasn't overly impressed."[161] A show several months later at Queen Elizabeth College saw their first national review in the *New Musical Express* (*NME*) by Kate Phillips, who called them the "next big thing."[162] The second mention in *NME* came from Neil Spencer, who saw them at the Marquee club opening for Eddie and the Hot Rods, an R&B group. The image used in the review to illustrate the chaos of their live performance was a close-up of a sneering Lydon. Jones said in an interview with Spencer, "We're into chaos." The cover of that edition also had Patti Smith.[163] McLaren believed that national media attention from live shows was a key factor in his plans for the band. He did not want widespread acceptance from the media. Rather, he hoped the Sex

Pistols would garner hate from the mainstream but adoration from youth increasingly alienated by the economic crisis of the 1970s. The way McLaren shaped the band was an attempt to implement core Situationist theory of détournement, the act of turning the culture of capitalism against itself. At these early shows, they displayed the key factors of punk culture such as "non-conformity, an expressive DIY stance, and a chaotic outcome."[164] The positive reviews were at odds with McLaren's attempt to make the band notorious. He was not entirely alone in this endeavor. Other artists were also beginning to challenge established norms, such as Throbbing Gristle, who were invited to stage an art exhibit and musical performance at the Institution of Contemporary Arts in London (ICA). The exhibition and performance inspired MP Nicholas Fairbairn to call the band "the wreckers of civilization."[165] An article in *The Guardian* about the exhibit noted that the ICA "had anxieties" about the exhibit, called "Prostitution," with the possibility that the group's funding could have been pulled. The article also noted that a band called Death Rock would perform, which was in fact one of the earliest performances of Throbbing Gristle.[166] Rebellion via music was definitely in the air in 1976.

The attention the British media gave punk started with the Sex Pistols but soon covered other bands. This meshed with McLaren's long-term goal of creating a disruptive youth culture. He even tried to facilitate other bands, which was hit or miss. He tried to put Chrissie Hynde, later of the Pretenders, together with Dave Vanian, Captain Sensible, and Rat Scabies, who later formed the Damned. Hynde failed to gel with the other members of the band.[167] McLaren encouraged Sid Vicious to play drums with Siouxsie Sioux in an early incarnation of the Siouxsie and the Banshees. The Damned and the Banshees played with the Sex Pistols and the French band Stinky Toys at a punk festival organized by McLaren in 1976.[168] At a Ramones and Talking Heads gig that year, McLaren told Vic Napper and friends to start a band since they looked the part. They formed Subway Sect, which would also be part of the punk festival at the 100 Club.[169] It was at this punk festival where Sid Vicious accidentally put out someone's eye when he threw a glass at the Damned. McLaren waved the injury off as unimportant in the grand scheme of things. But he was happy about the notoriety the incident got the band and the growing British punk scene. It made international papers, with an article about British punk in the West German teen magazine *Bravo*, including a five-page spread on the Sex Pistols.[170] By the mid-1970s, punk was gaining international stature as the "next big youth rebellion."

The more dangerous the subculture seemed, the more media attention it received, which generated even more media panic. But this vicious circle allowed McLaren to secure a deal with EMI after a short bidding war from the major labels in Britain.[171] To cover his own interests, McLaren convinced the band to sign a questionable contract with his new management company, Glitterbest. It advantaged McLaren financially but later contributed to the bad blood between him and the band. The EMI deal he negotiated included an advance for three years with a renewal option. While many British punk bands were signing with independent labels, McLaren was "dead set against signing with the new independent labels such as Stiff and Chiswick."[172] Some of that was practical, as these new independents had fewer options for distribution. Signing with an independent clashed with his plan of maximum social disruption of the capitalist system. In his own words, "the idea was to demystify the pop music establishment,"[173] a reoccurring theme in punk history. He believe that if successful, the Pistols could "broaden things out, make them literary and more political, more international."[174] Savage said that "it seemed the Sex Pistols were an enemy within, entering the music industry in order to destroy it."[175] It deepened and coincided with a wave of youth radicalization in the face of the ongoing economic crisis. Savage said of the public backlash to punk: "if you were Punk, you suddenly found yourself a scapegoat, an outsider. This realization—part delicious, part terrifying—radicalized a small but significant part of a generation."[176] McLaren's goal of disrupting an industry that promoted itself as representing youth culture did help peel back the curtain a bit on the mainstream music industry. That revelation coupled with the studious lack of interest in second-wave punk bands in the United States would drive a wave of new independent labels that catered to punk music in the 1980s. Along with the emergence of punk zines, it helped create a punk counterpublic that existed outside the mainstream culture industries.

Thanks to a controversial interview with Bill Grundy on the show *Today*, the Sex Pistols' EMI deal barely lasted into the new year of 1977. The Sex Pistols showed up to the teatime program broadcast in London with some of the Bromley Contingent, a group of their friends and fans, including Siouxsie Sioux. The fifty-three-year-old Grundy flirted with the nineteen-year-old Sioux after she gushed about how she loved the show. In response, Steve Jones called him a "dirty old man" and then a "dirty fucker." Lydon also cursed at Grundy. The media storm the next day ignored Grundy's flirting and focused on the foul language the band used. McLaren was over the moon, as the negative attention was far more than he could have hoped for in terms of creating notoriety. It eventually lost them their contract with EMI. Savage showed that there were factions in the company that wanted to keep the band on the roster, so they stayed on the label for a while after the Grundy incident.[177] A major blow came when the group was banned from many venues across Britain. They continued with a tour anyway, with EMI's support.[178] After EMI finally dropped them, the Sex Pistols released their first single and then album on Virgin Records, a label that started as a record shop that imported krautrock bands.[179] McLaren had also secured contracts in the United States with Arista and Warner Bros., which survived the Grundy controversy.[180] Their ill-fated trip down the Thames to "celebrate" the Queen's Silver Jubilee with a performance of "God Save the Queen" had more dire consequences. It resulted in McLaren's arrest. After this, the members of the Sex Pistols suffered random attacks on the streets.[181]

The Sex Pistols' American tour put the final nail in the coffin of what was the most high-profile punk band in the world at the time. *Never Mind the Bollocks* was released in the United States in November 1977. Some record shops saw lines to get the album. Savage said that with some exceptions, "America was ready for it, whatever 'it' was."[182] Unfortunately for their US distribution partner Warner Bros., FM radio stations across the country were pretty conservative. Industry insider Bill Drake said at the time that "new wave" music (meaning punk and postpunk bands) "won't amount to much." Both Ramones and the Talking Heads were playing to packed shows but could not get even minimal radio airplay. America had a more fragmented media environment compared to the United Kingdom, which had the BBC. This worked against punk in America in general and against the Sex Pistols specifically. McLaren's strategy just wasn't as workable in that fragmented media landscape.[183] Drumming up media hype for the tour proved difficult. They ignored the size of the country when planning the tour, said Savage.[184] Much like with the New York Dolls tour a few years earlier, McLaren planned a blitz of the Southern United States rather than bringing them to New York, Chicago, and LA. The only exception was a planned December 17, 1977, performance on *Saturday Night Live*. Unfortunately, visa issues prevented them from making it. The slot was given to Elvis Costello, who caused his own trouble. SNL producers banned Costello when he played the forbidden single "Radio, Radio."[185] The Sex Pistols' tour kicked off in January 1978 under strict supervision by representatives from Warner Bros., starting in Atlanta, Georgia. The music associated with Georgia at the time was made by artists like James Brown,

Ray Charles, and rock acts like the Allman Brothers Band. The Sex Pistols were booked at a club called the Great Southeast Music Hall. Savage gave the total attendance of fans as around 500, which was the capacity of the venue. Local and regional media showed up in force, as did the vice squads from Atlanta and Memphis, TN.[186] The national media had a field day with the show. Reporter Jack Perkins covered the show for NBC. He attempted to interview Vicious and Cook, showed off the destruction of their hotel room, and derisively noted the relatively small size of the audience while ignoring the size of the venue. In one crowd shot, a young man in a leather jacket with thick glasses might have be the infamous Atlanta punk Chris Wood, lead singer of the Restraints (who went on to die in prison after being convicted of manslaughter).[187]

Arguably Atlanta was the most successful date of the tour. But Savage said of the performance that "they stank." He described Vicious's downward spiral during the tour. He "was uncontrollable and had to be watched twenty-four hours a day"[188] as he struggled with heroin withdrawal. Cook said "that [the] American tour was so heavy with paranoia" because of McLaren's behavior and the presence of the armed guards hired by Warner Bros.[189] The publisher of the magazine *High Times* joined the tour and witnessed the bodyguards physically assaulting the detoxing Vicious. The band believed the publisher was a CIA plant. By the time they arrived in Memphis for their second concert, no one was talking to anyone else.[190] At their Dallas show in January, LA punks made a strong showing when scene member Hellin Killer headbutted Vicious in the nose. He continued the show with blood flowing down his face and later slashed his chest with a broken bottle.[191] In San Francisco, the band was set to play at Bill Graham's venue Winterland. Graham was the rock promoter associated with the rise of the San Francisco sound in the 1960s. Later, we will see how he got no real love from the second-wave punk scene in the Bay area. Local bands the Nuns and Avengers opened for the Sex Pistols at midnight.[192] The Sex Pistols' performance was an utter disaster. Legs McNeil declared that the Pistols' performance that night "destroyed punk" because they dismantled the mystique he argued the Ramones had created around it.[193] Ironically, the demystification of popular music and youth culture was one of McLaren's central goals with his intervention into punk rock.

Whether McLaren succeeded remains up for debate. What is not is the demise of the Sex Pistols that night. The group split up after the performance. Cook and Jones joined McLaren on a trip to Rio to work on a new project. They recorded songs with Ronnie Biggs, a notorious criminal figure in the United Kingdom. Lydon and Vicious ended up in New York, where Vicious landed in the hospital due to his drug use.[194] Lydon headed to Jamaica to help Virgin Records develop some reggae groups there.[195] Vicious moved full-time to New York City with his girlfriend, Nancy Spungen. They secured a room at the Chelsea Hotel, saying they were looking for a fresh start. Unfortunately, they deteriorated into heavy and constant drug use. This ended in the stabbing death of Spungen on October 12, 1978. The exact details of her death remain in dispute. Neon Leon lived at the Chelsea at the same time as the couple. He claimed he saw them the night that Spungen was stabbed. Vicious showed him the knife Spungen bought for him and then gave Leon one of his jackets and some newspaper clippings. Leon also claimed they called him for pot. They had gotten a drug known as Tuinol from a dealer named Steve Cinotti, who gave a conflicting account of the events of that night to the *New York Post*. We know that Vicious found the twenty year-old Spungen dead the next day, curled up on the bathroom floor. He believed he had done it and turned himself in to police. He was deep in shock and never really recovered from her death. After Spungen's death, McLaren flew over and took control of organizing a defense for the strung-out Vicious, as did Vicious's mother.[196] The case never went to trial, as Vicious died of a drug overdose with heroin bought for him by his mother on February 2, 1979.[197]

The story of the Sex Pistols illustrates several important points about punk that explains why it went "underground." First was the hostility and contempt from much of the press, first in the United Kingdom, then in the United States. It highlights the conservative cultural turn in both countries. The 1970s and 1980s saw the ascendancy of more conservative politics. In the United Kingdom, Margaret Thatcher became prime minister in 1979. In the United States, the Ronald Reagan became president in 1980. Both leaders became prime targets of more political punk bands' derision. The press and popular media would help rev up a "punk panic" that would keep punk bands largely out of the mainstream until the 1990s. This was a two-way street, as many punks rejected any engagement with the mainstream music industry. Instead, they built their own distribution networks and globally circulating alternative media that connected punk scenes all around the world. Punk became a translocal subculture as a result. Punk also splintered into several different subculture during the 1980s, with varying levels of inclusion into the musical mainstream. Hardcore punk became the working definition of punk for many, but other subgenres used the same structures as hardcore punks. The members of these scenes had varying levels of contempt for mainstream success. Although the Sex Pistols were not the only punk band to receive mainstream attention, how the band was treated tells us much about why many punks went underground in the 1980s.

There were other bands from the British wave of punk rock who were directly influenced by the Sex Pistols. Word spread in the wake of their early performances. Some who frequented McLaren's and Westwood's store started their own bands, such as Siouxsie Sioux and Steven Bailey of Siouxsie and the Banshees.[198] Viv Albertine and Mick Jones were in the audience for the Sex Pistols' first show. Jones auditioned to be the Sex Pistols' second guitarist and later formed the Clash. Albertine played guitar for the Slits.[199] The Sex Pistols inspired a similar reaction when they played in Manchester. Their influence preceded them. On a trip to the northern city, McLaren met Howard Devoto and Pete Shelley and convinced them to organize gigs for the Sex Pistols in Manchester. The origins of Joy Division was at that Sex Pistols gig. Gorman quoted Peter Hook, who said, "I wanted to tell the world to fuck off, just like Johnny Rotten."[200] Steven Morrissey, the singer for the Smiths, also decided to get involved in music because of seeing the band play.[201] This dynamic was another critical aspect of punk rock—people seeing a punk show and realizing that they could also start a band.

The bands inspired by the Sex Pistols found their own success. The first punk singles to reach stores was not from *Never Mind the Bollocks*. Rather, The Damned's single, "New Rose," appeared in record shops first, followed closely by their album *Damned, Damned, Damned*.[202] They arrived in the United States before the Sex Pistols and played in major cities with well-established punk scenes. The Damned's guitarist, Brian James, wrongly claimed that LA had no punk scene at the time they played the city. But punks from that scene crashed the in-store event held at the Bomp! Records shop. This included John Denney of the Weirdos, Darby Crash, Pat Smear, and Lorna Doom of the Germs. They (unsuccessfully) attempted to get a show with the Damned.[203] Unlike the Sex Pistols, who McLaren set up for maximum cultural jamming via the established music industry, the Damned went with an independent label that was trying to support the growing punk scene. Stiff Records was started in 1976 by Jake Riveria and Dave Robinson, who was a former tour manager for Jimi Hendrix and the Animals. They first put out a Nick Lowe single before signing the Damned. Stiff also signed Elvis Costello in 1977. To get Costello more attention in the US market after the release of his first album, *My Aim Is True*, they staged a busking event with a flatbed truck outside of a convention for CBS Records executives in London. Robinson phoned in an anonymous tip to the police, and Costello spent the night in jail. Angry as he was about it, the stunt worked and he signed a contract with CBS for US distribution.[204] For the Damned and other punk bands, independent labels were the way to go. Marcus Gray compared labels like Stiff and Chiswick that signed many of the first-wave punk bands to the early rock labels of the 1940s and 1950s. He argued that by the 1970s, the "powerful multinational majors" dominated the production of popular music. But the British wave of indie labels associated with punk grew out of the work of Stiff and Chiswick.[205] The rise of indies in the rock era and then in the punk era were part of a larger pattern of fragmentation and consolidation in the record business.[206]

The Clash were another key British band who were influenced by the Sex Pistols and inspired a new generation of musicians. The band stuck around longer than their more anarchic counterpart and made a broader impact on US audiences. In his biography of the Clash, Gray showed they had some of the same musical influences as the Sex Pistols. Mick Jones was a fan of glam and the New York Dolls, having seen them in 1972 on their first UK tour.[207] Bassist Paul Simonon embraced skinhead culture as a teen-ager while growing up in a predominantly Black neighborhood in Brixton. Violence at the football pitch proved as much an influence on Simonon's worldview as the ska and reggae that was popular in his neighborhood.[208] Joe Strummer (born John Mellor) had a much more eclectic and privileged upbringing as the son of a civil servant who served around the world. This was sometimes a point of controversy as the band presented an explicitly working-class identity to their audiences.[209] He also had more wide-ranging musical taste than his bandmates, such as an interest in weirder albums like Captain Beefheart's LP *Trout Mask Replica*. For a short while, Strummer went by the name Woody as an homage to American folk singer Woody Guthrie. Like Guthrie, Strummer made a strong connection between politics and popular music.[210] Another influence on Strummer was his time spent in London squats. He shared space with immigrants from Latin America at a time when the Cold War was shaping politics in that region. Gray argued that the people that Strummer lived among were not themselves particularly political, but the plight of Latin American countries as a battleground in the Cold War showed up in the themes of the band's music later.[211]

Strummer's pre-Clash band, pub rock act the 101ers, shared a bill with the Sex Pistols at the 100 Club on Oxford Street. This brought Strummer into contact with the scene around the Sex Pistols, including members of a band known as London SS, which included Mick Jones. In one (now mythol-ogized) encounter, Strummer ran into Jones, Simonon, Rhodes, and Matlock.

They called his band the 101ers "shit" but said that his performance was awesome. The 101ers had secured a contract with Chiswick, but Strummer had a waning interest in that band and a growing interest in punk. After several meetings with guitarist Keith Levene and manager Bernie Rhodes, they offered him a slot with the Clash and he agreed within a day.[212] They opened for the Sex Pistols at a Sheffield club within a month.[213] There were more line-up changes, most notably Levene getting fired due to drug use, which he denied.[214] Levene was not out of the music scene for good as he formed Public Image Ltd (PiL), with John Lydon, Jah Wobble, and Jim Walker in 1978.[215] The Clash played a few dozen gigs before signing to CBS Records in early 1977 for £100,000. Some, like Mark Perry who started the punk zine *Sniffin' Glue*, proclaimed that moment the death of punk rock. But the editor who took over at the zine, Danny Baker, penned a measured defense of signing with a major label. He noted that "there's no point screamin' to the converted on privately owned/distributed labels that could see about two hundred, is there? You wanna be heard, fuck being a cult [*sic*]."[216]

These higher profile punk bands get the lion's share of the attention in punk histories. There is good reason for that: the influence they exerted on others. The proto-punk and first-wave punk bands are generally universally cited as inspiring a new generation of musicians to make music, too. These bands also kicked off debates that shape our discussions of popular music today. The definition of who was a punk ended up rather broad and inclusive. It was not just those playing in bands that qualified. Take some of the early supporters of the Sex Pistols, called the Bromley Contingent by music journalist Caroline Coon. A group of friends from southeast London, they discovered McLaren's shop SEX and supported the Sex Pistols at their earliest performances. Some members of the group ended up in bands, such as Siouxsie Sioux and Billy Idol. But not everyone from that group ended up in a band. Pamela Rooke, known as Jordan, worked at SEX and was known for her confrontational fashions. She appeared in the film *Jubilee* and briefly managed and sometimes performed with Adam and the Ants. But she did not form a band that had the same influence of these other bands. There was also Sue Lucas, or Soo Catwoman, known for her outlandish styles. She only occasionally worked with bands.[217]

Figures like Rodney Bingenheimer, Kim Fowley, Lester Bangs, McLaren, and Westwood were older individuals that made important contributions that helped set the direction of punk rock. Bernie Rhodes was another person who made important contributions to how punk shaped up in Britain. Often in McLaren's shadow, Rhodes was just as influential as his counterpart. He discovered John Lydon, for example, who said of the Clash's manager, he "was important to me in so many ways . . . He would sow a seed and then wait to see if I would pick up on it."[218] According to Don Letts, Rhodes's influence on the Clash was critical to giving the band more "depth. They could see the tradition they were following, and they made music as a way of communicating ideas as a protest thing, rather than just having an agenda of making music to sell records."[219]Punk in the United Kingdom inspired many young people to form a band. Some of the bands ended up being quite influential, if short-lived. The Slits formed in 1976 with Ari Up (Ariane Foster) and Palmolive (Paloma Romero), later joined by Viv Albertine and Tessa Pollitt. All of them were in other bands prior to the Slits, such as Palmolive and Albertine playing in Flowers of Romance with Sid Vicious.[220] Others not known for being musicians also were inspired by punk. Before Neil Gaiman wrote beloved works of fantasy, he was a teenage punk with his friend Geoff Notkin. Leah Schnelbach said that "punk shaped Gaiman's attitude toward art and creativity. The idea that you just get up and do it, and don't worry if your work isn't any good at first, but just keep at it until you get better, clearly shaped his writing career."[221] His short story "How to Talk to Girls at Parties" was about a shy boy at a party full of odd punk girls who turn out to be aliens.[222] Gaiman's other work has included characters influenced by punk culture, such as his version of Death in the comic *Sandman*. Probably his most beloved character, Death's likeness was inspired by Cinamon Hadley, who was a friend of illustrator Mike Dringenberg.[223] Gaiman was not the only British creative inspired by their days as a punk. Comedian and TV host Craig Ferguson was in a punk band called the Dreamboys with his fellow Glaswegian Peter Capaldi. Capaldi has had a long acting career, most notably recognized from the long-running British science fiction series *Doctor Who*, where he played the twelfth Doctor.[224]

In New York City there were scene members who made music but never made it as big as bands like Ramones, Blondie, or the Talking Heads. Jayne County was another regular on the New York City punk scene who never made quite the splash in the American public imagination as some of her contemporaries. But County was a globe-trotting artist whose career helped connect punk across national boundaries and broke new ground in popular music. Originally from Georgia, she first went to Atlanta, where she discovered drag culture in the gay clubs. She arrived in New York City only slightly ahead of the Stonewall riots, which she participated in. Here she began to come to terms with her gender identity. Doing so limited the opportunities she had to become a bigger star in the United States. She said that "in a lot of ways, I was [aware of being trans], but I wasn't able to make the records because I was in over my head."[225] She also performed in off-Broadway plays, including *Pork*, written by Andy Warhol. David Bowie saw her in that play in 1971 and offered to manage her. It did not work out well for her. She said that "her ideas were 'stolen, whitewashed,' and repackaged by Bowie himself."[226] County, who came out in 1979, might have been the first openly trans musician, with pioneering electronic musician Wendy Carlos also coming out the same year. Carlos said once she came out, most people were either accepting or indifferent and that hiding her identity "had proven a monstrous waste of years of my life."[227] But punk had a long history of being welcomed to some degree in LGBQT+ spaces. In addition to the club Mother's in New York, the Damned practiced in a gay club in the late 1970s.[228] The London punk scene included plenty of crossover with the LGBQT+ community. Debbie Wilson and Siouxsie Sioux of the Bromley Contingent discussed the interconnections between the nascent punk scene and the LGBQT+ community. According to Wilson, "it was the Bromley Contingent who introduced the Pistols to the gay scene."[229] Siouxsie said of the club where Wilson first saw the Sex Pistols "before it got a label it was a club for misfits. . . . Waifs, male gays, female gays, bisexuals, non-sexuals, everything. No one was criticized for their sexual preferences."[230] Vivienne Westwood was partly responsible for bringing this diversity of sexual orientation and gender to the early punk scene, as she cultivated many of the connections via SEX. According to Savage, "the women and men Vivienne collected acted out their wildest fantasies. By doing so, they became part of the Sex Pistols and gave Punk its Warholian edge."[231]

Finally, I conclude this chapter with an acknowledgment that from its inception, punk was not just restricted to New York and London, but incubated in other locations as well. Los Angeles and San Francisco had interconnected scenes early on. The Motels were originally from Berkeley but came to LA for better opportunities with no luck. Lead singer Martha Davis said that lack of airplay on the radio meant that music venues were not interested. Along with other bands like the Pop and the Dogs, they sought a grassroots solution to their collective problem. They split the cost of renting a location called Troupers Hall and started a night called "Radio Free Hollywood," a twist on the anticommunist shortwave stations broadcasting in Europe at the time. They had a packed house, and Davis called those events "a turning point." Journalist Gene Sculatti said flyers and a newsletter were the primary means of promotion. Plus, they gave away numerous free passes. They lost only $90, she said.[232] This artist-centered DIY approach became central to building punk communities. This was in early 1976, around the same time that Rodney Bingenheimer began his radio program on KROQ, a staple of LA rock culture since the 1960s. He was hired by the station to play glam and bring in famous artists from that scene. But Bingenheimer played punk instead. "The first thing I played was the Ramones," he later recalled.[233] He played local bands such as the Berlin Brats, the Dils, and the Motels. By 1977, he was playing demos from other local punks.[234] Most consider Rodney Bingenheimer and Kim Fowley as key figures in the early LA punk scene, but others felt they held the scene back. Mary Kay of the Dogs said, "Rodney and Kim had this town sewn up if you were an unsigned band. Without their endorsement you were cut out from airplay on KROQ and from playing the Whiskey."[235]

Other bands were forming on the West Coast, with influence from New York and London becoming apparent. Black Randy, later of Black Randy and the Metro Squad and cofounder of the independent label Dangerhouse, brought a copy of the British paper *Sunday Times* with punks on the cover to his friends in the Screamers. He told the band, which he called the first punk band in town, "This is going to be what happens next." Others also were reading about the events in the United Kingdom, especially the infamous Grundy interview with the Sex Pistols. Hal Negro of Hal Negro and the Satin Tones said of the Sex Pistols after that "it was the big band. And we felt it here."[236] In 1977, several new bands formed around the Hollywood scene, including the Screamers, the Weirdos, and the Germs. Like in other scenes, live shows provided an inspiration for others. A series of early punk shows at the Orpheum with the Weirdos, Nerves, Screamers, and the Germs, plus the Damned show at the Starwood proved influential. The guitarist for the Zeros, Robert Lopez, said of the Damned show that "everybody in the audience [it seemed] started their own band."[237] The LA scene also had DIY media pretty early. Claude Bessy, a French national later in the band Catholic Discipline, had been writing a reggae zine named *Angeleno Dread*. He switched to writing a punk zine on advice from his friend Steve Samiof after he had visited the United Kingdom, which became *Slash*. Bessy worked with Samiof and Philomena Winstanely. They convinced Bob Biggs to invest and expanded into a label, which Biggs eventually ran.[238] *Flipside* began publication around the same time. Hal Negro preferred it because he believed it was more grassroots.[239] Scene member Pleasant Gehman started her own zine, *Lobotomy*, which she described as "a lot of work."[240] Their general focus was on the more social aspects of the growing punk scene, especially drug use, while she called *Slash* more political.[241]

LA also had locations that allowed the first-wave scene to develop. Unlike punks in New York, who benefited from friendly clubs that gave new bands an chance to play live, some of the key clubs in Hollywood were not interested in showcasing unsigned acts. The Whiskey and Starwood eventually opened their doors to punk music, but it was only after they got KROQ airplay and built their own clubs for shows. Punks created their own spaces for performances and community building, which became a key element for second-wave punk scenes. Brendan Mullen got a great deal on renting out the Hollywood Center building, "as is" he noted, in the summer of 1977. "We were literally dead center in the bowels of Hollywood," he recalled.[242] Much like Hilly Kristal in New York, Mullen noted that when he rented the building, "punk rock, British, American, or otherwise, was not the main agenda." He wanted to rent out rehearsal rooms. But soon, it "quickly morphed into probably the first illegal club space . . . since prohibition."[243] Once he began advertising the space for rehearsals, bands with very little to spend got in touch.[244] These bands began to play free shows. Soon, they wanted to charge a cover to make a little money. Thus began the legendary club the Masque. John Doe said of the Masque that it was "the real turning point" for the LA punk scene.[245] By the end of the year, two hundred people packed the makeshift club to see shows there. Scene member Hellin Killer recalled it as a "club house" and that it was always a place you could go. "Such a dive, but it was our dive," she said.[246] Killer and several other scene members made their apartment into a punk hangout. Dubbed the Plunger Pit, many ended up there after the clubs closed to drink and have a good time. The Masque closed temporarily to get their license straightened out, but upon reopening, the venue provided space for the scene to continue growing in the late 1970s.[247]

Other scenes emerged in the communist world. Tim Mohr described how Britta, known as Major, discovered punk despite living in a society supposedly cut off from the rest of the world. Her half-sister's father, who lived in West Berlin, brought magazines from the West when he was allowed to visit. She heard the Sex Pistols' "Pretty Vacant" on Radio Luxembourg.[248] Young people in the more Western-friendly communist state of Yugoslavia had an even easier time accessing culture like punk rock. Led by Josip "Tito" Broz since its inception, the country had been expelled from the Warsaw Pact and Cominform by Stalin in 1948. As a result, unlike the Eastern Bloc countries, Yugoslavs was more Western-oriented. They had more freedom to travel to the West, and the regime had a bit more tolerance for Western culture like rock music. Shortwave radio from the West was still the primary means of accessing Western bands.[249] Punk had a wider audience than just those who identified as punks, with a large percentage of young people listening to punk in Slovenia, one of the federal republics that made up the country.[250] Early punk bands in Yugoslavia were able to record in the increasingly market-oriented music industry in the Balkan country, according to Igor Vidmar, an early participant in the Yugoslav punk scene.[251] The Ljubljana Student Cultural Center distributed the first single by first-wave punk band Pankrti. They garnered enough sales to get their next LPs released on a regional label.[252] In 1978, after seeing another early punk band, Paraf, in Zagreb, Vidmar began to play punk music that he imported from the West on Radio Študent. He also began to write about punk in Yugoslav magazines.[253] The punk subculture in Yugoslavia grew over the end of the 1970s in part due to the lighter touch on such issues under Tito. His death in 1980 and the rise of hardline nationalism changed the relationship between the state and punk youths, as we will see when we discuss hardcore punk.

These are just a few of the punk scenes that emerged between 1975 and 1980. But punks appeared in many other places around the world during the end of the 1970s. The globalized nature of punk stemmed from the spread of US and British popular music, a by-product of the Cultural Cold War. There was far more musical and social diversity than hardcore punk scenes later. Although there was a very strong language of cultural disruption, most of the early punks did not reject being signed by major labels or more established independent labels. Until the controversy caused by the Sex Pistols in 1977, punk was generally a marginal and tolerated part of the music industry and youth culture. The 1980s would see punk become more countercultural. These later scenes were on the receiving end of harsher and stronger reactions from the mainstream culture, which sometimes meant serious consequences for punks. We will see how in the 1980s punks built underground subculture that created a translocal counterpublic that shaped how many think about their relationship to popular music.

Chapter 3

Second Wave

From Subculture to Underground Globalization:
1980 to 1990

Scene: Ljubljana, Yugoslavia, early 1983.

The scene had grown and changed in the past few years since punk first appeared in Yugoslavia. New (hardcore, underground) bands were appearing while some older ones broke up or went commercial. People were making tapes and zines and sharing them with each other and with punks in other countries. The student center in Ljubljana had become an important ally and a champion of noncommercial music and culture. They had even begun to act as a de facto record label. Technically it was still a state-run entity, but recently lunatics took over that asylum—probably more in line with the spirit of real socialism. Yugoslavia was changing, and so was Yugoslav punk.

For you, the last few months flew by in a flurry of activity. You and your mates crafted a scene report over beers and smokes down at the local pub that was now done. Everyone agreed it was an important milestone for any local scene and that you were point person on this. But it proved difficult to pull together, given the turbulent nature of the punk spectacle in post-Tito Yugoslavia. The changes in the country—set off less by Tito's death and more by the economic malaise making itself felt as of late—made forging a coherent narrative of the interconnected local scenes even more difficult. Cities like Ljubljana, Zagreb, Belgrade, and Rijeka all had their own dynamics, but in many ways, they were looking more alike than ever before because everyone was plugged into the hardcore scenes in the United States. You continued to pursue connections with other Yugoslav punks in the spirit of "unity and brotherhood" even as that old slogan seemed to be failing. Your scene report shows an attempt at expressing unity in Yugoslav punk and solidarity with punks all over the world.

You take pride in recounting the number of recent shows from the past couple of months, the two new zines put out by your friends, and the three new bands that appeared on the scene, among other highlights. The report, which included pictures of one of the most recent shows, was wrapped around a sampler tape put together by several local bands. After several years of reading scene reports from all over the world, you finally feel like you can share and contribute to the rest of the global punk community. Then it was a trip to the post to send it to a zine in California.

Everyone waited to see it in print a couple of months later. Finally the issue arrived. Pretty much everyone got their copies the same week. Not too long after that, letters began to arrive from across Europe and the United States—from West Berlin, Amsterdam, Dublin, London, New York, LA, São Paolo, among other places. You got some new tapes from bands in those cities (with explicit directions to dub and send on), some zines, and some artwork. There were also requests to write back and letters inquiring about the possibility of including Yugoslavia on upcoming tours. It felt good to be part of a community and to be reaching out across the world to share in one's interests. If nothing else, it showed that you weren't quite the entirely singular misfit, but you shared your status with plenty of others!

The Adolescents	Anti-Nowhere League	Anti Cimex	Armia
Bad Brains	The Teen Idles	Black Flag	ChaosUK
Circle Jerks	Crass	Destructors	Vice Squad
Dayglo Abortions	The Bags	Dead Kennedys	Discharge
DOA	The Exploited	Subhumans	T.S.O.L.
Flipper	G.I.S.M.	Government Issue	Kaaos
Hüsker Dü	MDC	Middle Class	Niet
Minor Threat	White Noise	Abrasive Wheels	Patareni
Negazione	Cro-Mags	Agnostic Front	Fear
Ratos de Porão	The Subs	Die Kreuzen	
Tožibabe	Social Distortion	Murphy's Law	

We saw how punk began as a transnational phenomenon. The first major punk scenes were transatlantic, a cultural scene shared between the North America and Western Europe. The American proto-punk and punk artists touring Great Britain and Western Europe created a mutually constructive event for punk's development in both places. Punk followed along with the cultural flow of the Cold War era. The mainstream culture industries (such as recording companies, Hollywood film studios, and publishers) materially benefited from the cultural Cold War. It gave them state support for opening new markets. British culture also had a global reach, thanks in part to the long-term consequences of British imperialism. As such, the United States and Britain shaped global musical tastes and gave some a target for their cultural rebellion during the rock era. During that time, looking for the "next big thing" became a key music industry strategy. It drove a search for musical novelty and high sales from the 1950s to the 1970s. As we saw earlier, this led to some unlikely signings of confrontational proto-punk bands to either majors or subsidiary labels that were owned by a major. Several artists did not do nearly as well as expected partly because the goal sought by the labels was superstardom, replicating the path of the Beatles or the Rolling Stones. These proto-punk bands were not appealing to a mass audience. They did influence first-wave punk bands on both sides of the Atlantic Ocean as they toured North America and Western Europe. This was the groundwork for the bottom-up translocal communities that emerged with hardcore punk. Plenty of connections were made during this period outside the normal channels of the recording industry. It was not a conscious strategy of community building at first, but an outcome of shared interests.

That changed in the 1980s. Second-wave or hardcore punk became underground and inclined toward the countercultural. Many hardcore punks came to believe that to be punk one should reject "selling out" to the major labels and create translocal, actively democratic communities. Punks in the hardcore era leaned into the creation of a shared identity based on their ideas about music production and consumption. They actively adopted a mode of production that was artist-centered and self-consciously at odds with the major labels. In doing so, they fundamentally changed the nature of punk to be much more about consumerist community-building across national borders. Although punks often derided older subcultures, they shared a sense of alienation from the mainstream culture. Cassette tapes and easy access to photocopiers helped facilitate their underground culture.

Many hardcore punks came to see getting a major label deal as synonymous with selling out. This comes down to two primary reasons. First, by the early 1980s, the mainstream music industry was paying little attention to punk bands. Alan O'Connor breaks down the variety of reasoning for punks starting independent labels. A band's motivating factors included lack of attention from the industry, seeking artistic integrity, autonomy, and political integrity. He noted the control the majors had in the late 1970s (around 90 percent of the market). He also showed the difficulty of getting albums into major retail chains.[1] They sometimes turned to making small runs of singles to be sold at shows or in zines, and sometimes made dubbed cassettes at home with handmade inserts.[2] O'Connor also described how discussions on the appropriate relationship to record labels (large or small) are part of the ongoing internalized debates over what punk means.[3] The more punks had some sort of interaction with major labels in the late 1970s, the more they turned to politicized justifications for independent production. O'Connor points to another practical reason for independence: the experiences of the guitarists for the British band The Subs. The band originally signed to GEM records, a subsidiary of major label RCA. Now band members have no access to their earlier material because GEM controlled the physical masters and control publishing rights to those works.[4] For these and other reasons, punks came to see the recording industry as problematic during the 1980s.

As we shall see in the next chapter, by the early 1990s a general distrust of the mainstream music industry became more normalized in mainstream discussions about the popular music. A 1993 article in *The Baffler* by independent producer Steve Albini, widely republished, typified how many punks and others came to understand the mainstream recording industry.[5] He was building off arguments made in punk zines in the 1980s. The rant focused on the exploitative recording contracts typically offered to young artists. Albini had a high profile at the time, so the essay brought the issue to greater public attention. Musically he came up in Chicago's underground music scenes in the 1980s. These discussions were not confined to the Anglo-American industry in the 1980s nor even to punks in capitalist nations. Punks behind the Iron Curtain and in Yugoslavia, writing in to zines published in the United States, likewise railed against how the state-run recording industry kept out certain genres or particular (nonpolitical) ideas. It may seem like a very different critique on the surface. I argue that this is a shared issue of power and access to culture production happening on both sides of the Iron Curtain, which should tell us that in some ways, there were shared strategies of control. In one case, the "free market" is supposedly catering to the whims of popular taste, and in the other, the state is dictating cultural production (with some response to popular tastes imported from the West). In both cases, this is more about power and who is allowed access to the marketplace of (musical) ideas and youth identity formation via consumer culture.

Through the 1980s, punk scenes faced several internal and external pressures that splintered scenes and brought punks around the world closer together. Other problems arose within punk circles. Despite having a unified front and positioning itself as outside of the social problems of mainstream culture, racism, misogyny, and homophobia were not unknown in punk spaces. Hardcore punk scenes became whiter and generally dominated by young, white, straight men. People of color, women, and LGBQT+ were often made to feel like outsiders. This created new splinters in the late 1980s and early 1990s, which are explored here and in a later chapter. Here we look at how hardcore punks leaned into a white, masculine identity and how that caused a right-wing, racist splinter genre to form. When more explicitly racist elements emerged in punk scenes, it often forced people to take sides. Some punks who held racist views formed their own communities and joined white power movements, often embracing a skinhead identity. Other punks embraced antiracist positions and became more politically active because of their engagement with racists in their midst. There was also a crackdown by authorities around the world, which created a "punk panic," which also pushed punk into a more countercultural position.

During this period, punk came to be more than just a genre of music. It became a social refuge of sorts that gave many a sense of community they were lacking in their lives. It provided an alternative, more artist- and fan-centered method of producing popular culture that was far more democratic in nature. Moreover, the global nature of punk helped fragment the global music industry and give artists and fans a sense that artists should be in greater control, even if one was not a punk. Punk helped change the mode of production for the mainstream music industry, in part because it created a global discussion among young people about how music should be made. This included the production of music, but also the creation of punk media such as zines, including the New York–based zine *The Big Takeover* (see figure 3.1).

Building the Translocal Underground

In the 1980s, punks built a translocal culture that connected people around the world in a shared, imagined community. These connections were made

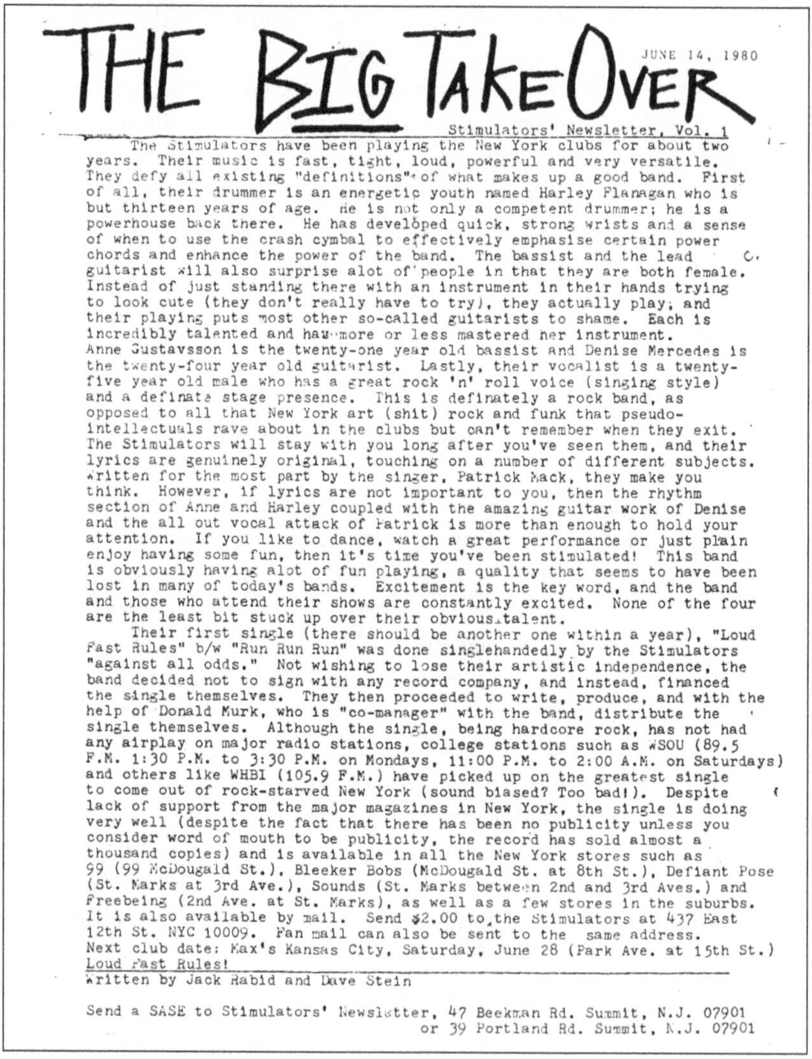

THE BIG TakeOver

JUNE 14, 1980

Stimulators' Newsletter, Vol. 1

The Stimulators have been playing the New York clubs for about two years. Their music is fast, tight, loud, powerful and very versatile. They defy all existing "definitions" of what makes up a good band. First of all, their drummer is an energetic youth named Harley Flanagan who is but thirteen years of age. He is not only a competent drummer; he is a powerhouse back there. He has developed quick, strong wrists and a sense of when to use the crash cymbal to effectively emphasise certain power chords and enhance the power of the band. The bassist and the lead guitarist will also surprise alot of people in that they are both female. Instead of just standing there with an instrument in their hands trying to look cute (they don't really have to try), they actually play; and their playing puts most other so-called guitarists to shame. Each is incredibly talented and has more or less mastered her instrument. Anne Gustavsson is the twenty-one year old bassist and Denise Mercedes is the twenty-four year old guitarist. Lastly, their vocalist is a twenty-five year old male who has a great rock 'n' roll voice (singing style) and a definate stage presence. This is definately a rock band, as opposed to all that New York art (shit) rock and funk that pseudo-intellectuals rave about in the clubs but can't remember when they exit. The Stimulators will stay with you long after you've seen them, and their lyrics are genuinely original, touching on a number of different subjects. Written for the most part by the singer, Patrick Mack, they make you think. However, if lyrics are not important to you, then the rhythm section of Anne and Harley coupled with the amazing guitar work of Denise and the all out vocal attack of Patrick is more than enough to hold your attention. If you like to dance, watch a great performance or just plain enjoy having some fun, then it's time you've been stimulated! This band is obviously having alot of fun playing, a quality that seems to have been lost in many of today's bands. Excitement is the key word, and the band and those who attend their shows are constantly excited. None of the four are the least bit stuck up over their obvious talent.

Their first single (there should be another one within a year), "Loud Fast Rules" b/w "Run Run Run" was done singlehandedly by the Stimulators "against all odds." Not wishing to lose their artistic independence, the band decided not to sign with any record company, and instead, financed the single themselves. They then proceeded to write, produce, and with the help of Donald Murk, who is "co-manager" with the band, distribute the single themselves. Although the single, being hardcore rock, has not had any airplay on major radio stations, college stations such as WSOU (89.5 F.M. 1:30 P.M. to 3:30 P.M. on Mondays, 11:00 P.M. to 2:00 A.M. on Saturdays) and others like WHBI (105.9 F.M.) have picked up on the greatest single to come out of rock-starved New York (sound biased? Too bad!). Despite lack of support from the major magazines in New York, the single is doing very well (despite the fact that there has been no publicity unless you consider word of mouth to be publicity, the record has sold almost a thousand copies) and is available in all the New York stores such as 99 (99 McDougald St.), Bleeker Bobs (McDougald St. at 8th St.), Defiant Pose (St. Marks at 3rd Ave.), Sounds (St. Marks between 2nd and 3rd Aves.) and Freebeing (2nd Ave. at St. Marks), as well as a few stores in the suburbs. It is also available by mail. Send $2.00 to the Stimulators at 437 East 12th St. NYC 10009. Fan mail can also be sent to the same address. Next club date: Max's Kansas City, Saturday, June 28 (Park Ave. at 15th St.) Loud Fast Rules!

Written by Jack Rabid and Dave Stein

Send a SASE to Stimulators' Newsletter, 47 Beekman Rd. Summit, N.J. 07901 or 39 Portland Rd. Summit, N.J. 07901

Figure 3.1. Issue 1 of *The Big Takeover* zine, June 1980. (Used by permission of Jack Rabid)

most importantly by sound recordings and fanzines that circulated globally. Through the circulation of this alternative media, punks around the world shaped a shared identity in part through patterns of consumption in their leisure time. Zines helped punks craft their shared identity via democratic consumption but also standardized punk during the 1980s. In other words, there emerged a democratic, yet sometimes exclusionary punk identity, which led to a backlash (explored in a later chapter).

We saw earlier that the origins and growth of the punk scenes during the 1970s in cities such as New York, London, and Los Angeles. First-wave LA punk—like New York and London—was relatively diverse musically, culturally, ethnically, racially, and with regard to gender and sexual orientation. In contrast, punk in the 1980s got a reputation for being much more dominated by white suburban young men. By the late 1970s, punk shows in Hollywood began to attract kids from Los Angeles's numerous suburban communities. One of the original bands from the Hollywood scene, the Germs, helped bring in new kids to the shows.[6] What drew many young people to the band was their aggressive stage shows. Singer Darby Crash had an aggressive performing style that include using food in unexpected ways, such as sticking the mic in peanut butter, and antagonizing the audience.[7] Later bands took the Germs' template and amplified it. The band Fear was another big influence on the development of hardcore punk. They came from Van Nuys, led by Lee Ving (Lee Capallero). The original line-up consisted of Derf (Fred) Scratch, Philo Cramer, and Spit Stix (Tim Leitch). The band's loud, fast, and aggressive style of playing, coupled with Ving's angry and cynical lyrics, appealed to suburban young men stewing with anger and resentment. Ving sought to inject a harder musical edge into the music after being turned off by the first-wave punk bands.[8] Their shows brought out more intense violence, which turned some punks off.[9] Their controversial appearance on *Saturday Night Live* in 1981 cemented their legendary among hardcore punks.[10] Many of the members of the Washington, DC, punk scene were in the audience that night. The whole lot were kicked out for "causing a riot" with stage diving and slamming. These hardcore bands attracted a suburban crowd that would make up the hardcore wave of punk. Communities like Huntington Beach and Costa Mesa proved to be fertile ground for hardcore.[11]

Many of these punks went on to form their own bands, much like punks in the first wave. The earliest hardcore band might have been Middle Class out of Santa Ana in Orange County, according to guitarist Mike Atta. They got along well with people in the Hollywood scene, with the more established bands being supportive.[12] Later in 1979, when bands like Black Flag, the Descendents, Redd Kross, and The Last began to play shows alongside the more established bands, attitudes began to change. Billy Zoom of the band X stated, "I thought the suburban beach hardcore thing ruined a good scene."[13] Brendan Mullen noted that "female attendance plummeted."[14]

But the punk scene in Los Angeles continued to grow in size and reputation. The bands from suburban communities near LA tended to be louder, faster, and more aggressive, as were their fans. This shift to more aggression in music and by participants at live shows contributed to an exodus from the original Hollywood scene. At the same time, some of the original bands ended up with a somewhat more traditional career in music. For most people, the Go-Go's were a fun pop girl group that got regular airplay on MTV in the early days. However, some of their first shows were played alongside bands such as Black Flag. The 1982 film *Ladies and Gentlemen, the Fabulous Stains* was loosely based on the trajectory of the band from nihilistic punks to optimistic pop group. Black Randy and the Metrosquad even make a brief appearance in the film, playing their first single, "I Slept in an Arcade."[15] It seems unlikely that these younger punks were trying to push out the bands they admired. They were excited by the idea that they did not need to just be passive consumers of music; rather, they could be active participants in the spectacle. Much like the earlier bands, the new hardcore bands were seeking to express themselves through music to build communal bonds with like-minded individuals.

The shift to hardcore was happening in punk scenes around the world. The Yugoslav punk scene had the same sorts of tensions between first- and second-wave punks. Much like the United States and United Kingdom, the early bands were a marginal part of the state-run music industry. By the mid-1980s, independent labels emerged in Yugoslavia, which coincide with market-based reforms in the socialist state. Forming independent labels was prompted out of necessity and by the desire to retain independence from the state-run industry. Younger punks in the early 1980s aligned themselves with the hardcore wave out of US cities like Washington, DC, and LA. In one scene report in *Maximum Rocknroll* (*MRR*) published in 1984, Tomi, David, and Gregor characterized older punks as "reactionary" and complained that [they] "hate us because we are all younger, and because we've developed our own ways. They want us to listen to only their reggae/post punk, etc., and we are BORED with that."[16] The implication here is that first-wave punks rejected the changes to the scenes in Yugoslavia and disliked hardcore. Tensions between younger and older punks were shared across national boundaries as younger punks were taking punk and making it their own.

Hardcore punk became associated with a rise in independent music labels that shaped the mainstream music industry from the 1980s to today. David Hesmondhalgh described this as a "democratization" of popular music in his study of the British postpunk label Rough Trade.[17] The labels associated with hardcore were part of the creation of a punk counterpublic that was connected by global circulating independent media. These helped create the translocal nature of punk in the 1980s. Michael Azerad pinpointed the postpunk wave of independent labels as essentially pioneering the "American indie movement."[18] He included hardcore under the umbrella of postpunk. Punk was becoming more than just a genre of music; it was also becoming a way of thinking about music production. O'Connor said, "It is a mistake to regard punk as a *thing* and then to argue about its true spirit or meaning. Punk is an activity or a series of activities that take place in time."[19] O'Connor argued that "many first-generation bands issued their records themselves or were on small labels. . . . Other than a small number of famous bands in England most of the early punks existed on the margins of the record industry."[20] The relationship between labels and musicians was never really a binary but existed as a "cultural field," as theorized by Pierre Bourdieu.[21] Punk exists in a cultural field of music production, and this "field" was never level. It was and remains heavily tilted in favor of the large, multinational record labels with deep reserves of cash and cultural capital. Punks attempted to maintain their cultural vision in that field. They worked to balance their vision of independent music production and sustain their labels as businesses. Many of these labels were not market-oriented, preferring to embraced the vision of the artists. Other punk labels embraced a more market-oriented path that replicated the model of the mainstream industry, just scaled down.

Bands in places like LA started their own labels primarily due to lack of attention from the major labels. By the early 1980s, creative control became the driving factor for many punks. Members of the LA band Black Randy and the Metrosquad formed Dangerhouse to put out some of the first-wave punk recordings. This became a model for Greg Ginn of Black Flag, who formed SST. In San Francisco, Jello Biafra of Dead Kennedys formed Alternative Tentacles. Dischord Records from Washington, DC, provides another example of punk going independent. Founder Ian MacKaye of the Teen Idles was directly influenced by Dangerhouse, according to O'Connor.[22] From the start, MacKaye opted for the noncommercial model. He started the label because "nobody else was going to put it out."[23] The band glued together the album covers by hand. Even that decision was controversial among some punks at the time. MacKaye recalled that "releasing a record . . . some people looked at a little askance."[24] But Guy Picciotto of Fugazi said doing so "demystified the process" of producing an album.[25] MacKaye said that the label was run by volunteers until eight years into the project. The first three years, all proceeds went directly back to sustaining the label. Around the time Nirvana went big, Atlantic Records attempted to woo Fugazi with a $10 million contract, but the band continued their own label, "charging

$5 for gigs."[26] The label operates without contracts with their bands and over its history, only two bands left for a major label contract.[27] Artist-run independent labels became a translocal phenomenon early on, with the band Crass starting their own label in the United Kingdom. This anarchist collective even advocated for a boycott of British major label EMI in their promotional materials, primarily because the label charged more for their records than was necessary.[28]

O'Connor notes the additional problem of the commercial viability of hardcore music, which he describes correctly as a "fast, aggressive" form of punk rock.[29] However, it was not long after the rise of hardcore punk that heavy metal bands started to gain traction on MTV. Other labels emerged specifically to produce and distribute hardcore bands. O'Connor discussed several of the British labels, such as Crass, Rough Trade, Factory, and Riot City. The first three he called "explicitly 'political' in how they operated. Crass insisted on low-cost records, Rough Trade operated as a collective, and Factory offered bands a 50:50 split of revenue after expenses."[30] He said of Riot City, started by Simon Edwards, and some other labels at the time that they "behaved more like ordinary businesses."[31] If there was a difference between Edwards's hardcore label and Dischord in DC, it would be that Edwards was not a punk or even a musician. O'Connor gave some general characteristics of what he called these "commercial punk labels." He noted that they tended to be run by men in their thirties who "grew up on punk rock" and had friends in bands. "All these people learned how to run a record label by doing it themselves," he argued, noting a singular example of a label owner with an MBA, John Janick, but in that case he had already run the label for a while.[32] These commercial-oriented punk labels run by entrepreneurs tended to avoid "serious political involvement."[33]

Bands in other genres also turned to smaller, artist-run labels. Daniel Miller founded Mute Records to put out his electronic band the Normal. He connected his music to punk rock. He said of punk, "like many of my generation, I was inspired by the raw noise, the attitudes and the DIY ethos of punk. The music didn't always interest me that much—though I loved the energy, I found a lot of it quite conservative."[34] He felt electronic music was "more punk than punk: you didn't have to learn any chords but could just press down on the keyboard and an interesting sound would come out."[35] It lowered the bar to entry into making music even further than guitar-based punk had done. After recording a single at home, he set up Mute to "shift" it. He secured a distribution deal with Rough Trade and ended up selling fifteen thousand copies of his single.[36] In his biography of Mute band Depeche Mode, Dave Thompson argued that punk was not a specific genre of music, but a way of thinking about popular music. He said, "punk did more than liberate music, it also liberated the means by which music could be distributed."[37] Los Angeles also had a wave of independent labels that followed in punk's wake. Lisa Fancher started Frontier Records in 1979, responding in part to how punks were being ignored. She was influenced by Dangerhouse Records, which lasted from 1977 to 1980. Frontier reissued two Dangerhouse collections in the early 1990s.[38] Fancher said she missed the boat on the first-wave LA punk bands, but caught up with hardcore and other postpunk bands. She put out albums by Flyboys, Circle Jerks, the Adolescents, and China White. The label's best-seller ended up being the first Suicidal Tendencies album whose single "Institutionalized" got play on MTV. She did not focus on genre, putting out albums by death rock pioneers Christian Death.[39] Independent labels also sprung up in more out-of-the-way places. K Records was founded in Olympia, Washington, by Calvin Johnson of Beat Happening. K Records was known for putting out cheaper cassettes rather than vinyl. The label was a driving force in the riot girl movement and carried a variety of bands that did not fit neatly into punk.[40] He was not the only one interested in independent music production in the Pacific Northwest. He was friendly with Bruce Pavitt, who ran the fanzine *Subterranean Pop*, which later became Sub Pop Records.[41]

Punks around the world championed independent production during this period. Tony Nitwit, a punk from Holland, touted the number of local record labels there and stressed the importance of independent production. This included cost control for punk fans. In Brazil, a record shop in São Paolo sold locally and independently produced singles by punk artists. According to Fábio of the band Olho Seco, a Rio de Janeiro shop acted as a distribution hub for punk recordings, in addition to the São Paolo shop.[42] In Yugoslavia, the state-run label dominated music production into the late 1970s, but alternatives were available for punks there. They benefited from the ease of travel to neighboring Italy. Foundational punk band Pankrti crossed the border to record there. Later they recorded an album on the label set up by the Student Cultural Center of Ljubljana (ŠKUC).[43] Though technically still a state-aligned operation, ŠKUC became a center for art and alternative music in the Socialist Republic of Slovenia (a federal republic in socialist Yugoslavia) from the early 1970s. As such, they championed punk bands in the 1980s, including acting as a de facto label. They hosted international artists and supported fanzines, too.[44] During the 1980s, punks put a greater emphasis on producing recordings on their own, often sharing resources via zines. Many scene reports in zines like *MRR* wrapped up with an address soliciting letters, scene reports, or recordings to play on local radio stations such as one from Italy in December 1983.[45] O'Connor describes DIY punk labels as labors of love as much as a means of making a living, stating that "everyone who runs a DIY punk label also say [*sic*] they love the music."[46]

It was not as simple as starting a label, though. O'Connor defined distribution as one of the major problems for punks concerned with autonomous music production. This was critical if seeking to reach a wider audience outside of the local scene. During the 1980s, he said several independent distributors were formed to get punk albums to independent record shops, but getting those albums into more corporate stores proved difficult.[47] One alternative distribution chains was via person-to-person relationships forged in the pages of punk zines. Punks used scene reports as a means of telling others about their scenes and the bands there. They used these reports to build networks for sharing music. As such, these solicitations functioned as a sort of informal distribution network. As long as one could get a copy of a zine like *MRR*, one could find out about new punk bands and bands could access new listeners for their own music. Independent distribution of punk in the 1980s primarily reached independent record shops that specialized in harder-to-find music. In a 1982 issue of *MRR*, Ruth Schwartz, a DJ and wholesaler for Rough Trade, advocated seeking alternatives to the majors or subsidiary independents that had working relationships with major labels. She called labels such as Jello Biafra's Alternative Tentacles or Ian MacKaye's Dischord Records, whose business practices were more in line with the punk ethos, as truly independent.[48] Distribution continued to be an ongoing problem for punks in the 1980s. Outside of zines and shows, punks relied on a patchwork of independent distributors that got smaller label releases only into smaller record shops, with college radio providing the bulk of airplay for most punk and underground music. For a good decade, punks hashed out a means of catering to their communities in a democratic way to help preserve their autonomy and sense of identity. The goal was to produce music with integrity that had meaning and relevance to their community. Being able to make a living while doing so was the ideal, but not an all-consuming goal for many. Punk identity flourished as a subculture during the 1980s despite mainstream opposition, primarily because it was based on the production of a specific kind of music in a particular way.

Zines hosted debates about how one should go about supporting a local scene outside of the issue of label. A tension existed in these discussions over who benefited from for-profit institutions and about profiting from punk music. In a 1983 issue of *MRR*, New York punk Jack Rabid—founder of the zine *The Big Takeover* and drummer for the band Even Worse—lamented the state of the punk scene in the city in the previous year. He made the argument that to support the scene, one must do so financially. Paying for gigs, zines, and shows was critical to ensuring that the scene could continue. I quote him at length because his comments get to the heart of the debates happening in various punk spaces during this time:

> Want to put out a record? A magazine? Put on a show? Do anything of this nature? You need the capital to start. Once you've started you must at least make back your investment to continue, and if you make more than that, chances are the incentive will be there *to* continue, *and*, you are also in a position to turn that profit into more capital, that is *more* records, *more* good shows, and *more* magazines, etc., which is what people want. And, even if someone pockets the profits, he is just making his living (within reason of course), because he risked his money doing something you would benefit from, so you consumed it. He is providing you with a service. No one complains about greedy grocery store owners or greedy coffee shops just because these people want to make a living. (And certainly one doesn't go to a grocery store or coffee shop and say, "Hey, I know it's $5 a piece, but my friend and I only have 32 between us. Can you let us slide?" or "Let me in free" the way they do at punk shows.) (This is ruling out true greed, which is not profit, but instead exploitative profit, which is what is being confused here). People around here (and other punk scenes I've visited) seem to think they have a right to shows and other like services without supporting them, and seem genuinely shocked when the economic forces involved spit that notion back in their faces [meaning when punk-friendly venues stop booking punk bands or close] [*sic*].[49]

Rabid laid out the argument for putting money on the line to show support for the scene. The editorial received a response in the next issue of *MRR* from another local NYC punk, John Wendel. He took issue with Rabid's characterization of a boycott that a group called NY B.Y.O. had organized against a venue that booked hardcore bands, the Great Gildersleeves. They were concerned that the venue started checking IDs at the door and keeping out underage punks. Wendel argued that the new policy kept out a large number of punks. They also advocated for firing a bouncer who had harassed punks. He rejected profitability as important to the punk scene at all.[50] The issues around Gildersleeves and the NY B.Y.O boycott also found its way into the editorial section of Rabid's zine, *The Big Takeover* (see figure 3.2).[51] Rabid recounted how critical Gildersleeves had been for

Figure 3.2. Issue 12 of *The Big Takeover* zine, December 1982. (Used by permission of Jack Rabid)

booking punk bands from NYC and from nearby scenes like Boston. He attended the B.Y.O meeting after the boycott had been organized, proclaiming himself "unimpressed" by what he heard. He noted alternative venues for shows for younger punks. He spoke up, and the group decided to discuss the matter with the club and managed to win some concessions.[52] What matters for our understanding here is not that everyone agreed with how to best support the scene; rather, the overall goal of Rabid and Wendel was to create a self-sustaining scene.

In both the capitalist West and the communist East, punks sought to produce music and sustain their scenes on their own terms, although what those terms were was often debated among punks. Several models emerged to facilitate the production of sound records of punk music. This included person-to-person direct sharing of recordings, forming noncommercial labels, or commercial independent labels. In all three cases, autonomy was an important organizing principle.

Who's the *Real* Punk: Politics, Racism, and Other Ills

Although punk scenes during the 1980s were grassroots and democratic, these scenes dealt with various kinds of social problems. The expansion of punk scenes brought some unintended consequences. We saw how tensions occurred between first-wave and second-wave punks. First-wave punks felt that some of the second-wave punks were too aggressive and violent. But bands that played hardcore started to become the primary working definition of punk in the early 1980s. Violence was a recurring feature after the rise of hardcore and created controversies in punk scenes. Violence in punk spaces had multiple purposes. Slam dancing replaced pogoing at shows. It was more aggressive as more young men used the pit to take out their pent-up aggression. Slamming at shows in other American punk scenes was a point of contention into the 1980s. Jack Rabid expressed dissatisfaction with the prevalence of slamming at shows. He cited an article in *People* magazine when they called slamming "a new phenomenon." Rabid said that "slamming is insignificant. It's a few kids having fun."[53] Despite mainstream culture getting punk practices wrong, Rabid argued that punks themselves contribute to the mischaracterization of the slam dancing. He said, "how can I really blame the press, when at every show, the slammers, go too far, and end up distracting, hitting, annoying, and sometimes injuring people who just want to stand on the side and watch the show [*sic*]?"[54] He explained that in the New York scene some slammers attempted to "take over the whole club," which he found "not very considerate."[55] For Rabid this was part of a larger problem in New York, noting that "people here are getting more narrow minded by the day."[56] He saw this as part of a larger problem of stagnation in the New York punk scene. Rabid argued that slamming reflexively went along with what he thought of as the lack of musical diversity of hardcore bands and the unwillingness to experiment.[57] Slamming was more than just a violent practice. According to Dewar MacLeod, such acts of violence were also about "policing the subcultural borders" of punk scenes intended to keep out "latecomers" attracted by the media circus aimed at hardcore.[58] Not everyone came to punk shows to participate in that ritual, which made it controversial. Violence was seen as solving a problem but it also caused problems.

Another major difference between the first and second wave of punk rock was the role of politics, which became a subject of controversy. Some first-wave punks, especially in Britain, certainly made music with political content, such as the Clash. The Sex Pistols were created as an act of corporate disruption. The second wave of punk made politics a much more direct aspect of punk. The late 1970s was a period of growing mistrust in various institutions that had been built up during the first half of the Cold War, which drove political content.[59] According to Kevin Mattson, punk was one of the key locations of the 1980s Cold War–driven "culture wars."[60] That translated into embracing do-it-yourself modes of production and to more punks embracing politics in their work. In the United States and United Kingdom, the conservative governments of Ronald Reagan and Margaret Thatcher began the process of dismantling the strong state institutions that had been built since the Great Depression. They advocated for a more bellicose foreign policy. Both were prime targets for punk anger and parody. Other punks defended them and figures even further on the political right. The injection of political content ended up splitting the punk scene in the 1980s. This was often expressed via a stylistic or semantic split. Early on, there was a fair amount of cross-over between skinhead and punk culture, especially in the United Kingdom. Tensions emerged between the two groups as some skinheads embraced racial politics. They began to cause a greater degree of trouble than the usual brawling on the dance floor as they went after punks of color or bands that expressed left-wing political views.

Greater political content began to show up in punk zines with *MRR* leading the charge on a more political stance. Reagan and Margaret Thatcher were prime targets of punk anger. One antiwar op-ed in an early issue of

MRR included the use of corporate logos juxtaposed with fighter planes and bombs. On the second page was a picture of Reagan with the phrase "America knows a real turkey when it sees one."[61] In an *MRR* issue from 1982, New York punk Dave Insurgent of the band Reagan Youth called himself a reluctant anarchist.[62] The use of "Reagan" in his band's name was meant to invoke Hitler Youth of Nazi Germany.[63] Insurgent was the child of Jewish survivors of World War II. His mother survived the Lodz ghetto and his father was a Polish prisoner of war in the Soviet Union.[64] In 1984 the anarcho-punk band Crass created a fake recording of a conversation between Thatcher and Reagan. The State Department and CIA believed it was Soviet propaganda. The two-minute tape was actually spliced together from found sounds by Andy Palmer and Pete Right of Crass. In the March 1984 issue of *MRR*, there was a reprinted article from the *San Francisco Chronicle* quoting Palmer, who said that "it is a hoax, we intended it to be a hoax, but what we said in the tape we believe to be true." In the doctored tape, the leaders discussed blowing up a ship to justify further escalation in the Falkland conflict and nuking Europe to intimidate the Soviets.[65] In an 1985 issue of *MRR*, Sara Diamond wrote about connections between the "new right" and the intelligence community. It included references to the organizations like the Heritage Foundation (a right-wing think-tank), the *Washington Times* newspaper, and Thatcher. The cover of that issue was a collage of a little girl holding "God Bless America" sheet music, surrounded by imagery such as Reagan, Pat Robertson of the 700 Club, swastikas, and cameras.[66]

Political content in punk culture was evident not just in the capitalist West. Behind the Iron Curtain and in socialist Yugoslavia, state repression and problems in the economy were driving greater resistance to the state even as some communist countries undertook much-needed reforms. Mykel Board was interviewed in *MRR* in September 1983 about his time in the Eastern Bloc. He believed that West German punks had a harder time than those in East Germany.[67] East German punks had a different perspective. Tim Mohr's history of the East German punk scene, *Burning Down the Haus*, highlighted just how much of a threat the regime found punks. As such, it drove many in the scene to political activism.[68] During the 1980s, Punks became a major focus of the police and the notorious Stasi in the German Democratic Republic (GDR). One of the earliest punks form East Berlin, Major (whose real name was Britta Bergmann) saw her punk activities as inherently political.[69] Mohr said that "Major and her friends were being politicized by having fun."[70] They faced regular harassment and beatings by the police starting in 1980. Once the police beat other punks staying in Major's apartment so badly that blood was splattered all over the kitchen, even on the ceiling.[71] By mid-1982, Major was expelled to West Berlin after being arrested multiple times, the ultimate solution for someone unwilling to conform to the dictates of the state.[72] Punks, the police, and the Stasi considered punk to be political music. Before embracing a punk identity, Speiche would record songs off the radio and listen to them at his overnight job at a bakery. While listening to one of his tapes on an East Berlin tram, he encountered several punks who told him what he was listening to was "protest music."[73]

The reaction of the political arm of the police was telling, too. According to Mohr, they "had expected to dismantle the punk scene by April 1981. It had not worked out that way."[74] The Stasi got more deeply involved in watching the growing punk scene.[75] When punks started hanging out at churches as a safe space, Stasi snitches kept a close eye on them.[76] By 1983, the Stasi was increasing efforts on reining in the punk scene beginning with the band Wutanfall.[77] Even entirely acceptable political acts in the GDR were considered suspect when carried out by punks. Several attempted to lay a wreath at Sachsenhausen, a concentration camp site—an overtly antifascist gesture that was perfectly acceptable to the regime. But it led to a round of violence as the police attempted to shut the gesture down.[78] In 1983, a punk known as Pankow, whom the Stasi considered a punk leader, was being subjected to constant surveillance.[79] Mohr argued that the actions taken against punks by the state "far exceeded that undertaken against any other opposition group since the installation of dictator Erich Honecker in 1971."[80] Even so, some punks attempted to work within the system. The band Feeling B was a sort of party punk band rather than a political one. They applied for and received *Einstufung*, an amateur license that permitted them to legally play in clubs and bars across East Germany. Even so, Feeling B refused to play state-sponsored events sanctioned by the official youth organization known as the Free German Youth. Other punks still saw this as a betrayal of the rest of the scene experiencing high levels of state violence for their activities. But the members of Feeling B were interested in fun, not political action.[81] Many of the punks of this scene continued their political activities after reunification.

In many ways Yugoslavia was far more open than the Eastern Bloc countries. However, even here, punks dealt with overt acts of oppression. After a period of general toleration of punk in the late 1970s, the authorities became more inclined to crack down after the death of longtime leader of Yugoslavia, Josip "Tito" Broz, in 1980. Scene reports from Yugoslavia first appeared in *MRR* in 1983 and covered Ljubljana and Belgrade. The Ljubljana report by Dario Cortese discussed how the media in Yugoslavia was interpreting punk. It recounted an event known as the Nazi Punk Affair. Twelve punks had been part of writing a "Nazi manifesto." Cortese said that only two of them were arrested and spent a short time in jail. He argued that the media magnified the issue and many people now "viewed [punks] as 'scum of the earth'."[82] Cortese believed that the situation had improved since then. But other punks had also been associated with Nazis, and as a result had been on the receiving end of police harassment.[83]

Other artists tangential to punk were also targeted by the state. This illustrated a growing sense of nationalism in the country. The industrial band Laibach formed not long after Tito's death and soon became a pariah in their home republic of Slovenia. The use of the name Laibach was provocative, as it was the German name of the Slovene capital, Ljubljana (Germans had occupied the country during World War II). Between 1983 and 1987, the band was banned from using their name to perform in Slovenia.[84] The powerful and well-respected Partisan Veterans Group lobbied to get Laibach banned after a controversial TV interview.[85] This was due to their perceived attack on Slovene rather than Yugoslav identity.[86] Alexei Monroe argued that by 1987, the band had largely been accepted as part of the Slovene cultural landscape despite objections from the Partisans. They received full backing from student organizations in Slovenia.[87] They engaged in further provocative actions, such as when they compared the Serbian nationalist leader Slobodan Milošević to Hitler prior to the outbreak of war in 1989.[88] The emergence of Laibach unfolded against the backdrop of punk in Slovenia and Yugoslavia. Monroe argued that "punk's impact in Slovenia was as much ideological as musical."[89] Further, he argued that maybe "punk in Slovenia had even more concrete political effects than the movement in Britain."[90] The rise of punk unfolded across a landscape of rising nationalism in a socialist state that touted itself as living out the ideal of "brotherhood and unity."[91]

During the 1980s, some punks embraced political activism and connected it directly with their punk identity. Some found inspiration in *MRR*, which began publication in 1982. The first issue compared punks with the earlier counterculture of the hippies, and both were found wanting. It began, "what has two legs, hangs out on street corners, panhandles, sells dope, says 'That's cool, man,' is apolitical, anti-historical, anti-intellectual, and just wants to get fucked up and have a good time? A hippie? Nope, a punk!"[92] They looked different but acted in a similar manner. The op-ed discussed how the 1960s counterculture was co-opted and how punk began in part as a reaction to that co-option. However, history was beginning to repeat itself. The op-ed advocated for unity and true rebellion to mainstream culture. The important part of punk was not the image but the ideas that underpin the culture.[93] Later in that issue, the editors proposed organizing a punk contingent to join larger demonstrations for various political issues.[94] Despite their advocacy for a more political angle to punk rock, the editors showed the diversity of opinion on the issue of political punk. Maria had a conversation about whether punk bands with political messages were "telling people how to act" in a two-page conversation with several punks, including the drummer from the Dead Kennedys, Darren (D. H. Peligro), the singer from Bad Posture, Jeff Miller, and the lead singer from MDC, Dave Dictor. They ultimately agreed that everyone should do their own thing with regard to political content.[95] Although the tensions here were never fully worked out, a more political strain of punk emerged over this period for a variety of reasons both internal and external. The rebellious nature of the subculture attracted politically minded individuals. The realities of life in the 1980s also drove politicization of the scene.

The political content in punk culture included discussions on race, misogyny, and homophobia. The image of punk was relatively white and male in part due to how punk has been portrayed in the popular media over the years. Several documentaries that have been released since the 2000s reinforced that stereotype of punk. The 2007 documentary on the Chicago punk scene *You Weren't There* was an example. The earlier, more diverse nature of the scene apparently gave way to the more masculine hardcore wave in the early 1980s. In the late 1970s, the clubs that allowed punk to flourish were situated in the South Side of Chicago, a largely Black community. The punks of the early scene highlighted the diversity of the crowd at punk night at the gay club La Mere Vipere. John Molini and Mike Rivers managed Sounds Good Records and started the punk night at La Mere in 1977. The first night they opened the show, around a hundred people showed up, and it grew from there. Eventually, the club burned down. Later in the documentary, the hardcore bands interviewed tended to be white men. As hardcore took hold, many of the people involved in those bands seemed to reject other kinds of music. Lead singer of Naked Raygun, Jeff Pezzati, complained about Wax Trax! Records becoming the primary label for the Chicago industrial scene although the first release on the label was the punk hardcore band Strike Under.[96] Another documentary released the same year, *Punk's Not Dead*, tread similar ground. It focused on the underground hardcore bands, their relationship with the pop punk explosion of the 1990s and early 2000s. It also explored underground hardcore scenes of the early 2000s that were thriving outside the spotlight. Director Susan Dynner illustrated the very real split that emerged where some punks had mainstream success while others continued to adhere to the underground. Once again, the primary interviewees were mostly white men with D. H. Peligro of the Dead Kennedys as one of the few exceptions.[97]

Is this depiction of hardcore accurate? Women were not entirely out of the picture, even if their participation in the 1980s has been overlooked. First-wave punk was in part built by young women. Lauraine LeBlanc argued that women were just as critical to the construction of punk as a genre as were their male counterparts. Patti Smith, Debbie Harry, Jayne County, and Tina Weymouth all were key figures in New York punk, while the British scene included scene members like Jordan, Siouxsie Sioux, and Soo Catwoman as well as bands like the Slits, the Raincoats, and X-Ray Spex.[98] Women also built the LA and San Francisco scenes. Hellin Killer and the other members of the Plungers, Alice Bag and the Bags, Lorna Doom as bass player for the Germs, the early days of the Go-Go's, and Exene Cervenka (singer of X), among others, played important roles in LA punk.[99] San Francisco's scene had the Nuns and the Avengers, fronted by Jennifer Miro and Penelope Houston, respectively. LeBlanc called the Nuns and the Avengers the "premier" bands of that first-wave scene. They secured opening slots for the Sex Pistols in their final show, held in San Francisco.[100] Despite first-wave punk including many women, LeBlanc argued that young women struggled to make room for themselves in the "male-dominated youth subculture" of the 1980s. She said that "the [hardcore] punk subculture highly valorizes the norms of adolescent masculinity."[101] But young women in hardcore actively fashioned their own "strategies of resistance to both mainstream and subcultural norms of femininity."[102] But LeBlanc also noted that "the all-male bands of the West Coast became leaders in the new US punk scene. While some of these bands rhetorically espoused egalitarianism, self-respect, and social change, in reality, they edged women out of the scene."[103] She pointed to the San Francisco thrash scene and the Southern California hardcore scene, with their harder and faster music, not to mention slam dancing, which some took to extremes.[104] Although women were important figures in the first-wave punk scenes, young women found less acceptance as part of the second-wave punk scenes.

In LA, the first bands that made up the Southern California hardcore wave started to show up at the Hollywood clubs. These young, suburban teens, mostly young men, came from the suburban areas of Los Angeles, such as Hermosa Beach. Raymond Pettibon said of the Hollywood punks that "the original Masque scene in Hollywood were turned off by hardcore."[105] Brendan Mullen disagreed with Pettibon's assessment, saying that "many key people from the Hollywood scene embraced Black Flag and were totally supportive, even went out on a limb for them."[106] Audiences became more aggressive according to the roadie for Black Flag, Mugger. He differentiated pogoing, which meant "kids just jumping up and down, and if you fell, somebody picked you up," from slamming, where "kids [were] smashing into each other full-on football style with nobody picking you up anymore."[107] He called it "a bit more radical." He noted that a "football playing friend said he would just go to the Fleetwood [a punk club] 'cause it was all a football game to him."[108] He blamed people from the metal scene for the change rather than punks.[109] John Doe of X also noted this shift in temperament. He told one story of a punk named Mike the Marine swinging a ten-foot chain in the audience, which shocked Doe.[110] Punk started to attract people interested in violence, such as Jack Grisham of Vicious Circle and T.S.O.L. He said of the members of his first band that "Vicious Circle was more like a gang than a band."[111] Some women felt targeted by those enacting violence. Exene Cervenka said that when invited to play a birthday party, they stopped the show because the South Bay audience were throwing rocks. She said of the hardcore bands that "I stopped going to the hardcore shows because I was threatened too much."[112] They saw her as a "rock star," not a fellow punk.[113] During the rise of hardcore, slamming and other forms of violence became a regular part of punk practices. It had the effect of making some punk spaces less friendly to young women. Despite the harder edge to the hardcore scenes, some women stuck with it and made important contributions. Amy Pickering was part of the DC hardcore scene. She worked at Dischord Records for twenty-two years. She said in an interview that on the day she started, she removed a "no skirts allowed" sign that was hanging in the Dischord house.[114]

The US hardcore scene had no proprietary claim to forms of misogyny. Women were made to feel alienated in other scenes, too, and in other ways. UK hardcore band the Destructors had a single called "Jailbait" on their debut album, *Exorcise the Demons of Youth*.[115] Ian Glasper included few bands with women in his book. One was Beki Bondage of Vice Squad. In the overview of the band's history, Glasper called her vocals powerful but also described her as "punk's first real pin-up."[116] The Ejected at first sought a young women to provide vocals for their first band, which Glasper described as a practical decision because they were seeking "an edge" in a crowded field. Before settling on Dawn Payne as their singer, they auditioned several other young women who were subjected to sexual advances by guitarist Jim Brooks. Once Payne joined the band, Brooks and Payne dated. When it turned out that Payne had little interest in monogamy, Brooks and bassist Gary Sandbrook left Dawn Patrol to form the Ejected. Their debut LP, *A Touch of Class*, included three "punkettes" in heels and leather skirts lined up beside the band.[117] Like Payne, many young women in punk were subjected to this kind of double standard. Women in punk rock's first wave pushed to be seen as more than eye candy. In hardcore, women were once again being positioned as sex objects for a largely male audience, while being held to different standards of behavior than their male peers.

Racism has always been part of the production of popular music, and punk was no exception. People of color were important figures in the history of punk rock. The exploitation of Black musicians and the music associated with Black culture have been well documented.[118] Many of the proto-punk bands were influenced by R&B and blues which were some of the genres that influenced rock music. Amiri Baraka called rock "a flagrant commercialization of rhythm & blues."[119] Punk did not start as an all-white subculture. It developed alongside hip-hop, which was incubating in the Bronx at the same time. The connections between hip-hop and punk in New York during the 1970s have gotten attention, but not nearly enough. Jeff Chang noted how by 1981, hip-hop pioneer Afrika Bambaataa was bringing his ground-breaking sound to punk clubs in Lower Manhattan. Chang argued that this was a major step in taking hip-hop global.[120] Fab 5 Freddy also forged connections between various scenes around New York. Freddy brought Bambaataa to perform at a Keith Haring exhibit in 1981. He curated an art show at the Mudd Club, a favorite performance space of the postpunk No Wave scene. Chang described it as an era of "cultural crossover" between punks, postpunks, the hip-hop scene, and the art world.[121] For their parts, some punks were interested in aligning with hip-hop. In 1981 the Clash invited Grandmaster Flash and the Treacherous Three to open for them during their Broadway residency. They invited graffiti artist Futura 2000 to spray paint a backdrop during the show and perform with the band. Not everyone who bought tickets to see the Clash were appreciative of their efforts. Some members of the audience threw garbage at the opening acts, which infuriated Mick Jones. "We wanted to turn the crowd onto something," he fumed. "They're too narrow-minded to open up to something new."[122] In both the United States and United Kingdom, punks of color were part of the landscape during the first wave.

Neon Leon came up in the previous chapter. There was also Poly Styrene of X-Ray Spex in the United Kingdom.[123] In LA, Alice Bag, the daughter of Mexican immigrants, started The Bags, which regularly played at the Masque.[124] Just as women were an important part of the first wave, punk scenes included people of color, not just white people.

As hardcore became the dominant strain of punk rock, it became more associated with white men. Biracial James Spooner, the director of the *Afro-Punk* documentary, described how his punk identity was often put at odds with his Black identity in the foreword to the book *White Riot*. On his first day at a new school, he met another Black punk, Travis, who took Spooner under his wing. They had lunch with a white punk, Mason, who used racist language to describe other Black students at the school. Spooner felt like on "that day I was asked to make a choice: punk or black."[125] Stephen Duncombe said that during the 1980s, "punk offered a space for young whites growing up in a multicultural world to figure out what it meant to be White."[126] His band White Noise put swastikas on their faces with eyeliner. They were inspired by first-wave punks who used swastikas as a symbol that could "resist appropriation and commodification; it's political content was meaningless to us. But not for all of us, not entirely. Our lead singer was flirting with something else."[127] The singer later became a white supremacist.[128] Punk was in part about bringing new meaning to white identity that could and did go either way. Rock critic Greil Marcus wrote about the problems of "othering" in the LA punk scene. Othering is the process by which certain groups are imagined to be outsiders based on race, gender, or sexual orientation. It has been used to naturalize a white, Eurocentric identity and exclude nonwhites from much of public life. This process was described in the work of Edward Said in his book *Orientalism*.[129] In the United States, that tactic has often been employed to exclude Black Americans from the definition of "American." W. E. B. Du Bois wrote about that process in *The Souls of Black Folk* in 1903. In it, he explored the concept of double consciousness that was a common experience among Black Americans. "One ever feels his two-ness—an American, a Negro; two souls, two thoughts, two unreconciled strivings; two warring ideals in one dark body, whose dogged strength alone keeps it from being torn asunder."[130] Marcus showed that some punk songs othered people who were not white, male, and straight. He criticized the band X for employing a racial slur in their song "Los Angeles." Hardcore bands Black Flag and the Adolescents were the main focus of his critique, along with the Penelope Spheeris's film *The Decline of Western Civilization*.[131] Although Marcus liked the sound of their music, the Adolescents, "if their songs are to be believed, hate everything," he noted.[132] He quoted his colleague Robert Christgau, who argued that punks in 1977 turned their ire against the establishment. In contrast, LA punks had turned on "the other, the powerless—and that is a stance no less American than a happy barbarism."[133] Rather than rebel against the powers that be, some punks embraced aspects of the power structure and punched down at marginalized people.

British punks also had racism in their scenes, which led to a split. One of the earliest examples of punks engaging with racism was with Rock Against Racism. This movement was not led by punks, but many punks actively participated in the concerts that supported the organization. In 1976, Eric Clapton and David Bowie made controversial statements about racism and fascism. Clapton publicly supported Enoch Powell, a controversial politician who promoted anti-immigrant positions many interpreted as racist, as a Member of Parliament.[134] Bowie made statements about the "benefits" of fascism. Photographer and artist Red Saunders was a member of the radical theater group Kartoon Klowns. He showed the group Clapton's comments. In response, Saunders and Roger Huddle wrote a letter and sent it to the music presses. When *Melody Maker* printed it, they received hundreds of letters in response. Saunders and Huddle decided to stage a show with the help of blues singer Carol Grimes to promote antiracism in British culture. This became the first Rock Against Racism benefit. "It snowballed quickly," Saunders recalled. Around the same time he was covering the first-wave British punk bands for *New Musical Express* (*NME*). He began to include punk bands on the Rock Against Racism benefits. At one in Hackney Town Hall, reggae band the Cimarons played with Generation X. At the end, "everyone jammed together."[135] Soon the movement spread, with people across the country holding their own benefit shows. Some were held in places where racial tensions were running high, such as in Leeds. Saunders said, "that was an area where the Nazi National Front were really strong."[136] These concerts inspired other demonstrations and organizations, such as in Lewisham, where activists launched the Anti-Nazi League in 1977, which partnered with Rock Against Racism for a carnival that was initially expected to bring out 10,000 but ended up drawing 100,000 people.[137] Second-wave punk bands played Rock Against Racism gigs. Abrasive Wheels from Leeds played a Rock Against Racism show at Leeds Polytechnic in 1977 not long after their debut. Later, they were excluded because they were deemed too aggressive musically.[138] The movement even went international with a Rock Against Racism concert organized in Toronto in 1981.[139]

Many punks participated in these antiracist activities, but not everyone agreed with the aims of Rock Against Racism even if they agreed with antiracism. In a zine published in 1980, *New Crimes*, editor Jah Ovjam penned a criticism of the movement. He quoted a 1979 Crass song, "White Punks on Hope," which criticized "white liberal shit." Ovjam said he was in support of the movement until he examined the literature put out by Rock Against Racism. He felt that they only offered "patronising generalisations every bit as racist as much of the NF/BM [National Front and British Movement] propaganda currently floating around."[140] He pointed to Black-organized protests against racism in Depsford as a counterexample of "needing" white help. Ovjam objected to the top-down nature of the approach,[141] which he believed was infantilizing to already oppressed Black Britons. Other objections were simply grounded in racism. In his history of the genre Oi!, Garry Johnson called it a mix of punk and skinhead culture, that was "working class thru and thru [*sic*]."[142] Johnson connected Oi! directly to ska which had long been popular with skinheads. Oi! became the music of choice in this skinhead revival. Sham 69 was the first of these bands, followed by the Angelic Upstarts and Cockney Rejects. Punks also listened to these bands, according to Johnson.[143] Music journalist Gary Bushell began covering punk for *Sounds* magazine in the late 1970s. According to Ian Glasper, he was a key figure in the popularization of Oi!. Bushell started the Gonads in late 1976 and wrote extensively on the Oi! scene as an insider.[144] By 1981, the genre became associated with racism even though some Oi! bands had played Rock Against Racism gigs. Glasper noted that bands like the Business rejected being categorized as racist. However, the cover of the one of the earliest Oi! compilations included Nicky Crane who Glasper called "a notorious nazi skinhead."[145]

Not all Oi! bands and fans were racist, as many also embraced the two-tone wave of ska popular at the same time. But racists saw an opportunity in punk and Oi!. Eddy Morrison was an organizer for the National Front (NF) for Leeds and had a taste for punk rock. NF was a racist organization. Morrison recognized the organizing power of punk music. He said that punk "would be a 'powerful weapon for anyone who could turn it politically'."[146] When some punk and Oi! bands embraced Rock Against Racism, Morrison was propelled to action. "We could either condemn Punk or we could use it. I chose the latter option and started a spoof fanzine called *Punk Front* which featured a NF logo with a safety pin in it. To my surprise, *Punk Front* was a huge success."[147] As a result, NF dominated the Leeds punk scene with bands like the Ventz and the Dentists. They organized a response to Rock Against

Racism, known as Rock Against Communism. NF had 400 members by 1978 due to their engagement with the local punk scene.[148] People took notice. An article in *NME* discussed the *Punk Front* zine's anti-Semitic claims such as that the Anti-Nazi League was "controlled by Jews." The article also discussed an incident in Leeds involving Sham 69 fans. Their supporters were angry that the band had pulled out of a live show to be on the British TV show *Top of the Pops*. So they showed up at the venue singing "Tomorrow Belongs to Me" from the musical *Cabaret*, a song performed by young Nazis in the play. This led to a brawl with the remaining bands and their supporters.[149] Morrison supported the formation of Rock Against Communism in 1978. Some claimed it was "apolitical." However, it was formed specifically to "show up Rock Against Racism for what it is—a puppet of the extreme left."[150] Violence associated with the racist right spread from Leeds. The Lurkers, Penetration, Crass, and the Satellites all had shows disrupted that year by skinheads aligned with the NF and the British Movement.[151]

Even if not all who participated in Rock Against Communism were racist and anti-Semitic, it was associated with the now global neo-Nazi skinhead movement. Despite claims of anticommunism only, the Anti-Defamation League, an antihate organization, defined Rock Against Communism as racist and anti-Semitic. Rock Against Communism became an umbrella term for pro–white supremacist and neo-Nazi bands.[152] Racist bands with ties to Rock Against Communism appeared in Australia in the early 1980s. Blogger Slackbastard said that the first Australian Rock Against Communism band was Quick and the Dead from Perth.[153] Kurt Brecht of the band D.R.I. remembered "a handful" of neo-Nazi skins at a show the band played in Canberra, Australia.[154] Communist East Germany became a haven of right-wing skinheads in the 1980s because of the government's fear of punk. The East German government began paying attention to skinheads and neo-Nazis as early as 1983. But they maintained that Nazis could not exist in such a staunchly antifascist country, despite there being an estimated 800 skinheads in East Germany by the late 1980s. This was even as many skinhead gangs like the Ostkreuz skinheads actively identified as neo-Nazi and became vocal supporters for reunification with the West.[155] By 1987, the tensions between the skins and punks came to violence. The Ostkreuz skins went on the offensive. One night, they attacked a crowd leaving a show for a West Berlin New Wave band held at a church. The Stasi and police let it happen.[156]

American punks also struggled with the skinhead problem. In DC, skinhead violence contributed the break-up of Minor Threat, according to drummer Jeff Nelson.[157] Henry Rollins recalled how skinheads mugged Black

Flag's sound man in 1986. Thor Harris of Swans recalled how skinheads in Austin tried to take over shows for bands like Scratch Acid. There were problems with skinheads even in progressive Berkeley, California. They began showing up to the 924 Gilman Street club in 1988. Dave Dictor of MDC said that "we literally had open clashes for an hour and a half" one night they showed up in 1988.[158] One of his friends came away with a broken collarbone that night.[159] The punk scene in Portland, Oregon, also struggled with neo-Nazis during the 1980s. A recent podcast, *It Did Happen Here*, explored how Portland went from a haven for white supremacist skinheads to a far more progressive city. Ethiopian immigrant Mulugeta Seraw was killed by racist skinheads. His death became the fulcrum of the transformation of the city.[160] Police had done little to end the racist violence in Portland. Instead, activists, including some punk and Skinheads Against Racial Prejudice, made racists feel far less welcome on the streets of Portland.[161] The modern antifascist movement in the Pacific Northwest, colloquially known as "Antifa," grew out of that work.[162]

Punk scenes also struggled with homophobia. The hardcore scene that emerged in the Lower East Side in New York City in the early 1980s later became a "violent and insular scene," according to Ben Nadler.[163] In this scene, punk intersected with spirituality and a violent strain of skinhead culture. Bad Brains moved from Washington, DC, in 1981, which Nadler argued "changed the entire direction of New York City punk rock."[164] In addition to harder and faster music, they brought along their Rastafarianism.[165] The British anarcho-punk band Crass also influenced this scene with their embrace of anarchist philosophy. Both bands had a major influence on the worldview of Dave Insurgent, among others.[166] Insurgent's songwriting showed an interest in spirituality and anarchism. He joined an organization called the United Freedom Fighters, started by HR of Bad Brains. Nadler said that "the Bad Brain's drift into Rastafarianism is probably what opened the door for religiosity in the punk scene."[167] HR also espoused some homophobic and misogynistic views at times. Other bands embraced spiritual beliefs, including the Cro-Mags and Agnostic Front, who adopted aspects of Hare Krishna.[168] This greater interest in spiritual movements became coupled with a taste for violence. A very specific kind of skinhead culture became popular after 1984, associated with Cro-Mags and Agnostic Front. This scene had a strong focus on violence as a means of creating unity, Nadler argued.[169] The New York punk scene did not struggle as much with racism, however.[170] This did not hold for homophobia. The problem with skinheads committing acts of violence against gay men in the city got so bad that at one point a gay magazine had an image of two members of the Cro-Mags with the headline "GENTLEMEN . . . BEWARE OF THESE TWO SKINHEADS." Nadler described the skinhead scene as right wing but antiracist due to the scene including Latinos such as Roger Miret, the Cuban-born lead singer of Agnostic Front.[171] Misogyny, racism, and homophobia were issues that shaped punk scenes during the 1980s.

Punk Panic

Crackdowns against punks on both sides of the Iron Curtain during the 1980s also politicized the scene. If violence, misogyny, homophobia, or racism created rifts that split punk scenes, punk panic brought the scenes together. It created a stronger, shared sense of alienation among punks in different places that helped consolidate a translocal punk identity. An underground counterculture identity was built in part by the shared cultural activities that punks undertook—a constructive set of activities. This was in part a reaction to the antipunk attitudes of the recording industry. Punk panic also made punks more disdainful of mainstream culture. As such, punk was both constructive and reactive.

Depending on the type of government, punk was dealt with by different sets of institutions. In the capitalist West, rebellious punks were understood as a private family matter that should largely be dealt with via private institutions, such as churches and medical professionals. Schools and police were expected to bring rebellious punks in line. The federal government seemed to have little say in such matters. The only caveat to that was the attempt censor popular music in general via the Parents Music Resource Center. This was an organization started by Tipper Gore, then wife of Senator Al Gore, among other Washington insiders.[172] During this time, the Dead Kennedys were sued over their use of an H. R. Giger painting in the *Frankenchrist* album artwork.[173] American mass media reinforced this messaged of a "privatized" response to the punk "threat." In communist states, punk was a topic of conversation at Communist Party conferences. Public institutions were called on to control these problematic youths, from local police to national organizations charged with keeping public order. This split in how the capitalist West and communist East dealt with social problems goes back to the early days of the Cold War. Uta Poiger discussed the contrasting approaches in West and East Germany in the 1950s in her book *Jazz, Rock, and Rebels*.[174]

The East German and Yugoslav governments cracked down on their punk scenes to various degrees. These were robust, state-based reactions to youth cultures that were understood as a threat to the social order, and hence to the state. Punk panic started early in the British punk scene and influenced it in the United States. The dismissive US media attitude toward the Sex Pistols in 1978 was shaped by the British media's view of the band. British tabloids like the *Daily Mirror* were key factors in driving outrage against the band back in the United Kingdom.[175] As discussed already, Malcolm McLaren's strategy of driving the media outrage cycle had consequences for the band, who suffered physical retaliation from the public. They were not the only punks to face violence in public. Viv Albertine of the Slits recounted the violence aimed at the band's singer, Ari Up. Twice she was stabbed by strangers. She told Alexis Petridis in the *Guardian* that "people didn't know whether to fuck us or to kill us . . . we put them off kilter."[176] Paul Cobley noted how British punks outside of the major cities dealt with regular violence against them. "The kind of punk subculture that existed in the provinces . . . did not have to work as hard [as punks in London] to provoke onlookers."[177] One punk in the city of Wigan "reports the way that 'the entire deck of a passing bus gave me "the finger" as I set out to see Slaughter and the Dogs at Wigan Casino'."[178]After a Sex Pistols gig was canceled at the last minute on September 3, 1977, punks from nearby towns who had lined up for the show were attacked by a group of "Northern Soul" locals (fans of that genre of music). The violence put several punks in the hospital.[179] Though celebrated now, at the time punk was associated with acts of violence, argued Adrian Goldberg and Jim Frank in 2015.[180] Much of that active violence was aimed at punks rather than committed by punks. Still, many in the British public believed that punk itself was inherently violent and thus in need of a strong response from the police and other authorities.

As US media followed the British media's line on punk, the US public began to agree with their British counterparts. In LA, the "St. Patrick's Day Massacre" in 1979 marked a turning point in local punk history. Previously, police and punk interactions had been relatively easygoing. But on that evening, a punk show at the Elk's Lodge saw a major response from the LAPD. They deployed riot gear and arrested punks after a complaint was called in about someone throwing a bottle in the stairway of the building. From that point on, there were regular incidences between the LAPD and punks. The size of the crowds at punk clubs in LA steadily grew, and some of the younger punks acted out more aggressively. Black Flag had their shows overbooked, which led to police coming in to clear the streets of angry punks.[181] It was a big enough problem that Black Flag wrote a song about: 1981's single "Police Story" referenced tensions between the police and punks.[182] This was mirrored by a general nationwide "punk panic" on American mass media, which helped reinforce these overreactions by authorities. Daytime talk shows and nightly news programs began producing stories about the punk phenomenon. Much of this coverage was negative and sensationalistic, similar to the "satanic panic" and "stranger danger" themes in this same period. *The Phil Donahue Show* brought punks into discussion with critics of punk like Serena Dank, a psychologist who founded a support group known as Parents of Punkers.[183] Television dramas like the medical procedural *Quincy, M.E.*, produced episodes about the "dangers" of the punk subculture.[184] Donahue kept returning to the problem of punk rock in 1986, when he interviewed members of the New York hardcore scene. Natalie Jacobson was a panelist. When asked what drew her to the hardcore scene, she pointed out that the music drew her to the subculture. Once again, such points were ignored in favor of the more sensational concerns such as how the punk panelists and audience members were dressed. Another panelist, Jimmy Gestapo of the band Murphy's Law, told Donahue that they were just looking to enjoy themselves. He also said that they were friends playing for friends. The focus on music, community, or political messaging was consistently glossed over in favor of more sensationalistic concerns.[185] Jacobson also appeared on an episode of the *Morning Show* that same year. Regis Philbin gave the punks a bit more time to explain themselves. Jacobson accused Donahue of putting words in their mouth on their appearance on his show. Another panelist on Philbin's show called punks a family that takes care of each other. Philbin brought in a psychologist, Joy Browne, to offer some analysis of the movement, which was a bit more nuanced than Dank's views of punks. She asked them what they were rebelling against, and the punks bristled a bit at this notion. Attempts to get the kids to give her a single sentence to describe "hardcore" failed to get any traction, as they argued that hardcore was not something that could be easily summed up.[186]

The news media focused on the danger that punk supposedly posed to the general public. A search on YouTube yields several old news reports from across America. Not all local news reports made punk out to be a threat. In one video from Oklahoma, City 5 Alive covered the scene there in 1980. The report on "New Wave," as it was introduced, began with reporter Bill Vincent walking next to a pond with some ducks serenely floating behind him. He told the audience that Oklahoma City "is a quiet little place." But he then intones in an ominous voice that "under the cover of darkness, while the city sleeps, there's a force that is growing, unnoticed and unhindered. Growing until it is too late to stop it. And becomes . . ." The phrase "punk rock" was projected on the screen against the Oklahoma City skyline. Vincent said that he has no interest in defining it for the audience, but instead lets the punks at a show do it for him. The tone of the report seemed to be attempting to match the tone of the interviewees, which was often sarcastic.[187] Others stories were less ambiguous. A clip from a 1980 news report included Black Flag and interviews with police who claimed they could not discern slamming from real violence. The band defended the shows and blamed the police for the violence.[188] Another undated video (from the early 1980s) from CNN warned that punk was "not just a new look, but a pathway to drugs." The clinical psychologist asked to explain the scene to the audience claimed punk had "no social value" compared with earlier youth subcultures.[189]

A particularly notorious entry in antipunk news reports was called "We Destroy the Family," named after a song from Fear's debut album, *The Record*. The LA station KABC aired the documentary on the LA punk scene in 1982 and apparently won an award for it. It argued that the punk subculture was far more problematic than earlier forms of rebellion. The reported admitted that Fear's music was satirical. Still, parents might worry over their kids embracing punk rock. The Hodges family was interviewed as an example of punk tearing families apart. The parents expressed dismay that Ron Jr. and his sister, Rhonda, considered themselves punks after previously being a football player and cheerleader. For their part, Ron Jr. and Rhonda were upset that their parents were regularly violating their privacy because of their concern. Ron Jr. said, "we never had their trust." Mother Caroline said she was experiencing "diminished love" for her children as a result of their unruly behavior, which included drinking. The father denied that he was projecting his desires on his son. In the third uploaded clip, Serena Dank makes an appearance hosting a group therapy session for punks and their families. For her part, she explained that she was not trying to "stamp out punk" but trying to bridge the gap between parents and children. If punks were sometimes nihilistic, there might have been a good reason for that. One young punk tells the group that death by the atomic bomb was preferable to dying by mustard gas, indicating that perhaps he was seriously struggling to make sense of the geopolitical situation in the early 1980s. In the conclusion, the reporter gave little consideration to the concerns the wayward youth expressed in their interview.[190] Such news programs helped promote an erroneous or at least one-sided punk views of punk.

Punks all over the world were subject to social rejection, ridicule, and political pressure from the state, and it created a greater sense of shared identity that crossed national boundaries. As a sense of disillusionment with both capitalist and socialist modernity descended on the youth of the 1980s, some sought a new kind of self-selecting community to pledge their allegiance. But the overreaction by authorities might have partially been driven by increasingly political content of punk rock. Punk in the 1980s seemed to worry those in power enough to at least rail against it and at worst deploy state power to suppress it. Antipunk sentiment in the United States steadily waned after the end of the Cold War, though elements of it hung around into the 1990s. The crackdowns in capitalist and communist countries helped reinforce a translocal punk identity.

During the 1980s, punks became more committed to creating an oppositional identity to mainstream culture. Scene reports from all over the world started to appear in American punk zines. Those who wrote scene reports discussed shared cultural practices, such as going to shows, clothing styles, struggles against authorities, opposition to mainstream culture, problems getting attention from the music industry, and events in punk history. They would put their addresses at the end in the hopes of getting punks from other scenes to make connections to organize tape trading, letter writing, sharing zines, and even getting bands to come play. These shared realities worked to bring hardcore punks in line with each other. The hardcore bands from North America tended to set the tone and were seen as the progenitors of this shared cultural identity. These discussions found in the page of punk zines and in person between self-described punks helped define hardcore punk.

There were several ways that punks created and reinforced this translocal community. First, there was a growing emphasis on independent, artist-centered production of sound recordings that circulated by independent distribution channels. Some of this was eventually colonized by the major labels. But for a time, punk labels were able to find a niche outside of the mainstream recording industry and its distribution channels. The critiques that punks brought to the table about the mainstream recording industry eventually ended up "going mainstream" and shaping how artists today think about the production of music and their rights in the industry. Second, punks made community via the music and zines they produced and circulated globally, as well as by their local activities, which mirrored the activities in other scenes. Many actively discussed and debated the meaning of punk in these spaces. As such, it became an evolving discussion shared across national boundaries that helped create a imagined community world-wide. During this period punks sought to build their translocal communities by independently producing music and the building an identity based on those activities. These communities were locally enacted but with ties that stretched around the world, facilitated by a grassroots punk counterpublic that tended toward democratic structures in which inclusion rested on active participation.

Chapter 4

New Underground Scenes and the Rise of Alternative Music

1990 to 2000

Scene: Portland, Oregon, Backyard Punk Show, May 1992

Since age fifteen, you've been attending weekend shows in the backyard of this punk house known as The Pitz. This was partly because many of the local venues that hosted punk bands were not open to all ages. The shows here are usually local bands, but the occasional national (or a couple of times, international) touring acts sometimes play there. It took a while before the crowd of mostly white boys accepted you. Some instantly made you feel welcome, such as Spastic Steve, who always defended you against the racists and misogynists. Others were not so kind, and Steve was not always there. One guy demanded you list off the punk records you had in your collection when he first met you. Another leered each time he saw you in a crowd and tried to corner you in the kitchen once. You heard racial slurs at times when you made your way through the house. Some of that had changed, since many in the scene had come together to make sure that kind of thing was stomped out after the death of that Ethiopian guy a few years ago. Pretty much all the racist skins who had been part of the scene had been made to feel unwelcome, sometimes violently. Since then, the scene had become a bit more attentive to racism in Portland, even if some racist sentiment still lingered.

But not so much with misogyny. There were few women at shows, and the ones that came (like yourself) were not always treated as equal members of the scene. Women were seen as girlfriend material, rather than as active members on their own merits. Of course, many of the men who held this view listened to plenty of bands with women. Other young women were coming to these shows and you had found each other. Many of you wanted to do more than just passively consume punk, you wanted to actively participate. Last year, you and your friend Jackie started a zine that you put out bimonthly. You had about fifty local readers and sent out another fifty in the mail. You'd also begun to organize shows at The Pitz with bands you met via your zine. You and Jackie moved in with Dotty. You started a "riot girl" meeting night once a week. It was a great space to share radical ideas and music that put women front and center. But after hearing Revolution Girl Style Now! *by Bikini Kill, Dotty insisted that you do more than just organize and talk. She wanted to start a band to express the anger and frustration of life in America.*

Tonight will be the first time the band performs in front of a crowd. You brought a good half of the current audience with you, a rowdy bunch of angry young women. As you begin your set (the second band in a night of six bands), you call the girls to the front. They come up as you kick into several originals ("Damaged Girl," "Kicking Melons," "En mi quinceañera") and then a cover of Dead Kennedys ("Nazi Punks Fuck off"). Partway through the Kennedys song, Rooster, a tall antiracist skinhead, shows up. Clearly irritated at the lack of testosterone in the pit, he waded into the fray, busting heads, purposefully going against the flow. He aimed a direct blow to your friend Lucian's face, and then attempted to shove down Janie. An enraged Dotty shouted behind you "enough you fuck." She dropped her guitar with a wave of feedback, launching herself into the air straight at Rooster's head, fist raised, connecting to the side of his head. They both went down to gasps, applause, and finally arms reaching down to pull the two part, with tough old Rooster weeping and Dotty angrily kicking her feet in his direction.

Feminine Protection	The Dishes	Bikini Kill	Bratmobile
Pansy Division	L7	Spitboy	Bread and Circuits
Sleater-Kinney	GG Allin	Billy Bragg	Dicks
Tribe 8	General Idea	Team Dresch	The Replacements
The Outnumbered	The Offspring	Rancid	Guttermouth
The Frogs	Fifth Column	God Is My Co-Pilot	Vaginal Davis
G.L.O.S.S.	Nirvana		

The previous chapter explored the 1980s underground punk scene. In the early 1990s, there were new splits in punk scenes. After more than a decade of being dominated by white men who identified as straight, some new subgenres emerged in the late 1980s and early 1990s. Riot girl combined the DIY ethos of punk rock with the third wave of feminism.[1] Queercore gave voice to LGBQT+ punks who often felt alienated from both gay and punk scenes. Both built social networks via zines and music. The bigger split came with a new mainstreaming of punk rock. The success of grunge bands from the Pacific Northwest kicked off a new round of corporate interest in underground music. The 1990s saw the erosion of the independent underground that was now celebrated as visionary by the mainstream culture industries. But a new wave of young people embraced punk and the punk mode of production. After coming to punk via Nirvana or pop punk bands like Green Day, many wanted to become a part of the underground punk scenes they had started to hear so much about. Grace Elizabeth Hale argued that the 1990s did not sound the death knell of indie culture. Instead, the energies generated from music scenes in places like Athens, Georgia, brought about a "cultural autonomy imagined as local and egalitarian," that became an "everyday practice" for many.[2] While many independent labels were bought up by majors, a whole new generation of young people ended up enacting the punk mode of production in the digital age. As Penny Rimbaud of Crass noted in the trailer for a documentary about the anarchist band Chumbawumba, "I don't think we should be modest about the effects we had."[3] The struggles over maintaining independence during the "alternative" 1990s brought punk into the mainstream industry more firmly, and large corporations certainly profited from underground cultures. But the concept of building an independent culture made its way into the mainstream, influencing how the cultural producers thought about what they made and how they made it. Moreover, punk persisted as an underground phenomenon right up to the present day.

Riot Girl and Queercore: Make Punk Inclusive Again

In the previous chapter, we saw how hardcore punk scenes became dominated by white, straight young men. By the late 1980s and early 1990s, women still sought to be included in these scenes. During the 1980s, this issue was discussed in the pages of punk zines. In the December 1985 issue of *Maximum Rocknroll* (*MRR*), Robin Vote penned an essay about gendered violence in the United States. She called it a "war against women being waged in this country." She laid out statistics of violence against women and discussed other ways that a toxic masculine culture affects the daily lives of women. She also explained some of the ways men are negatively affected by this culture. She argued that the Reagan administration played a role in further eroding freedom and opportunities for women through their policies. She addressed what she saw as the failures of feminism in previous years. It was an article that bridged the second and third waves of feminism.[4]

MRR received responses to Vote's essay for at least the next three issues. In issue 32, V. Verdi took exception with her positions in regard to equality. He argued that the genders were "fundamentally different." Furthermore, men were not really free, as he believed women manipulate men with their sexuality. He concluded that the "sexual revolution made things worse." He also believed that social problems were not just caused by men being in political power, pointing to Prime Minister Thatcher and vice presidential candidate Geraldine Ferraro as a counterexamples. Erikka, listed on the inside cover as one of the "shitworkers" of the zine, responded directly to Verdi. She compared his take on women having "special status" under the "traditional" gender roles as the same as enslavement for African Americans in the antebellum South. Barbara Quinn was a new reader who picked up the previous issue specifically because of the cover story. To further explore feminism in punk, she recommended a Boston-based band called Feminine Protection.[5]

The conversation continued in the next couple of issues. In issue 33, E. Jones felt that Vote's essay was an unfair attack on all men. Rueben Dann was initially angered by the essay, but took some time to process it before responding. He still felt she merely repeated unfair stereotypes about men while ignoring bad behavior in women. But they seemed in the minority in that month's letters. Others were appreciative of the article and the conversation it started. Lili Feingold, a women's studies graduate, liked the article enough to share it with her professors. Jodi Gran chimed in that she hoped people believed Vote's arguments. A member of the DC-based Dischord House Dug also expressed support. He wanted punk to be part of the solution, as it "gave men and women a golden opportunity to overcome bullshit in their lives." But he asked "why do we continue to play games with ourselves." Vote responded to the letters received so far. She noted that the people who disagreed with her position did not actually engage with her points but made assumptions about what she was arguing. She noted that they accused her of making blanket statements about men, when in fact her article addressed how men were also harmed by misogynistic culture.[6] In issue 34, European punk Maus Gossens noted how the punk scene was getting more "masculine." He wanted punks to look at their own behavior in their local scenes for evidence of that. Rikki Sender from LA felt that Vote's article was not radical enough and merely reified a biological view of gender, "what [French literary theorist Roland] Barthes would call a 'myth'." They also took exception with the violent images in the article, which reinforced the idea of women as "objects of physical abuse." In contrast, George Monk appreciated the connection drawn between violence against women and military violence.[7] The heat of the debate found in the letters section about Vote's essay indicated that these issues were found in punk scenes all around the world. If there was an increasing macho attitude among some men in various scenes, it would stand to reason that punks like Vote felt a need to address the issue with the general punk public.

Although it was clear that discussions of feminism caused controversy, punk scenes became locations for the emergence of the feminist riot girl movement by the early 1990s. Women were part of the first wave of punk. Iain Chambers said that with punk, "a space for women as active protagonists within the production of music."[8] Many young women were drawn to hardcore punk in the 1980s even as they struggled to make space for themselves among the misogynistic attitudes. Lauraine LeBlanc noted that with regard to being in the action at shows, "hardcore and thrash bands had a decidedly masculine emphasis and girls were discouraged from entering the pit."[9] LeBlanc noted that the split between hardcore and new wave included women being pushed into the new wave category.[10] Despite the real obstacles thrown in their path by the harsher tendencies of the hardcore scene, "pit girls," as LeBlanc dubbed them, persevered and embraced hardcore and wanted more than just to "be a girlfriend."[11] Although riot girl came out of punk scenes on the West and East Coasts of the United States, LeBlanc noted how riot girl was considered a "break-away faction" of that scene.[12] She argued that women in punk who embraced the riot girl ethos ended up feeling "marginalized [in punk], indeed, have formed their own subculture now quite distinct from punk."[13] LeBlanc said the young women she interviewed for her book might have objected to that characterization of their relationship to punk and to riot girls' place in it.[14] Even as they were pushed to the margins, women refused to be pushed out of the scene entirely. Riot girl pioneer Kathleen Hanna of Bikini Kill recalled being obsessed with "going to punk shows" in addition to "weed" and "drinking alcohol."[15] Riot girls embraced the ideas that animated many punks—that they could make their own music like other bands they saw at shows. Carrie Brownstein of Sleater-Kinney recalled how seeing local punk bands in high school contributed to her decision to start a band. "Here

I could get close enough to the players themselves. I could see how the drums worked with guitars and bass, I could watch fingers move along the frets and feet stomp down on effects pedals."[16] She noted that "it seems obvious, but it was the first time I realized that music was playable, not just performable."[17] Janice Radway argued that although many of the first riot girl bands were from Olympia, such as Bikini Kill and Bratmobile, the real spark was when members of those bands moved to DC. Women from these scenes sought to "organize conversations among 'like-minded female punks' by calling meetings at a space in Arlington, VA occupied by Positive Force, an organization aiming to channel punk disaffection into action and community service."[18] This spread up the East Coast. In a New York City scene report in *MRR* in April 1993, the author noted that riot girls and Positive Force were using the space offered by Reconstruction Records to hold meetings.[19] The movement continued out west as well. That August, K Records put together the International Pop Underground Convention in Olympia. K Records founder Calvin Johnson said they dubbed it a "convention" primarily because the artists and fans had "an agenda." According to Mark Baumgarten, they "couched the invitation in a call to action." It was "a celebration of the underground for the fans and bands that, for the most part, weren't interested in 'making it'."[20] Women who were part of planning the event demanded their own spaces, as they felt like women were being marginalized. Olympia feminist and artist Stella Marrs was one of those women. She recalled that one of the events was screening cartoons. They planned to show cartoons that had boys or men rather than girls or women as the main characters, as the latter would alienate men.[21] Marrs and Tobi Vail of Bikini Kill insisted on the necessity of a women-only night at the convention even though it added an additional day to the schedule.[22] Baumgarten characterized the women's night as a success, but Radway argued it was controversial within punk circles.[23]

Stella Marrs was a pioneer of a feminist punk attitude that many punk women would embrace in the coming years. Emily White noted that Marrs opened a store, Her Girl City in Olympia in the 1980s. It became one of the epicenters of the movement. She sold clothing and artwork, White noted. She also embraced public performance, such as when she organized the 50 Girls 50 States/Women for World Peace in 1986. White found it a remarkable performance. This "punk debutante parade" had fifty women dressed up in DIY dresses that represented each state and the concept of world peace. They marched down the streets of Olympia. One participant described it as "political march and craft show."[24] Marrs told Baumgarten that she was "driven to make this mini-universe of girl production."[25] She was also a major influence on Calvin Johnson, who founded K Records.[26] Like other waves of punk, art and music intersected as forms of expression for people in the scene. Following in the footsteps of Marrs, many other women went on to express themselves in bands and in an active zine culture. Zines gave riot girls a space to express themselves and share their views with each. White also connected the rise of these feminist zines to the rise of punk queercore zines.[27] Women were taking space in the more traditional zine culture of punk rock. Beginning with the September 1991 issue of *MRR*, a call was posted asking girls and women to write in to discuss problems they face as women.[28] In the December 1991 issue, Christy Colcord started an ongoing column in *MRR* dedicated to discussing feminist issues. In her first essay, she said that women were active in punk but "were viewed as uncommitted." But she argued that many young women put in a great deal of work for their local scenes. They edited zines, ran radio shows, made fliers, and booked tours, often for their boyfriends' bands. But when women expressed interest in being in a band themselves, they were often ridiculed. Some bands had misogynistic lyrics. In the marginalia for the essay, she reprinted the lyrics of a Guttermouth song, "Just a Fuck."[29] Leslie from Ontario shared her experiences in her local scene. The reason she became part of the scene was the exhilaration she felt attending her first punk show. She recalled, "I was angry, and an important part of this anger came from my frustration of being female in a world of invisible rules and fences. I could never succeed at fulfilling the roles of passive and submissive girlfriend, daughter or girl-citizen." The hardcore scene gave her some space from the norms of society. She was still met with some of the same oppressive expectations. She called the partnerships she had with punk guys "scarily traditional." These expectations caused her to move "further and further away from the hardcore community." She hoped to get reinvolved if the situation improved for women in the scene, but she expected to find the same sexist attitudes. Leslie suggested a list bands with "femayl members," including Bikini Kill, L7, and the Avengers.[30] In February 1992, the editors asked if the community would like the expansion of what they were calling "*MRR* 'Girl Stuff,'" soliciting material from both men and women.[31]

Letters came in response to this new section on women in punk. In February 1992, Tina Spatford from Ontario hoped the article would show men in the scene that "we can have strong opinions and beliefs." Jane Hseu of Laguna Niguel, California, discussed misogyny in American culture, such as the reaction to the allegations made by Anita Hill during the Clarence

Thomas Supreme Court confirmation hearings. She dismissed the media depictions of Hill as lying to further her career as "absolutely ridiculous."[32] Many responses reflected the frustrations that punk women felt in society at large and within the punk scene itself. Allie from Hadley, Massachusetts, described herself as a riot girl and complained about the "feeble minded" January column and wanted a continued specific focus on women. By way of contrast, Andria Lisle of Memphis, Tennessee, was upset about what she called "separatism" in the magazine. From her perspective, if women were feeling left out of their local scene, the solution was to "persevere." She drew on her own experiences in Memphis and touted her new label, Sugarditch. People took her seriously because she was serious in her work for the local scene.[33] Some believed that *MRR* was being hypocritical in printing this feminist content. Sean from Laguna Beach called *MRR*'s prochoice stance hypocritical because they allow ads from artists like GG Allin, known for violently assaulting women. They also had ads by the band Slapshot, who he described as racist. Meanwhile, he complained that a prolife material was being rejected.[34] The columns in the zine were not free of sexist attitudes. In Jeff Bale's April 1992 column, he posted a "punk-rock cheesecake" recipe that included "1 bodacious, verbose blonde in a bikini." He suggested that you "take the remaining 1/2 bottle Amaretto and use it to ply the blonde into helping you wile away the 2 hours of cooking time."[35]By the early 1990s, riot girl was being seen as the stand-in for feminism in punk scenes. In a *MRR* interview with Sarah Zimmerman of the zine *Sour Mash*, she discussed the impact of riot girl. She said that the movement was generating more contributions from women in punk scenes. "When I got into the scene 3 years ago you were the girlfriend of a boy in a band. I wasn't at the time (my best friend was) and that's how we got into it."[36] That was less common after riot girl.[37] In a letter, another Sarah, who had a zine called *Action Girl*, discussed the backlash against riot girl. She argued it stemmed from people misunderstanding what it meant. She said, "Riot Grrrl has transcended its original roots to become an inspiration to girls internationally to take charge of their lives."[38]

Not all discussion of riot girl was positive. Mykel Board's column in February 1993 addressed the rise of riot girl. He began by sarcastically advocating for self-castration, and it went downhill from there. He argued that women in modern society had the real power, as men were merely driven by their sexual urges. He compared men identifying as feminist as "a Negro wanting to get into the Klan!" He also insisted that women who "positioned themselves" as victims of sexual assault actual had the real power in society.[39] Board's positions were called out. Donny the Punk responded to his belief that rape victims were in control, bringing up victims of sexual assault in prisons. He said, "Mykel, I got news for you: those who suffer rape in jail and are subsequently inducted into a form of sexual slavery which ends only with their release from incarceration do *not* 'call the shots.'" But Lisa from Bellingham, Washington, was inclined to agree with at least part of Board's argument, calling "Riot Grrldom" "counterproductive." She was also "troubled" by his dismissive attitude toward date rape and sexual harassment. "The majority of date rapes and harassments aren't ever reported. A lot of women, especially younger ones, keep the rape to themselves and just let it eat away at their brain and take away whatever self respect they once had."[40] In the same issue as Board's anti–riot girl rant, a classified ad ran for a "Riot Boy Zine" out of Nashville, Tennessee. It said, "Anti-revolution contributions needed immed. 'Well, what are we supposed to do without jackets while we mosh? Everybody knows punk klubs [*sic*] don't got not coat racks!'[*sic*]."[41]

This focus took a toll on those at the forefront of riot girl. Many considered Hanna of Bikini Kill to be the primary leader of the movement, just as they focused on riot girl as representative of all punk feminism. Hanna published a zine, *Bikini Kill*, and formed a band of the same name. She became the focus of much discussion in punk circles and in the main-stream media. Her high profile shaped her approach to music production. Her solo project, The Julie Ruin, was an attempt to put some distance between that media scrutiny and her work. It was also a means to fight her own objectification. "Some people think that anybody who is ever in the public eye becomes an object that they can banter about like you're not a person," she told Daniel Sinker of the zine *Punk Planet* in 1998.[42] In his introduction to the interview, Sinker indicated two problems for riot girl as a movement and for Hanna personally. First was how the mass media sought to commodify riot girl, which some in the movement believed would be a problem early on. He quoted one young woman as saying that the movement was important to her and she feared it being exploited. But just as problematic was the reaction from other punks in the pages of various zines. He noted how Hanna and others were labeled "'bitches,' 'cunts,' 'man-haters,' and 'dykes'" by editors of other zines. "Kathleen Hanna received the brunt of this criticism, often being harassed verbally at shows, yet she appeared unshakable."[43] Sinker pointed to *MRR*'s lack of attention to riot girl and emo as a primary reason he decided to start *Punk Planet* in 1994.[44] He believed that there was a concerted effort to exclude riot girl from the category of punk rock.

Not all women in punk considered themselves to be riot girls, even those who embraced feminism. In the November 1992 issue of *MRR*, LS Downing wrote in from Washington state to note that she did not considered herself a riot girl, but "this idea of men being oppressed really has me perplexed . . . I just want to walk down a dark street at night without fear of rape."[45] In June 1993, Daisy Rooks of Bethesda, Maryland, wrote to discuss a review of the *Eureka* fanzine from the April 1993 issue that covered "Chicks up front." The reviewer called it a riot girl subgroup. She was frustrated that a joke between her and her sister had spun out of control and that she was being associated with riot girl.[46] In her column in *MRR*, Karin Gembus discussed riot girl and what she perceived as their "separatist" stance. She understood the need for a safe space to grapple with misogyny. She also believed that men needed to be included in the conversation if anything was going to change for the better. She addressed the DC riot girl boycott of her band Spitboy. She called it "high school politics." "I cannot understand how the notion of disagreeing on a couple of principles, mainly the idea of separatism, has turned into a Spitboycott. To me, we are working towards a similar end. We can simultaneously disagree and understand." Generally speaking, she said, "I find it difficult to comply with the rigidity of dogmatic platforms."[47] In an *LA Weekly* article about riot girl, Emily White noted that many of the women in the scene were white and from a middle-class suburban background.[48] As such, whether fair or not, riot girl gained a reputation for speaking only for white middle-class women and their concerns. Nonwhite women in punk had different experiences, however. In her preface to Michelle Cruz Gonzales's memoir, *The Spitboy Rule*, Mimi Thu Nguyen discussed the impact that the feminist and anarchist band Spitboy had on her. They were one of her favorite bands. She said that she was excited by "its [punks] promise to fuck shit up."[49] Spitboy typified that promise.[50] Gonzales, a Mexican American women in a primarily white punk scene in the 1980s and 1990s, struggled with her growing feminism as the white, middle-class riot girl movement was seen as the primary mode of "punk feminism." She found punk feminist ideas outside of riot girl. Ian MacKaye was one such influence. She called Fugazi's song " 'Suggestion' one of the best feminist punk songs ever."[51] As discussed already, Spitboy found itself at odds with riot girls in DC. At a show there, Gonzales told the crowd that they were not riot girl when asked

if they wanted women up front at a show, a common practice at riot girl shows at the time. "I pulled my vocal mic up to my mouth, 'Before we play, we'd just like to say that we don't expect men in stand in the back of the room. We're not a riot grrrl band.' "[52] Lead singer Adrienne Droogas attempted to soften the perceived slight. But Gonzales recalled how that one comment "forever altered our relationship with one of the most influential women's movements in the punk rock scene nationwide and created an uneasy rivalry."[53] This division made her second-guess her artistic choices. The time came to choose artwork for their first seven-inch, and one image floated was a photograph of graffiti that said "kill white bitch." Gonzales, said the phrase "doesn't really apply to all of us," which got no response from her white bandmates. In the end, they went with a less controversial image.[54] Spitboy's 1994 release on Allied Records, *Mi cuerpo es mio* (My body is mine) caused controversy. One unnamed riot girl accused the band of cultural appropriation for giving the album a Spanish title. Gonzales quipped that "apparently my body was invisible."[55] At the time, the punks in the Bay Area were still "trying to be colorblind," so her race was rarely discussed. She was also known by her nickname, Todd Spitboy, rather than Michelle Gonzales, so those who only heard the album and never saw the band live might have thought she was a white man.[56]

By the late 1990s, many advocated for punk spaces to be more welcoming for women, not just riot girls. In his column for *MRR*, Jose Palafox of the band Bread and Circuits gave a city-by-city account of the band's 1999 tour. In Columbus, Ohio, they attended a three-day music fest called the More Than Music Festival. That year it was a "women-centered punk fest." The proceeds benefited the Central Ohio Abortion Access Fund and included a variety of informational panels in addition to bands playing. Some punks showed up for the Pride march, held on the last day of the festival. Palafox noted that "many [of the punks] really wanted to talk, listen and learn." He said some argued that allowing women and people of color spaces of their own was "self-segregating," to the detriment of punk unity. Palafox hoped that he had evolved since the early 1990s and the high point of riot girl. He said "some of us refused to listen and called them 'feminazis' and some of us were forced to take notice and really think hard about how our words and our actions affected others."[57] The festival planners did not necessarily identify themselves as riot girls. This speaks volumes to how many punks were seeing feminism as an important issue in all punk circles. Riot girls had connected their activism to punk, which built a model for future activism that anyone could embrace. Punk could

"reform" from within rather than needing to be torn down completely. The reform or tear down and rebuild has long been a debate among activists. Kathleen Hanna struggled with the issue of tearing the system down versus pushing for reform. With riot girl, she sought to create an alternative model for future changes to cultural communities and society in general. Although she was more interested in revolutionary action over reformism of the capitalist system, she argued that "but unless we build models—even small little Lego ones in our houses—we're not going to figure out how that's going to come about."[58] Riot girl was that little Lego house that modeled new gender relations in punk, which she and other riot girls hoped would translate to spaces in society.

Riot girl was not the only movement that sought greater space in punk scenes. Members of the LGBQT+ community had been part of punk since the beginning. Some of the earliest spaces that hosted (maybe tolerated) punks were LGBQT+ spaces. Much like with women in punk in the 1980s, many members of the LGBQT+ community sought to carve an "out" space in punk communities around the same time. But if members of the LGBQT+ community had long been part of punk scenes, why did some feel the need to create space for their own advocacy? Jayna Brown and Tavia Nyong'o discussed the history of queercore, a subgenre of punk from the late 1980s to the 1990s. They noted that the term "punk" itself had queer roots. It was an old word, used as far back as Shakespeare's era to mean a female prostitute. By the twentieth century, it evolved to mean a younger man selling sex to an older one. "Punk and queer are a match made in the gutter . . . punk is queer," they concluded.[59] Some punks also addressed aspects of gay life in their music. The British Celtic punk band the Pogues' 1985 song "The Old Main Drag" was a sympathetic story about male prostitution and drug abuse.[60] Queercore bands sought to carve out a distinctive space in punk.

In 1997, Michael du Plessis and Kathleen Chapman wrote about the queercore movement in the journal *College Literature*. Pushing against the tendency to use the term "queer" as a generic term for an outsider, they argued that it meant a specific subcultural identity. They said that as used by members of the subgenre " 'queer' did at one time indicate membership in a specific group in very particular ways. We understand 'queer' to have been the marker for a distinct subculture, whose members emphatically distinguished themselves from dominant straight culture and lesbian/gay parent culture alike."[61] Much like punk itself, they noted the creation of "fanzines, records, clubs, music, videos, and some novels even" as a "queer

counter-public sphere in opposition to the institutions of the lesbian and/
or gay public sphere already in existence."[62] They created "new positions in
the field of cultural production."[63] The queercore scene in punk emerged
because some felt alienated by the gay rights movement that emerged in
the midst of the AIDS crisis. Chapman and du Plessis said that "queercore
introduced or created a new position ahead of 'consecrated' . . . lesbian and
gay cultural and political monopolies."[64] The projects they cover drew from
across musical genres. They highlighted the band Coil, a industrial band
from the United Kingdom founded by Peter Christopherson of Throbbing
Gristle and his partner, Jhonn Balance.[65] The authors also discussed the work
of Vaginal Davis, an African American queer punk writer and performer.
Her work included references to hardcore bands like Black Flag and elec-
tro-industrial acts like Meat Beat Manifesto.[66] Punks in queercore sought
to differentiate themselves from what they considered the mainstream gay
scene. Jon Ginoli of Pansy Division felt out of place at many gay clubs
because he disliked the music they played. He struggled with what he saw
as a double life during this time. "My gay life and straight life were almost
totally separate; I didn't wish for such a distinction, but overlap was minimal."[67] He only met a few other gay punks during his five years with band
the Outnumbered while living in Champaign, Illinois. His experiences there
and later in LA did not include active discrimination against members of
the LGBQT+ community from punks. Rather, he had a sense of distinction
between the communities during the 1980s. He called his straight friends
"accepting," but he felt alienated from the gay scene.[68]

Queercore as a distinct punk subgenre emerged full force in the late
1980s. Cultural critic Sam Sunderland placed its origins much further back
with the Toronto band the Dishes. They formed in 1975 and managed to
get a week-long residency in 1976 at the Beverly Tavern.[69] The band broke
up by 1978, but their influence, and that of their contemporaries General
Idea, lingered on in the form of their "upfront sexuality."[70] Don Pyle, who
was in Crash Kills Five and Shadowy Men on a Shadowy Planet, noted
that "the roots [of the early punk scene] were very gay. Even the bands
that preceded the punk thing, like Martha and the Muffins, came out of
a gay-slash-arts sensibility."[71] Sunderland argued that "the Dishes built the
foundation for the punk scene in Toronto, establishing its rules and social
mores."[72] He argued that Toronto had a greater "prevalence of gay culture"
than London or New York.[73] These roots influenced the later queercore scene
in the mid-1980s. Bruce LaBruce, a filmmaker, came to Toronto because of
bands like the Dishes. There he met G. B. Jones and they began the *JDs*

zine. Jones was a member of the band Fifth Column. LaBruce said they embraced punk because "we felt rejected by an increasingly conservative gay scene."[74] Other cities in Canada, such as Calgary, had gay punks. Art Bergman from Vancouver remembered that "we had art bands, and artists playing guitars, and mixing with the gay scene and the punk scene. It was all mixed together into this great amalgam."[75] Still, Sunderland advocated for the uniqueness of Toronto's scene. "In other parts of the country, it appears to have been one of sympathetic tolerance. . . . In Toronto, the relationship was deeper and more symbiotic; punk might have ceased to exist without the involvement of groups like General Idea, but punk flourished because of it."[76] Ginoli cited the Toronto queercore scene as inspiring him to form Pansy Division. He landed a job at Rough Trade San Francisco in the mid-1980s. There he discovered the queer punk community he sought through two zines, *Homocore* (see figure 4.1) out of San Francisco (started by Tom Jennings) and *JDs* out of Toronto. Ginoli characterized Fifth Column as "low profile" with regard to the band being "out," but that might just have been his perspective from the United States. He discovered some of his new coworkers at Rough Trade were out with their music, such as Donna Dresch of the band Team Dresch.[77]

Other punk scenes included LGBQT+ punks. In Adam Rathe's oral history of gay punks in *Out* magazine, Gary Floyd of the Dicks said that Austin in 1979 "always had lots of queers in the scene."[78] Contrary to Sunderland, writer and artist Dennis Cooper (writing from an American perspective) believed the origin of queercore was in 1985.[79] Despite these claims of inclusion, some felt there were limits to straight toleration of gay punks. Ginoli said he never felt active discrimination from his straight punk peers. But he also felt like he needed to obscure his sexual orientation to the larger punk public. In songs from his band the Outnumbered, he hinted at his sexual orientation. But his friend Dena warned against making it explicit as "we'd be known as 'that gay band,' immediately consigned and filed away."[80] Some punk bands were less welcoming and mocked the LGBQT+ community. In 1989, Rough Trade put out an album by the Frogs, who described themselves as a "gay supremacist" band. It turned out the band was made up of straight men pretending to be gay. Ginoli characterized them as "exploitative, making fun of the idea of being gay."[81] In a telling turn of events, they later wore blackface for another project. Still, Ginoli felt that the Frogs actually showed that the world might be ready for some out and aggressive gay punk rock music. In 1991, British punk-folk artist Billy Bragg had a hit single, "Sexuality," which expressed acceptance of the gay community, which Ginoli appreciated.[82]

Issue #1   September 1988   *limited reprints* May 91   TJ $1.00 / $2.00

Figure 4.1. Issue 1 of *Homocore* zine, September 1988. (Used by permission of Tom Jennings)

The LGBQT+ community in punk scenes were becoming more organized and connected by the late 1980s. As with other punk scenes, zines were a key element in bringing this community together. Queer zines predated queercore punk zines. In the wake of the Stonewall riots in 1969, there was one called *Faggots and Faggotry* from New York City. It was put together by Ralph Hall, who was a member of the Gay Activists Alliance. A wave of zines that catered directly to the gay community in Canada followed. Another similarly named zine, *Fags and Faggotry* from London, Ontario, published an interview with John Lydon in its August 1981 issue. In 1984, a new zine from Toronto began publication called *Dr. Smith*, which was produced by a woman named Candy.[83] According to the "Queer to the Core" oral history, the *Dr. Smith* zine "made up that there was a queer-punk underground" that predated the queercore scene.[84] It had a major influence on Jennings, who started the *Homocore* zine. He came to Toronto after discovering *JDs* zine. He also found Candy's zine via Bruce LaBruce. He started *Homocore* after arriving back home in San Francisco. He was influenced by his experiences at an anarchist gathering he attended in Toronto in the late 1980s. He said, "we were networking, realizing there are all these weirdo punk, queer, street culture people who are not particularly interested in the macho stuff."[85] At the same time networks were being built during the Toronto anarchist gathering, he noted that the "macho, dickhead punk-rock boys were off overturning mailboxes and getting into fights with the police."[86] Zines like *Homocore* and *JDs* received letters from all over North America, especially from small towns, according to Jena Von Brucker of the zine *Jane and Frankie*.[87]

Even more radical zines started to emerge, such as the incendiary *Bimbox*. This zine appeared in the early 1990s and took aim at "state of the gay and lesbian community," such as advocating for gay bashing against more conservative elements in the LGBQT+ community.[88] By the early 1990s, LGBQT+ punks were ever more vocal and making space for themselves in punk rock scenes. In 1991, Bill Hsu wrote about the queer punk fanzine convention SPEW. He argued that queer punks often felt marginalized by both gay communities and punks. "Letters from queer-identified punks began appearing in punk fanzines in the mid-80s, usually provoking responses from homophobic punks."[89] Hsu argued that the *MRR* "Sexuality" issue from April 1989 was "lip service" rather than a serious attempt at inclusion of LGBQT+ punks.[90] He said that "very few people from the traditional hardcore crowd were at SPEW for example. Instead, more of the attendees were from the 'new allies' of the queer punk movement: ACTUPers, Queer

Nationals, and radical queer artists and performers. Apparently, despite all the rhetoric about liberal/progressive politics, the hardcore establishment still has to come to terms with its homophobia."[91] The queercore zine culture sort of preceded people forming bands. These circulated widely and helped spread the idea of queercore. Vaginal Davis argued that zines built the foundation of a queercore in New York, including zines such as *My Comrade* and *Pansy Beat*. In Chicago, she noted the importance of Steve Lafreniere and "his clique," who put together the convention Hsu visited in 1991.[92]

Music eventually became the primary means of sharing the queercore scene and worldview, according to Rathe. Matt Wobensmith, who created the *Outpunk* zine and record label, said that zines created a "network of queer punks," but "they were creating a scene that existed in glimpses. In order to be realized, it needed bands."[93] Some who made up queercore discovered the connection between a queer identity and punk rock music early. Joanna Brown, who cofounded Homocore Chicago, discussed finding an issue of *New York Rocker* in her small town in Louisiana, where she discovered lesbian punks. "I realized, maybe it was OK to be queer if you were into punk."[94] Leslie Mah hitchhiked to San Francisco from Colorado to see punks and the gay scene. "A friend came back from San Francisco and said, 'Men were holding each others' hands in the street . . . it's so disgusting,' and I said, 'I wanna go'."[95] Mah went on to form Tribe 8.[96] In 1991, Ginoli recorded a demo and settled on the name Pansy Division for his new project.[97] He saw Pansy Division as his way to contribute to the wave of 1980s and 1990s gay activism around the AIDS crisis, which he said was "cultural rather than overtly political."[98] His first experience playing was at a benefit for Queer Nation, a gay activist group, where he "cleared the room." He performed at an underground gay club called cabaret Klubstitute, where he first met members of Tribe 8. He called them the "perfect female parallel to what I was trying to do."[99] Donna Dresch worked with Ginoli at Rough Trade. She moved to San Francisco from Olympia in 1989, eventually living in the *Homocore* warehouse.[100] Homocore Chicago was founded by Joanna Brown and Mark Freitas in 1992, which according to a 1995 article from the *Chicago Reader*, became a long-term project. They quoted Brown as saying that "it was just to entertain ourselves."[101] The first show they put on was with the feminist hardcore band Fifth Column at a gay bar. Over the years they hosted "dozens of shows each year," including bands like Bikini Kill, Pansy Division, Tribe 8, God Is My Co-Pilot, and Vaginal Davis. They even took the night on the road, organizing shows in New York and San Francisco.[102]

San Francisco—whose gay community has a long and vibrant history—became a center of the queercore scene according to Rathe, with bands like Pansy Division, Team Dresch, and Tribe 8.[103] Ironically, this was partly due to the rise of white supremacist activities in cities across the West. Brown and Nyong'o noted that white supremacist groups attempted to recruit punks and skinheads in northern California cities like San Francisco. "Queer and trans punks refused to concede ground, and so created scenes of their own."[104] There was crossover with the riot girl movement. Matt Wobensmith was directly influenced by riot girl. Jody Bleyle of Team Dresch said both scenes had feminists. But Donna Dresch said that they did not identify as riot girl since she felt "it was mostly a straight movement."[105] As late as 2002, a queercore festival was planned, Homo A Go Go. But the 2000s saw the movement "fizzling out," according to Dresch.[106] As Lynn Breedlove of Tribe 8 noted, "a long as we're not shutting up, we're still pressing the queer punk ethos."[107] Even today, there are bands inspired by the ethos of queercore. The band G.L.O.S.S. (Girls Living Outside Society's Shit) got together in Olympia, Washington, in 2014. Ari Perezdiez interviewed them for the May 2015 *MRR*, describing them as "future kids playing music from the past." Their music was "hardcore jams chronicling a trans/femme/queer existence that are as relentless, angry and inspiring as the people playing them."[108] The band promoted a radical queer agenda. When Perezdiez asked about the support they received from straight cis people, they were more than a little dismissive, calling the excitement "a narrative" of "boring, liberal values of 'inclusion' and all that being put on us."[109] But vocalist Sadie argued that "we're an intentionally intolerant band . . . we're not trying to cater to mainstream queer agendas."[110] She also argued that assimilation for trans people just meant that you ended up compromising your message. "Then you are actually making things worse for queer people."[111] G.L.O.S.S.'s debut album was called *Trans Day of Revenge*. Their unwillingness to compromise with the straight world puts them firmly in the category of queercore.

Both riot girl and queercore had a long-term influence on punk. These scenes made it clear that punk rock was not just for straight men, but for anyone who embraced it. The DIY nature of punk rock laid down a template for these scenes to emerge and shake up the status quo. They took the more radical elements of punk in the 1980s and sought to employ them to create their own spaces and challenge gender norms and those of sexual orientation. The scenes also revealed splits in the punk scene, but it also showed how powerful hardcore punk could be at creating space for activism. Hardcore punk survived women and the LGBQT+ community carving out space for themselves. Some within and outside these movements saw them as separate from punk. I would argue that they helped make punk more inclusive.

Alternative Nation

A more disruptive and divisive event of the 1990s was the rise of "alternative" music as a mainstream phenomenon. Nirvana's surprise success changed the relationship between independent music of the 1980s and the mainstream music industry. The mainstream music press became less antagonistic toward underground and independent music like punk, as did the recording industry. The first proto-punk bands were inducted into the Rock & Roll Hall of Fame in the 1990s. Major labels offered contracts to independent artists, including punk bands. There was a round of industry consolidation as larger labels gobbled up more commercially oriented independent labels. The pressure that resulted from the new attempt to co-opt punk would split the punk underground again. But it also reinforced the underground scene, as new kids discovered punk and other underground music thanks to the success of Nirvana and other bands.

Nirvana was considered the vanguard act of the alternative music movement. The popular narrative goes that the band's success with "Smells Like Teen Spirit" came out of nowhere and took the airwaves by storm, very much like Elvis or the Beatles before them. This trope was even found in the underground press of the day. *Propaganda* magazine ran an article about the band by Rene in the spring of 1992. She noted how their hit song took aim at the "Nintendo generation," who was entirely focused on sex and consumerism rather than music with anything critical to say about the world.[112] Another example of this was from the Nirvana biography by Brad Morrell. In his introduction, 1991 was positioned as the year punk either broke or fully sold out, depending on one's point of view. There was a dividing line before and after the mainstream success of Nirvana.[113] Many believed that there was a pure underground scene defined by punk rock and a tainted, exploitative mainstream industry. Nirvana's smash hit changed that. Others had a bit more nuanced take on the band's success. Gina Arnold argued that Nirvana built on the success of various indie rock artists from the 1980s. The band's success was built up prior to their single's popularity. She argued that "though MTV and Nirvana's record company, Geffen, like to claim that they 'created' Nevermind, in fact the album sold genuinely well from the second it was released, entirely on its own merits."[114] She argued that their success was "reflecting the public's true will and not just that of radio and the record industry."[115] Unlike "Mariah Carey, Def Leppard, Skid Row," Nirvana's music was an authentic expression of the underground that had been studiously ignored from the days of the Sex Pistols.[116] Despite showing how the band built their own success, there was still a division at play. Arnold's goal was to tell the prehistory of Nirvana, which included the punk underground. She said, "punk rock changed my world, and thanks to Nirvana, it's now changed a lot of other people's, too."[117] Overall, her experiences in punk were grounded in a similar generational narrative that has been told about the Beatles. She compared her experience with the Sex Pistols at Winterland to that of a friend's with the Beatles.[118] But Arnold still assumed that Nirvana was the dividing line that no independent bands had crossed before then.

Arnold was not wrong in noting that Nirvana opened a door for a new generation of underground music to move into the spotlight and shape the industry. But Nirvana was most certainly not the first band to come up through the underground to achieve some measure of mainstream success. Some managed to do so on independent labels. MTV had played at the edges of independent music for several years by that point. College radio had been incubating what became known as alternative music in the 1980s. Several other bands had breakout hits from smaller labels before Nirvana. After years of touring and several albums under their belt, R.E.M. was breaking through to the mainstream by the mid-1980s. In April 1985, they played a concert with Alex Chilton in Athens, Georgia. Around 12,000 people showed up for the free concert. Hale said that when "Peter Buck hit the first three notes of 'Feeling Gravity's Pull' on his black Rickenbacker, it felt like every single member in the record-breaking crowd of between 10,000 and 12,000 roared."[119] The success of the band helped put the small college town of Athens on the map as an important music city, a reputation it retains today. MTV helped build that reputation. That year, Bill Cody and Tony Gayton arrived from LA to put together a documentary about Athens and its eclectic music scene.[120] *Athens, GA: Inside/Out* included R.E.M. and other Athens bands. It premiered in Atlanta and was shown on MTV during its monthly program *The Cutting Edge*.[121] Independent labels were making inroads onto MTV early on. IRS (the label that had the Go-Go's and R.E.M.) curated the show on the network starting in 1983. According to Craig Marks and Rob Tannenbaum, the program aired the last Sunday of each month in 1983. *The Cutting Edge* was hosted by Peter

Zaremba of the Fleshtones, a garage rock band from New York.[122] Michael Stipe likened the show to the "island of misfit toys." He said that "all the miscreants and the outcasts and the punks and the fat girls and the kids with bad skin and the queers could gather together around this universe. Pre-internet, and before that instantaneous sharing of information and knowledge about music or about art, and that was it."[123] It included artists from the punk underground like the Minutemen and Henry Rollins doing his spoken word performances.[124]

The weekly show *120 Minutes*, which played independent music, followed in 1986. Dave Kendall, who had arrived in the United States from the United Kingdom on a student exchange program, was looking to stay in the country legally in the mid-1980s. He was a music journalist and was able to parlay that into a job writing for *120 Minutes*. The program further opened the floodgates of underground music to a wider audience across middle America. Kendall later became the VJ for the show when he "wrote himself into the script." Dave Grohl of Nirvana and Foo Fighters remembered the bands on *120 Minutes* being "pretty fucking cool" for making their own low-budget videos.[125] Because of this, by the mid-1980s, underground music was already getting a wider audience. MTV regularly played R.E.M., the Sugarcubes from Iceland (with singer Björk), and Sinéad O'Connor, among others. Bands like this, though not explicitly punk, laid the groundwork for the success of Nirvana in 1991.

The alternative label was an attempt by the industry to define a motley collection of different styles that included punk, industrial, goth, new wave, electric dance music (EDM), and hip-hop. Inclusion of hip-hop under the "alternative" umbrella was more common in the early part of the 1990s, before it became as dominant in the music industry as it is now. Stuart Kallen described the term "alternative" as anything that "differed from the straight-ahead, sing-along music by mainstream superstar acts like Michael Jackson, Britney Spears, and Taylor Swift."[126] It pulled from a variety of musical genres but existed as a category all its own in the industry, he argued.[127] Eric Weisbard's amorphous definition was built on cultural fragmentation and crossovers within the music industry, those artists who do not fit within a category. "Alternative rock . . . is anti-generational dystopian, subculturally *presuming* fragmentation; it's built on an often neurotic discomfort over massified and commodified culture, takes as its archetype bohemia far more than youth [in contrast to rock culture of the 60s], and never expects that its popular appeal, such as it is, will have much impact."[128] He drew a straight line between what he deemed "musical dissenters" of the

1960s to punk and right on through the 1980s.[129] For Weisbard, punk and what came after were the logical prehistory of Nirvana and grunge from Seattle. "Nirvana was the fulcrum," he argued, "because Kurt Cobain was able to make alternative conventions register with ordinary people as rock necessities; suddenly, the loose tradition defined in this book was cool's road map."[130] The implication here was that punk was not really a phenomenon outside of how it related to the mainstream music industry. Punk existed as a precursor to bringing "purity" back to the recording industry, rather than an attempt to create a less commercial mode of producing culture. Alternative music was the industry's attempt to impose commercial order on the messy underground music scenes that often derided commercial sensibilities. Given that punk continued to exist as a non-mainstream phenomenon, many would dispute that idea.

Not all punk bands believed that they should avoid commercial success and stay "pure" to their roots. Some courted mainstream success. This was nothing new, as bands like Ramones signed to the large independent label Sire Records. After all, it was Malcolm McLaren who injected political considerations into the act of signing with a major label. As hardcore came to dominate punk scenes, that political argument led some to pioneer a less commercial approach to music production, such as what we saw with Dischord and other hardcore labels. But not all the hardcore bands necessarily saw their inclusion in the genre, meaning that they had to remain "noncommercial" to qualify as punk. The trajectory of Hüsker Dü illustrated the growing divide in the hardcore punk scene about the commercial question. The band formed in Minnesota when Bob Mould (see figure 4.2 for a *TBT* cover with Mould) befriended Grant Hart, Greg Norton, and Charlie Pine in 1979 while attending Macalester University in St. Paul. The band had "lofty ambitions" from the get-go, according to Azerrad, who noted that "to them, a deal with punk-centric Sire Records seemed practically inevitable."[131] But they struggled to get a deal even from the local punk label, Twin/Tone. This forced them to form their own label, Reflex Records.[132] The reason was not an "ethical" choice but out of "necessity." However, Mould said that "when you start giving up parts of your independence . . . it gives off an impression, an illusion for people."[133] Hart felt that the decisions they made by forming their own label had them taking on so much that it "hurt the band in the long run." He said that "we should have been able to let go of and oversee [more aspects of being part of a working band]."[134] As the band became more popular, they were unable to keep up with the demands of their success. They could not afford to press ten thousand records. They

Figure 4.2. Issue 84 of *The Big Takeover* magazine. (Used by permission of Jack Rabid)

turned to Greg Ginn's SST label for help. Ginn was the guitarist for Black Flag.[135] Here we can see an important point about the history of punk. Humanity has spent its history building large-scale institutions for reasons other than the consolidation of power in the hands of a few. Many punks saw the recording industry as corrupt and exploitative, which was true. Many punks spent the 1980s building up alternative institutions because of the corruption found in the music industry. This institution building was key maintaining that independence. Labels like SST and Dischord were built on the notion of artistic autonomy. Punk was and remains an example of successful democratic institution building.

Not everyone wanted to think deeply about what these institutions meant to punk. The ongoing debate over the production of music alienated Hüsker Dü, but so did the hardcore scene in general. "Mould in particular was growing well tired of the hardcore scene," said Azerrad.[136] Mould perceived pressure to conform. "Basically, they were going 'Be different, be different. Be like us or we'll kill you,' Norton says of the hardcore crowd."[137] Azerrad concluded the band believed that "the scene was flooded with poseurs and violent thugs who knew and cared little for the music's original impulses."[138] But Hüsker Dü's popularity continued to grow, at the same time that Minneapolis was gaining attention for other artists, such as Soul Asylum and the Replacements, not to mention the now-legendary Prince.[139] Hüsker Dü recorded *Zen Arcade* in late 1983, a double disc concept album that went on to be their best seller up to that point and proved to be a major challenge to SST. The first run of five thousand units sold out. The album was a hit with music critics, which "expanded the [band's] music's audience beyond the punk underground."[140] Some considered that to be a betrayal of a pure punk ethos. But the band showed loyalty to the punk institutions that helped them. They deferred their royalties on the sale of the album to help SST stay afloat. By 1987, the label owed the band around $150,000, according to Hart.[141]

In 1985 the distributor JEM folded, which was one of the major independent record distributors that many punk labels depended on. As a result, the Hüsker Dü accepted an offer from Warner Bros. that year. They hoped that a well-established major would insulate them from the volatility that could upset the smaller punk labels. Warner Bros. had courted the band since *Zen Arcade*. Azerrad said, "It was a momentous move. Hüsker Dü was the first key American indie band to defect to a major . . . Some insiders were shocked and others outraged."[142] Warner Bros. was able to infuse more cash into the band's operations. But the band still ended up as a bad fit for a major label.[143] The label often insisted that the band play by the rules of the mainstream music industry. They demanded that the band fire their friend David Savoy as their office manager. Azerrad connected that demand to Savoy's suicide just before a major tour. "Hüsker Dü never got over the blow."[144] Mould insisted he take on the duties of manager, which Azerrad interpreted as Mould being "unwilling to relinquish control." Even though their first major label album—which ended up costing the band dearly in personal terms—sold 125,000 copies, "the band made little more than they would have with less sales on SST. The major label gambit had failed," Azerrad said.[145] He felt the core problem was the inability of Warner Bros. to properly market their music. One of their friends, Julie Panebianco, said their music was "too aggressive for regular radio."[146] The band became the "sacrificial pancake" for the industry to learn how to incorporate harder music like hardcore or heavy metal more fully into the industry.[147] The problems the band faced—interpersonal conflicts and drug abuse—were exacerbated by a system for music production that demanded too much say and not enough independence for the artist. Hüsker Dü's experiences on a major label reinforced the reasons for avoiding working in the mainstream industry for many punks. After Nirvana, that calculus changed to some degree.

The struggles Hüsker Dü had on a major label anticipated the debates about "selling out" in the 1990s, when some punks and other underground bands achieved mainstream success. Punk had created a means of existing outside of the major label system for musicians. There was some level of robustness to the independent networks that punks had built to a certain size. But the examples of how SST struggled to keep up with sales and a major independent distributor collapse showed that they struggled as punk grew during the 1980s. Even more new people were drawn to underground scenes thanks to their encounters with alternative music in the early 1990s. As a result, new pressures were put on those scenes by the mainstream music industry seeking to sign the next Nirvana. It changed how punk institutions thought about what music to include. To compensate for what they saw as an attack on their scenes, *MRR* settled on a new review and ad policy in 1993. The changes started in 1994. In the February 1994 issue, a note was added to front material indicating the new policy with regard to advertisements. It clarified to possible advertisers what they would prioritize, with music-related ads taking top priority. They noted that "we only have space to run ads for releases we're reviewing, so if your label is putting out many types of music, please tailor your ad towards what we will be covering." Artists on majors or " 'indie' majors wanna-bes with corporate ties" would no longer be accepted.[148] A further clarification was made in March 1994. The revised "note to advertisers" said, "Our focus is on punk rock, garage rock, hardcore punk, and other aggressive, energetic and raw blasts."[149] The shift to narrower coverage was addressed by *MRR*'s editor Tim Yohannan several times in 1993 and 1994. In the April 1994 issue, he began an editorial column where he listed himself as a "tyrant" in response to some of the criticism he received. It had been a change that Yohannan had wanted and pitched at a staff meeting, which included more than fifty people. "All but a few staffers felt they could live with it as long as it was stated in the zine."[150] The change did drive some out of the staff out of *MRR*.

In June 1994, in *MRR* Yohannan penned the opening editorial for a collection of essays about the mainstream music industry. He compared punk going mainstream to the problem of neo-Nazi violence six years prior. He described how the major labels had been interacting with the punk underground in the previous two years. Fifty underground bands had been "bought up," punk clubs were undermined, and radio shows and zines had been "bought off." While "they threaten to stifle and ultimately control this community, and little is being done to resist this threat." That entire issue was dedicated to making an argument in favor of retaining independence for the underground scene and rejecting working with the major labels. He said, "there can be no middle ground or grey area when you're under attack by forces alien to the fundamental principles of a community or society."[151] Later in the issue, Brian Zero discussed the connections major labels sometimes had with the military-industrial complex. He recalled an antinuclear demonstration he participated in on April 29, 1985. Part of the demonstration included calling out corporations who profited from wars. He quoted a Subhumans song, "Rats," was about a protest in the United Kingdom around the same time. Unfortunately, due to their distribution, the band had connections to the very same war profiteers via EMI. For the protest Zero attended, EMI did not make it on their list because it was locally focused. But many bands that were part of the underground were distributed by Caroline, which was owned by Virgin, who had recently become a subsidiary of EMI. Their parent company, Thorn-EMI was a electric company and a defense contractor.[152] Zero discussed how Kevin McCracken of Kirbdog Records challenged the general manager of Alternative Tentacles, Greg Werckman, about their continued connections to Mordam Records, who distributed through Caroline. Werckman argued that they stayed in that arrangement because it meant their music was being spread. He felt that made it worth the compromise. Zero called this a common argument, that "the corporate sources are better at getting your art or message out of harder to reach areas."[153] Zero wondered "where do we draw the line?" To him the attempt to bring punk into the corporate fold showed that the punk underground was viewed as a threat to the mainstream music industry.[154] Zero viewed punks as being on "strike against the bullshit of this world, that the corporations are the main source of bullshit in this world, and punk bands who deal with them are effectively strikebreakers."[155] He argued that punk provided a space for independent, noncorporate culture and that independence was under attack from the mainstream recording industry.[156]

Letters responding to this *MRR* issue appeared in the next few months. Much of these focused on the reader's experiences as punk became more popular in the mainstream. Megan from Seattle noted how strange it was to be a punk there since Nirvana. She was disappointed that the bands she had supported were now becoming "in-accessible" to her since a key aspect of punk was the communal connections and lack of distinction between fans and bands. She felt betrayed. But gaining understanding of how that "betrayal" worked helped her put what had happened into context. She said that "these articles connected the dots for me . . . understanding the context makes it less bewildering."[157] Michael Penne agreed with Steve Albini's take on how major labels treat artists. However, he also felt that some independent labels acted in the same exploitative manner, such as the label Dutch East. "You have to keep your guard up no matter who you deal with and remember the reason you make music."[158] The problem was commercialization of music, rather than just some stark division between the majors and independents. Joseph B. Raimond wrote in from Germany, where he ran a label called eMpTy Records. He saw European punks under the same kinds of corporate pressure discussed in the major labels issue. For example, Raimond noted that most major European music magazines link coverage to advertisements, which meant "no ads and they will not even review your releases."[159] One thing he found lacking in *MRR*'s coverage was discussing why bands might be signing to major labels in the first place. He speculated that perhaps "they feel that being on a major somehow legitimizes them as 'artists'."[160] Such realities illustrated just how much of a stranglehold major labels had on popular music in general, which had consequences. "The word 'independent' now has come to mean strictly a musical style, regardless of what label it is on," he concluded.[161] Labels like his were being forced to deal with the majors and the commercial industry, he concluded. Even when they do play ball, many of the independent labels are left "almost broke. I'm just bitter about the whole thing," he lamented.[162] Many people writing in to *MRR* appreciated the analysis and weighed in with their own opinions and experiences of how this pressure affected their experiences in the punk underground.

The fractures caused by the mainstream "invasion" of punk scenes resulted in two new zines with an eye toward a national or international punk audience. Daniel Sinker, a former writer for *MRR*, began publishing *Punk Planet* in 1994, which he called "an interesting year" for punk (see figure 4.3). The

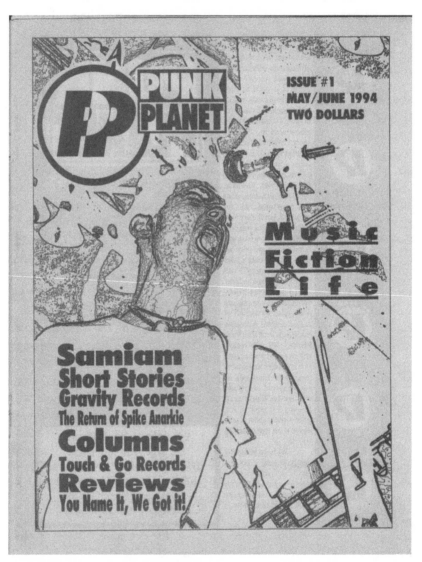

Figure 4.3. Issue 1 of *Punk Planet* zine, May/June 1994. (Used by permission of Dan Sinker)

success of Nirvana and "the signing frenzy that followed" had a major impact on underground music. He believed that *MRR* was being reactionary as they began to "tightly control what bands it would cover."[163] He argued that in doing so, they were attempting to police the meaning of punk and left many underground bands out in the cold. This meant genres like riot girl and emo (emotional hardcore) were not getting the support he believed they deserved from the punk community. He called them "two of the most exciting things to happen to the underground in the 90s."[164] The opening editorial speaks to the tensions around defining punk in the wake of Nirvana. "What does punk mean? Your guess is as good as ours," they published in the inaugural issue.[165] Cofounder Will Dandy laid out their motivation for founding *Punk Planet*. He called out *MRR* in all but name. He noted that only one zine had a national presence at the time and that "we want there to be at least two."[166] The goal was to "provide more to more people." He believed that *MRR* was essentially engaging in a form of gatekeeping censorship by attempting to pin down the definition of punk, hence their founding a new zine. "That is the main reason that this zine exists anyways: to stomp out the censorship that is going in zines that separates us."[167] The opening editorials by Dandy and Sinker made it clear that they disliked corporate music and the exploitation of punk rock as much as *MRR*. Dandy said, "the only rule we have here is no major labels or 'indie labels' that are just the corporate scum sweeping down on us like a bird of prey."[168] A letters section did not appear until the third issue. The first letter they printed was critical of the new zine. Andy Social called *Punk Planet* a reaction to the changes at *MRR*. He called their open-ended view of punk just as "piss poor" as Yohannan's narrow, genre-bound interpretation. He argued that the editors should "do some real thinking to come up with reasonable intelligent standards." Ultimately, he found *Punk Planet* "a waste of good trees."[169] Mike Beer City from Milwaukee agreed that the first issue seemed little more than a *MRR* clone. He did not see a problem with *MRR* narrowing their content to cover only hardcore and punk. Others disagreed and appreciated the efforts of Sinker and Dandy. Tyson McCreary and Dave Coker of the zine *Personal Politics* were excited about the new zine. McCreary found references to *MRR* tiresome, but was excited about the zine's potential. Coker called *Punk Planet* "*MRR* without all the shite being talked and negative attitudes."[170]

Another zine came out of the changes at *MRR*. Kent McClard who had also written for *MRR*, founded *HeartattaCk* in spring 1994 (see figure 4.4). He announced his new venture in *MRR* in the ad for his label Ebullition Records.[171] McClard laid out his justification for the new hardcore-centric zine in his column at *MRR*.[172] He penned the zine's opening editorial, arguing that hardcore was not just a strictly defined musical genre. He saw it as a "flowing word rather than a concretely defined word."[173] The zine published letters received for the first issue. Scott Something from Nevada City believed a new zine "was long in coming." He felt "*MRR*'s decision that only 'punk' material was worthy of review" merely reinforced the idea that "'punk' was essentially a long-ago established musical style." He concluded that "it seems like a willingness to stray from your conventionally accepted ideas, in the ones you hold about music, is one of the many thinks [*sic*] punk has been about."[174] Patrick Tutek agreed that the new zine was "a laudable venture." But he worried "if what is being created in the 'punk community' is not a dialogue but rather a schism that will further tear us apart." He said that lots of music "is trying to be passed off as 'punk' or 'hardcore'" when they do not fit the definition. He wondered if *MRR* was still a great means of filtering punk from nonpunk music.[175] In the second issue, McClard clarified his approach to his new zine. He noted that he wanted "to promote the ideology of do it yourself and to attempt to create a scene that I find interesting, exciting and stimulating." This would mean "less emphasis on covering the scene in general and more emphasis on covering those aspects that seem credible to me." As such, the zine "represents my interests and my tastes." He admitted that the zine would not be for everyone, but he encouraged people unhappy with his approach to "start your own zine," as he had done.[176]

The next few months, an interzine debate erupted about the split and what it meant. *Punk Planet* was reviewed in the August 1994 issue of *MRR*. Timojhen Mark noted that the zine was positioning itself as one of the "'alternatives' to this here rag." But he noted that "diversity is strength."[177] The review seemed fair if slightly snarky. Yohannan reiterated his support for new zines like *Punk Planet* and *HeartattaCk*. But he took both zines to task for mischaracterizing the changes to *MRR*'s policies with regard to the kind of music they covered. He rejected the idea that *MRR* was "banning" some artists. Rather, they were rejecting those that do not fit in with the core mission of the zine. He noted that "I reject at least 10 RECORDS A DAY."[178] Yohannan said that *MRR* always had two-pronged criteria—musical and political.[179] Rev. Nørb wrote a review for a zine called *Ninja* in the January 1995 issue of *MRR*, which seemed like an excuse to go after one of these new zines. He said it "kicks ass on *HeartattaCk*." He insisted that *Spin*, a corporate alternative magazine, was "a rod, a furlong, and a hearty Hi-yo silver above *HaCK*."[180] John Lacroix of the zine *Extent* thought *HeartattaCk* had "good stuff to read some times [*sic*], but the layout is so

Figure 4.4. Issue 1 of *HeartattaCk* zine, March 1994. (Used by permission of Kent McClard)

boring, and there is no humor in it."[181] Generally speaking, *HeartattaCk* got less attention in *MRR* than *Punk Planet* did. But neither was entirely exiled from the pages of *MRR*, though McClard and Sinker seemed to stop writing for *MRR*. It was clear that some at *MRR* were bitter about the split.

No doubt, many punks made a habit to read more than one of these zines despite the tensions between them—or perhaps because of them.

The pages of punk zines hosted debates about where the line was with regard to commercialization and easing access to punk music for a wider audience. In the second issue of *HeartattaCk*, Christopher Appelgren of Lookout Records wrote in to correct what he saw as a misconception around the UPC system. Contrary to McClard's statements about the barcode system in the previous issue, Appelgren argued that it was a technological tool and that "there are not sinister underlying meanings to the UPC systems."[182] He believed it was not intended to keep smaller labels out of chain stores or to compromise the autonomy of independent labels. He said, "I made the decision to utilize the UPC system after getting information that satisfied me that it was not some corporate plot to bring me into the establishment."[183] McClard argued that Appelgren missed his larger point. He believed that punk should remain underground and hard to get. He replied, "I am so tired of hearing people whine about getting better distribution."[184] He saw punk in exclusive terms. "I don't want every kid next door getting into punk rock. One of the biggest problems with punk today is that it is too easy to get into."[185] But when he started getting into punk, "we had to work for it. Now, thanks to labels trying to get bigger distribution and larger sales . . . every moron can go down to the mall and buy a flannel shirt and a Bad Religion record and pretend to be punk. Fuck that."[186] He reiterated his earlier argument that "punk rock is about ideology, ideals, and integrity."[187] McClard rejected the notion that punk should be easily accessible to everyone and hence rejected the use of barcodes on general principle.

Punks also debated the issue of bootlegging punk albums. In the fourth issue of *Punk Planet*, an organization called the German Label Allegiance wrote in to make readers aware of a problem with a label called Lost & Found. They argued that the label was profiting off illegal bootlegs, which they argued that punks should boycott. Rather than a dismissal of bootlegs in general, which they deemed fine when "sold for a non-profit price," they accused Lost & Found for profiting off "professionally" produced bootlegs.[188] Alex Sayf Cummings argued that such bootlegging existed along "a spectrum of unauthorized reproduction."[189] The label was not about reinforcing the punk community but about profiting from it, placing this in the "commercial" category, which many punks rejected.

Punks debated the merits of that success and whether it was punk rock. Sinker struggled with his zine's success. He said, "up until yesterday, I had

NO idea that punk rock had become so popular . . . all of a sudden, without even consulting me first, they've [major labels] up and made punk hip. That would explain the phenomenal distribution that *Punk Planet* managed to get with just three issues out."[190] He halfheartedly lamented that "we even have the word Punk in our title."[191] Sinker did not fully reject successful bands that came out of the punk scene. He praised the band Rancid but said many believed "it's not very punk to listen to Rancid."[192] He argued, however, that "those people are just DEAD WRONG. It's very punk to listen to Rancid."[193] *Punk Planet* interviewed the band in its second issue that summer. In it, guitarist Lars Frederiksen defended the band's video being on MTV.[194] Others defended the success of punk bands in mainstream culture. Punk label Epitaph Records was owned by Brett Gurewitz of Bad Religion. Several bands on the label achieved mainstream success, such as Offspring and Rancid. In an interview in *Punk Planet*, Sinker asked if Gurewitz had left Bad Religion because they moved to Atlantic Records, but he said it was for a variety of reasons that he did not list. However, he said that "there were certain artistic and creative decisions that were being made for the wrong reasons once we changed labels. The group was a bit too reluctant to rock the boat."[195] Sinker asked about MTV playing videos by Epitaph bands. Gurewitz said that he had been sending the network videos since 1987, but so did others such as Touch and Go and Alternative Tentacles. This was primarily at the discretion of the bands. NoFX did not want him to do so, while Down by Law did. "No matter what, I do what they ask me," he said of the bands.[196] He characterized it as "leveraging MTV" rather than "playing the game." The success of Offspring's single "Come Out and Play" had more to do with the radio, which led MTV to play their video. For radio, he said they mailed their band's CDs to college radio stations, but they rarely got play. He noted that Bad Religion's album *Generator* only got to sixty on the college charts (the *College Music Journal*), but for retail sales, for the album reached number nine. He believed that Epitaph was being blackballed.[197] The success of Offspring came from airplay they received from the commercial station KROQ in LA. Soon other "modern rock" stations picked up the song, and it spiraled from there. He rejected the notion that he or the bands on his label had "sold out." He noted that he turned down $20 million, though he did not say from whom he got that offer. He asked, "what's wrong with radio having good music on it?" and noted the success of the Sex Pistols in 1977.[198]

Other developments shaped the popularity of alternative music. During the 1990s, traveling music festivals came into vogue. Touring was central to building a fan base, and these festivals spread the popularity of the alternative genre. Perry Farrell started the Lollapalooza festival in 1991 as a good-bye tour for his band, Jane's Addiction. He included bands from across musical genres on the same stage and put less well-known acts alongside more well-established ones.[199] Although many see him as pioneering the touring festival format for the 1990s, some argued that Farrell modeled his idea on Ian Astbury's 1990 festival. A Gathering of the Tribes (AGotT) was created as a benefit concert for Native American peoples. Both festivals included a multigenre line-up, but Lollapalooza was planned as a national tour and AGotT was a weekend festival. The influence of AGotT on Farrell is up for the debate, but the influence of Lollapalooza is not. Other traveling music festivals followed in its wake, such as Ozzfest and the Warped Tour.[200] The skater punk festival Warped Tour was a long-term successor to Lollapalooza. It helped popularize the pop punk genre of music. It was founded by Kevin Lyman, who began organizing shows in college and turned it into a professional career. He partnered with Vans (a shoe company that marketed to skateboarders) and the Creative Artists Agency (a talent and artists agency). The tour has had corporate sponsorship from the start.[201] The Warped Tour went on hiatus in 2019 due to Lyman's retirement. In 2005, Lollapalooza was revived as a stationary festival in Chicago.[202] Both festivals played critical roles in the spread of alternative music and in more mainstream forms of punk.

Much of the punk public sphere was skeptical of these festivals, seeing them as a greater commercialization of punk culture. In one letter to *MRR* in 1992, Sal Manilla from Colonial Heights, Virginia, wrote about his experiences attending the previous year's Lollapalooza tour. He said the music was great, but he got "screwed over" due to long lines for food. It caused him to miss several of the bands he wanted to see, like Nine Inch Nails. He was also unhappy with the bouncers at the stage. They seemed unconcerned about people actually getting hurt in the crowd but policed people safely crowd surfing. He recommended that everyone skip the 1992 tour. He said, "if we don't keep the corporate hounds away from our music, starting with boycotting shit like Lollapalooza, there will be no more scene."[203] Manilla saw it as an existential crisis for punks. Jeremy McQueen of Jam Records pointed out in his letter that Lollapalooza tickets were $33 but sold out. The cost was too high in his mind. He advocated for boycotting the major label system that he saw as benefiting from the festival.[204] Lydia Lunch, when asked if she had been asked to participate in Lollapalooza, said, "I spat in their face."[205] The Warped Tour received some attention in *MRR* its first year. In October 1994, one of the columnists reprinted a review of the Swingin' Utters and L7 from the festival that August.[206] A year later, Ray Lujan explored the "punk rock explosion" in his column. He noted that for what was becoming known as "pop punk," he was finding it harder to "weed out the great stuff from the generic stuff or even the quality generic stuff."[207] He noted that he was no purist and had been to his share of "rock venue shows" and to the Warped Tour.[208] For the most part, *MRR* seemed to spare little space on discussing the Warped Tour, hewing to Yohannan's policy on avoiding reviewing or giving ad space to corporate-aligned punk music.

Punk Planet gave some coverage to the Warped Tour. It was mentioned in some music reviews in the magazine, such as for *Rumors from the Air-Conditioned Tiger Pit* (Rotten House Records, 1997). Reviewer Scott Yahtzee said, "I put this CD on and I feel like I'm at the Warped Tour. Actually none of these bands played at the Warped Tour but a lot of them sound like the bands that do."[209] It also got a couple of mentions in zine reviews, such as the zine *Sleestak*, which covered "skateboarding, Misfits, Warped Tour, Road Trips, Quick 66." In the review, Jim Connell joked, "notice 'Misfits and 'Warped Tour'. [Now] check your blood pressure and you'll know whether you'll like this."[210] The most sustained coverage came the fifth year of the tour in 1999, when the Warped Tour had become a well-established institution. *Punk Planet* had a cover article on the Warped Tour specifically calling out the corporatization of the punk scene. Dan Sinker quoted "PR flak" Charlie from Epitaph Records who explained that "we ain't in this business for our health. . . . I'm looking to pay my rent and make my bands as rich as fucking possible." Sinker lamented that "from punk rock ideology to factory workers' jobs, the Vans Warped tour seem to exploit everything it touches."[211] He argued that the tour began innocently enough at the intersection of skating and punk rock, with the skater punk wave of the 1980s.[212] After a lackluster first year, the organizers asked that the primary sponsor Vans attach their name to the marquee. They added additional sponsors the second year (1996). The tour was benefiting from the growing "alternative market." By 1998, a quarter of a million people attended. Sinker argued that the growing popularity put pressure on the creative side, such as "tapping into whatever the biggest trends are" at the time, but some of the organizers deny that this was a problem. As the popularity grew, it also drove a need for more corporate sponsorship.[213] In both zines, the Warped Tour, when mentioned, became a shorthand for unoriginal corporate punk.

If the rise of the alternative festival tour was seen as suspect, how about the bands that were considered the first major bands of the "alternative" genre? Early on in their career, Nirvana appeared in the pages of zines like *MRR*. They received positive reviews on a 1989 compilation they appeared on (*Teriyaki Asthma* on the Seattle label C/Z).[214] As the band's star rose, they popped up in interviews with other bands in the Pacific Northwest, such as in August 1990 issue of *MRR* where they were mentioned by both Mudhoney and Fitz of Depression.[215] In a Southern California scene report filed by Grungeboy in July 1991, he noted that Nirvana played a free gig at a local record shop, Sonic Records.[216] In the December 1991 issue, in the section where some of the contributors listed albums they were currently enjoying, two list Nirvana's *Nevermind* and two list one of their live albums.[217] Jeff Bale raved about *Nevermind* in his column that month.[218] One would see similar kinds of mentions and discussions of bands in the pages of zines. The tone began to change in the issue where Bale discussed Nirvana's major label studio album debut. Tim Yohannan "eulogized" well-known music promoter Bill Graham. He recalled how Graham tried to dominate the San Francisco punk scene as he did during the 1960s, "in his typically sterilized environment." Yohannan described the punk boycott that ensued. Even so, he said Graham "helped suck it [the music scene] dry" in his years as a promoter. He accused bands L7 and Nirvana working with Graham primarily to "ascend the corporate rock ladder."[219] By 1992, a full-on punk backlash against Nirvana was in the making in the pages of *MRR*. Bale received flak for his column praising Nirvana. A letter in the February 1992 issue called Bale out and was from the "What Happened to Jeff Bale" Committee. They felt he believed that "the music is more important than the message" and that "some of the greatest records in history are on major labels." They lamented that his "new attitude is saddening to us." They believed that his attitude was contributing to punk becoming "just another form of escapist entertainment" as opposed to "a genuine cultural alternative to mindless corporate rock."[220] Ben Weasel invoked Nirvana as a negative example of music he was listening to in his March 1992 column.[221]

Joey Vindictive of Franklin Park, Illinois, tied Lollapalooza and Nirvana together into a coherent argument about the corporate attack on the punk underground. He asked what the punk scene fears about the success of these newly popular bands. He said, "I believe it has something to do with a diluting of our 'punkness' or some such thing. Identification, maybe?" To counter that, he argued for punks to embrace materials that could invoke censorship because it would drive away the mainstream industry. "I am selfish," he said, "I do not want to share my little personal little secret subversive art forms with temporary losers." He was upset that "punk is losing its social stigma because of all this liberal rhetoric inside and outside the scene." He concluded that punks should "support censorship, record labeling and the whole bit. Let's see how many people will be left willing to take the risk of being an outcast instead of an admired untouchable."[222] His letter received a response in February 1993 asking what was wrong with him. Nick Giannone believed the mainstream tastes for alternative was a fad that would pass. The underground punk scene would persevere.[223] But Vindictive hit on an interesting point that he put in terms some found objectionable. What was the point of having a punk scene in the first place? Was it to incubate a musical genre that would end up in the mainstream industry? Or was it to create a space for like-minded individuals to share a love of culture that was not commercialized? Was it a form of upside-down elitism, keeping out the mainstream "riff-raff"? Or was it about maintaining an anticommercial space in a world that was increasingly commercialized and commoditized? That was at the heart of the ongoing debate happening in punk zines during the alternative music era. Of course, there was not one singular explanation for the attitude toward the success some punks achieved in the mainstream music industry. A good argument could be made for any and all of these. Overall, distaste for commercialized punk loomed large in the reaction to the mainstreaming of punk rock in the 1990s.

There are other cases to illustrate how the recording industry was attempting to incorporate punk as a musical genre into the mainstream. In 1996, the Velvet Underground were inducted into the Rock & Roll Hall of Fame. The archive and museum functions as the primary location of creating the preferred industry narrative about rock music and its role in modern society.[224] Inducting a band like the Velvet Underground was a tacit admission that the underground music scene was important in shaping popular music tastes more broadly. This coincided with punk being seen as more acceptable in the mainstream industry. Many in the punk underground rejected bands that reached mainstream popularity. Bands like Bad Religion and Green Day became seen as sell-outs for their commercial success by many punks. In the September 1989 issue of *MRR*, Green Day's new single was celebrated by Aaron in the Northern California scene report.[225] By the December 1993 issue, Kent McClard rejected Bad Religion and Green Day as being punk bands.[226] This reaction might seem irrational to people not familiar with punk as an underground phenomenon. Why condemn what many consider to be success as our society defined it? These strong rejections came from the experiences punks had with the mainstream culture, as we saw in the previous chapter. The mainstream culture in the 1980s positioned punk as a nihilistic and destructive subculture. But many punks found being part of a scene to be a positive and constructive force in their lives. Not surprisingly, they bristled at their community-building projects being turned into yet another money-making scheme. Despite the incursion and defections from the punk underground scenes, the punk underground carried on.

The End of Punk Panic?

Did the mainstream success of some punk bands mean an end to the 1980s punk panic? One might think so. But some amount of moral panic over punks and other cultural outsiders continued into the 1990s. This was often enacted on the local level as the culture industries were becoming invested in punk. This led to several high-profile stories related to punk and acts of violence that made headlines. The newfound popularity of punk in the mainstream might have caused some to double down on their attack on such subcultures. The incorporation of punk into mainstream culture meant a new kind of backlash that had two effects. First, it led to a continuation of punk panic often on a local level, which I explore here. Second, it led to some in the 2000s pushing far-right political platforms to claim that they were the "real" punk rockers as they opposed "mainstream" liberalism (discussed later).

One could still find news reports about the problems posed by punks into the 1990s. In 1995, the LA Fox affiliate had an undercover report on punk. It sounded much like news reports from the 1980s. The reporter, Chris Blatchford, focused on violence in his coverage of a punk festival in San Bernardino, which included a riot. He mentioned the heat, the expensive drinks, and the lack of shade, but still pinned the blame for the unrest on the punks. The show was finally shut down when the crowd ended up on stage. Blatchford attempted to define the various groups involved in the scene, included skinheads, punks, and what he deemed "straight" kids. In the second part of the clip from the second day of the report, focused on the differing skinhead subcultures, racists, SHARPS (Skinheads Against Racial Prejudice), and straight-edge. To their credit, they let the kids speak for themselves a good bit and worked to understand what must be seen as a confusing patchwork of identities to an outsider. Blatchford admitted that it was a "social movement" but still problematic. Everyone interviewed was put under the punk umbrella, however they might have understood themselves. Ignoring the social world they were covering, ultimately Blatchford found punk to be inherently "antisocial." For him, the primary force in the local punk scene seemed to be skinheads, ignoring that many people consider them different, if overlapping subcultures.[227] Another maybe less obvious case of punk panic in the 1990s was talk show *Jenny Jones* that aired in the late 1990s. She invited a panel of punks and their friends on the show to give the punks a makeover, indicating that how they dressed was a problem. The shocked audience response indicated that the fashion choices of the punks were still considered a bit too much for the mainstream audience.[228] Some level of punk panic still existed well into the 1990s.

It might be easy to dismiss this coverage of punk as missing the less nihilistic aspects of punk. They seem silly to many, even laughable, in retrospect. But the continued prevalence of punk panic in some parts of the media had real-world consequences for some. It shaped local events such as a murder in Amarillo, Texas, in 1997. Brian Deneke, a punk from Amarillo Texas, was killed in a deliberate hit-and-run. The popular football player who ran him over, Dustin Camp, ended up receiving a light sentence and fine for the murder. *Punk Planet* covered the story in 2000 (see figure 4.5). According to their article, punks were regularly targeted by the more popular kids from the local high school. The clique was primarily from a rich neighborhood and were identified by their white baseball caps. Camp was from a family of more modest means, but was well liked and popular among the in crowd. On December 6, Camp and his clique confronted a group of punks hanging out at the local IHOP, one of the few hangouts for all teenagers in town. Both groups moved to a parking lot across the street, but everyone backed off after Camp threatened the punks with his car.[229] Rumors of a planned fight the next Friday, December 12, circulated. A huge crowd ended up gathering at the IHOP that evening, which ended with Camp plowing his Cadillac into Deneke, running over his body, killing him instantly.[230]

The tight-knit members of Amarillo's punk scene recalled how they were routinely harassed prior to Deneke's death. But even Brian's brutal death could not moderate the negative views some held of punks. During Camp's trial in August 1999, his lawyer, Warren Clark, called the punk scene "a gang of young men who choose a lifestyle . . . designed to intimidate those around them, to challenge authority and to provoke reaction from others." Clark argued that despite professions of tolerance, punks exuded "pure naked aggression," and that "aggression has consequences." David Trew,

Figure 4.5. Issue 35 of *Punk Planet* zine. The cover issue with Brian Deneke. (Used by permission of Dan Sinker)

a local punk, said that "they didn't put Dustin on trail, they put Brian on trial."[231] Camp was convicted but only on a lesser manslaughter charge. The jury, who likely found Camp sympathetic and Deneke as a threat, gave him ten years' probation and a $10,000 fine. The prosecutor admitted that if the tables had been turned, Deneke would have gotten a harsher sentence. He concluded, "that's the way the world works."

Jeff Blackburn was a defense attorney that Camp attempted to hire but who ended up representing the Deneke family instead. He called what happened to Deneke a hate crime. "Dustin didn't know Brian. What animated him was who he thought Brian was." He worked with the family to set up the Brian Deneke Memorial Committee to "see that justice is done through the legal system."[232] Blackburn called Deneke's death a "punk lynching."[233] Given the deep racial meaning of the term "lynching" in US history, that statement is problematic. His argument that Deneke was killed because of who he was seems pretty accurate given the circumstances of his death. Other zines covered Deneke's death. *MRR* ran an article on the Deneke's death and Camp's trial in their April 2000 issue, which covered the same ground as the *Punk Planet* article.[234] In the following years, the Deneke family and the punks of Amarillo worked to keep Deneke's death fresh in the minds of the punk counterpublic. In April 2002, his family wrote to alert people that Camp, who had violated terms of his probation and was now serving time in June, was up for parole. They asked people to write the parole board and oppose his release.[235] Mykel Board wrote about an email he received from the Deneke Foundation in 2007 asking for support in planning a memorial show that would benefit the foundation. By this point the foundation put on yearly shows as fundraisers and was involved in organizing against racism and violence.[236] Though it has been over two decades since Deneke's murder and the committee that organized these events seems to have disbanded, Deneke is not entirely out of popular imagination. In 2017, a film called *Bomb City* dramatized his death and the aftermath.[237]

Brian Deneke's murder recently popped up in an interesting location. It was mentioned in a June 2019 issue of *Granma*, a publication of the Central Committee of the Communist Party of Cuba. Abel Prieto used Deneke's death to discuss a rise in hate crimes in the United States that he connected to President Donald Trump's use of violent language. Prieto characterized Deneke's murder as a hate crime. This puts his death on par with victims of other hate crimes based on race, sexual orientation, religion, or gender identity.[238] I would argue that throwing around the term "hate crime" could cheapen the notion to some degree. But it also seems accurate to say that some people truly hated punks and members of other countercultural groups. That hatred, in the right circumstances, can devolve into violence and murder, much as it did with Deneke and Camp. That being said, a punk identity is a choice one makes and not an inherent trait. On the other hand, there had been nearly two decades of antipunk propaganda on American TV by the time of Deneke's death. That shaped popular perceptions of punks that did not reverse with the rise of Nirvana. It seemed to have shaped the views of Camp's defense attorney. The mainstream success of some punk bands did not change every mind about punks and what they represented in the 1990s—a challenge to the norms of American modern society that was increasingly conservative since the Reagan era.

Other cases attest to the fear and hatred of cultural "outsiders" that circulated in the United States. Punk panic expanded to include people associated with other subcultures, such as goths and people who embraced neopagan religions. This included the West Memphis Three: Damien Echols, Jason Baldwin, and Jessie Misskelley Jr. In 1993, three eight-year-old boys were found murdered in West Memphis, Arkansas. Their bodies had been mutilated, leading some to believe that satanism was involved.[239] Suspicion soon focused on Echols, a high school drop-out who struggled with his mental health and had an interest in the neopagan Wiccan religion. The authorities believed he was a satanist.[240] Jerry Driver was an officer who worked with juvenile offenders; he had been assigned to work with Echols. Driver was primarily responsible for the shift to focus on the occult.[241] Driver characterized Echols as a satanist despite Echols calling himself a Wiccan.[242] Some saw no distinction between the two religions. Echols, along with Baldwin and Misskelley, were ultimately charged and convicted of the murders despite a lack of clear physical evidence. The arrests and conviction were based largely on the forced confession of Misskelley, who was mentally disabled and was interrogated for nearly twelve hours without parental consent.[243] In an editorial published in *MRR*, Mike Taylor recounted how their story reminded him of growing up in rural Alabama. The case reminded Taylor of the friends he left behind when he moved. One of the terms he and his friends were saddled with was "satanist." He went back for a visit and realized that he "had been yanked from the path of an ugly squall." One of his friends ended up being tried as an adult for having two joints, for example.[244] There was less discussion about the West Memphis Three in other punk zines. Most discussion was in connection with the benefit album of covers of Black Flag songs. Hardcore zine *Mosh Yankee* interviewed the Circle Jerks in their third issue that discussed Keith Morris's involvement with the project.[245] The Salt Lake City zine *SLUG* interviewed Henry Rollins about his reasons for contributing to the project. Rollins believed it was his duty as a US citizen to stand up to injustice when possible.[246] Some nonpunks joined Rollins in his crusade to correct this moral wrong, such as Chuck D of Public Enemy, Eddie Vedder of Pearl Jam, and actor Johnny Depp. The West Memphis Three were released in 2011 under an Alford plea, which allowed them to maintain their innocence while the state said they were still guilty.[247] In a telling coincidence, the original trial of the West Memphis Three was the same year as the trial and conviction of Varg Vikernes, a Norwegian black metal musician, for arson and murder. Unlike Echols, Vikernes identified at the time as a satanist and now regularly promotes a racist interpretation of Norse neopaganism.[248] The case illustrated how cultural outsiders like punks, goths, and Wiccans could be targeted for who they were rather than due to any threat they posed.

One more case illustrated how those who committed major crimes were thought to be associated with outsider subculturals like punk. The Columbine High School mass shooting was seen as being carried out by alienated outsiders. The shooters listened to some underground music like industrial band KMFDM and the Swans. Eric Harris and Dylan Klebold, seniors at Columbine High School in Littleton, Colorado, carried out a mass shooting at their school on April 20, 1999. They had planned a much larger massacre with bombs, but killed fifteen people (themselves included) and injured twenty-four more. Their actions shocked and terrorized the local community and the country.[249] Many consider it the first major school mass shooting that inspired others. Adam Lanza, the young man who killed twenty grade school children and six adults at Sandy Hook Elementary in December 2012, was apparently obsessed with Harris and Klebold.[250] Understandably, people attempted to come to terms with the horrific the actions of the young men. Most understood the shootings as stemming from the social exclusion Harris and Klebold experienced. Punk panic reared its head here, indicating that some believed the boys had no reason to be upset with mainstream society and should just conform. A few days after the shootings, *Time* published an article exploring the problem with cliques in US high schools. Adam Cohen argued that "the embittered outcasts against the popular kids on campus" helped drive the shootings. The shooting at Columbine was driven by the outcast's jealousy of the popular kids, he implied. He quoted several students from various high schools around the country. Two from suburban Atlanta argued that the "outcasts" were just engaging in attention-seeking behavior with their confrontational mode of dress. In Salt Lake City, straightedge punks were assumed to be white supremacists. Cohen failed to consult any outcasts themselves. He did quote psychoanalyst Leon Hoffman, who claimed that kids who "can't belong in a positive way, they'll find a way to belong to a marginal group like a cult or a gang."[251] The implication was that students who looked or acted different were a threat to the conforming students.

Some punks leaned into one of these erroneous explanations. In his *MRR* column in November 1999, Ted Rall took the school administration of Columbine to task for holding a pep rally during the summer after the shootings. He compared the pep rally to the Nazi rallies at Nuremberg in the 1930s. He argued that due to being "bullied repeatedly by asshole football players," that they "lost their minds and shot up a bunch of their classmates." "It's precisely this kind of pressure to conform that led to last spring's massacre." Of the shooters, he said that "they were kids—confused, angry, shortsighted, dumb kids."[252] Around the same time in *Punk Planet*, Leah Ryan discussed the events of Columbine via the lens of bullying of nonconformists. She was shocked not by the shootings but by the fact that such shootings were not a common occurrence. When she was in junior high back in the 1970s, she had a "hit list" herself and she was glad that she did not have access to weapons at the time. Looking back, she blamed "the machine that created" the people who hurt her at the time.[253] As late as 2005, the idea that the shooters were bullied misfits persisted, such as in Jeff Fox's article in the punk zine *Razorcake*. He said that in the wake of Columbine, many high schools turned to policing student's outfits, including banning trench coats, as it was rumored that the pair were part of the "trench coat mafia," a band of outsiders.[254]

Many at the time agreed that the shooters were driven by their status as social outcasts, which included subcultures like punk and goth. But as Caitlin Doughty explained on her show *Ask a Mortician*, this narrative was just flat wrong. Doughty said that Harris and Klebold had been understood by much of the media as "goth loner[s], unlucky with the ladies, racist revenge" shooters. After meeting Sue Klebold (Dylan Klebold's mother) at a TED Conference, Doughty became interested in the topic. She uncovered that in fact they were not bullied loners driven to violence by social alienation. Klebold suffered from depression and was susceptible to influence from Harris. Harris was most likely a garden-variety psychopath.[255] Psychologist Peter Langman, who studies younger mass shooters, argued that the phenomenon of school shootings were far more complicated than just outsiders taking revenge.[256] A more accurate version of events was known as early as 2004 and was recounted in an article on *Slate* by Dave Cullen.[257] Cullen went on to write a full-length book, *Columbine*, considered the authoritative account of this shooting.[258]

As we saw, there was some discussion of these three events in the punk counterpublic. But it seems that many punks might have come to believe that it was pointless to try and counter misinformation about underground music scenes. Rather, many were probably more interested in continuing to maintain their scenes instead of continuing to engage in the ongoing "culture war." The mainstream culture in general was beginning to split itself with the rise of twenty-four-hour cable news and the end of the fairness doctrine. The fairness doctrine was a policy of the Federal Communications Commission that said controversial issues that mattered to the public good should be treated in a balanced manner. The Reagan administration eliminated the policy in the late 1980s.[259] There was also a response to the misinformation found in the mainstream press that surrounded these high-profile events. The same day that *Time* posted their questionable article blaming cliques for Columbine, the *Chicago Tribune* published an article about the goth subculture. Some had believed the shooters were goths. Eric Lipton's primary argument was that the shooters were not goths at all. He knew because Lipton was himself interested in the subculture but not a member of it.[260] *MTV* pointed out the inaccuracy of calling the Columbine shooters goths, quoting other students from the school who knew the pair.[261] The rest of the media eventually caught up to these early attempts to correct the popular narrative about the Columbine shooters. In 2009, CNN posted an article about the post-Columbine backlash against goths and other cultural outsiders.[262] The underground scene had little focus on the shootings. In a review for the *Dimestore Rag* zine in *MRR*, Casey Ress wondered why they did not address the Columbine shootings since the zine was from Littleton, where the shootings took place. "I guess they're sick of hearing about it there," she surmised.[263] Punks in general might have cared less about these incidents because the shooters were not being labeled as violent punks but as violent goths. Some punks did take action on the West Memphis Three (the Black Flag tribute album to raise money and the ongoing Deneke benefit concerts) and wrote about Columbine.

Taken together, what do these three high-profile events say about changing perceptions of punk and related subculture in the 1990s? Although punk panic lingered to some degree in the mainstream culture, the late 1990s saw greater acceptance of subcultures like punk and goth. In the February 2000 issue of *MRR*, Josh Medsker reviewed a play by Barry Levine called *NYHC* which connected the 1970s New York punk scene with the 1990s hardcore scene.[264] Not all attempts to celebrate punk culture by the mainstream were appreciated. In 1998 the movie *SLC Punk!* (dir. James Merendino) was released and panned in punk zines. In Carolyn Keddy's review in *MRR*, she found a general lack of connection to deeper musical influences in the city. The soundtrack had "'new' bands doing old songs" but lacked local bands from Salt Lake City. She watched the film at a screening that included the director doing a Q&A, indicating that it was an event to publicize the film to the relevant press. She had been invited by Mike Millett of Broken Rekids, a punk label out of San Francisco. It is possible that the production company was attempting to burnish their credentials by inviting people associated with the punk subculture. This failed with Keddy.[265] In her *Punk Planet* review, Sarah Jacobson was even less appreciative of the film. She attended a press screening at the San Francisco Film Festival. Jacobson said she had "never written a negative review here before." Her primary complaint was that "it uses all this 'punk with cred' promotion to flaunt a move that is really conservative and pro-corporate." She was annoyed that the main character eventually took the same path as the father he was rebelling against, becoming a corporate lawyer. The "two old guys" sitting behind her during the film who "complained throughout the film about the loud music and drug references" decided they liked the film because of the ending. "These guys liked the film because in the end they weren't threatened by the film at all. The message is that rebellion is okay while you're young but when it's time to get serious, you step in line just like everyone else." She argued that the film was released only because "it ultimately rejects anything revolutionary in its content." It hammered home the message that punk was just a phase that "bored kids" passed through on the way to becoming adults. The film started off feeling authentic to her, but it "used authenticity only to blow it off later." She summarized the film as "a Bill Gates lecture dressed up in Doc Martens and a blue mohawk."[266]

The punk counterpublic seemed united in their disdain for a film selling an interpretation of their experiences back to them. Many felt they did not need to be told what punk meant, because they were participating in a punk scene. Likewise, the various mainstream media reactions to events like the death of Brian Deneke, the West Memphis Three, and the Columbine shootings did not ultimately matter for many punks. First, punks had developed a robust set of institutions that served the needs of their communities. By the end of the 1990s, these institutions were going digital, which would deepen the ability of punks to make connections. Second, in some cases, people in the mainstream culture were beginning to push back against "punk panic" narratives without the intervention of punks or people from other subcultures. Despite the splits that emerged in punk during the 1990s, punk as a coherent scene survived as a viable, underground subculture with a durable set of institutions. New people joined punk scenes across the country, even as punk was ever more incorporated into the mainstream culture. For many Americans who were not punks, the subculture had lost much of its shock value, and overall punks cared less about that anyway. In the next chapter, we will see how the punk underground continued into the digital age and shaped the modern use of the internet. New means of employing the term "punk" emerged in subgenres like Celtic punk or Taqwacore. More punks took a more serious look at race and racism in their scenes. Last, we'll see how the discussion punks had in the 1980s and 1990s affected the larger music industry going into the digital age, with people across genres more willing than ever to discuss the exploitative nature of the recording industry and demand greater control over their music and careers.

Chapter 5

Punk in the Twenty-First Century

2000 to 2021

Scene: Memphis, Tennessee, Negro Terror video shoot, 2018

    A bright afternoon in Memphis and you're headed to a film shoot for a new local favorite. You'd seen several of Omar's bands since he'd moved to Memphis. His latest Oi! project, Negro Terror, brings together all the elements you've struggled to reconcile—your love of Oi! and its association with violent racism. Those things are in tension here in the Deep South. You'd heard that the band had put together an EP of covers of Oi! and skinhead music, but then you realized the songs included tracks from Skrewdriver and Combat 84, known for their association with racism. Brilliant!

    The shoot started around noon at the skate park down the road from your apartment, so you walked down. You arrived and took note of the crowd of extras—the best of the Memphis underground, many of whom you know and greet with hugs. Older and younger punks, Black, white, Oi! boys, skaters, men, women, gay, straight, and so on, an impressive cross section of the local scene. Looking around, you realize that whenever anyone tries to pronounce punk as dead, scenes like this one just prove them wrong.

    Negro Terror arrives and you shake hands with Omar, Rico, and Ra'id, and help them set up their gear. They run through "Voice of Memphis" a couple of times while the film crew finishes setting up. It sounds aggressive and angry. The gathered extras love it. More people arrive to be part of the video. By 5 p.m., the film crew has several takes and has packed up and gone. But everyone is still there, hauling gear to the band's van, chatting, watching the

skaters shred, amped up from the music. Some ended up hanging out the rest of the day, as the sun began to set.
   Another day in the Memphis underground.

Negro Terror	Bloodplums	The Legendary Pink Dots	The Dresden Dolls
Redención 9-11	Operation Ivy	A Global Threat	Lost Cherrees
The Kominas	Secret Trial Five	Alien Kulture	The Rebel Riot Band
No U Turn	Stiff Little Fingers	The Pogues	Death Ridge Boys
Cipher	Dress Code	The Diders	Catcher in the Rye
Demerit	Gum Bleed	Joyride	The Ants
Little Debbie and the Crusaders		Ghostrider	The Bedstars

Punk continued to evolve in the twenty-first century. A major outcome of the alternative turn in popular music was recognition of first-wave punk bands by the recording industry. Several have been inducted into the Rock & Roll Hall of Fame. Ramones and the Talking Heads were inducted in 2002, the Clash in 2003. The Sex Pistols and Blondie were inducted in 2006, with the members of the Sex Pistols refusing to attend, sending a rude note instead.[1] Green Day, who came out of the punk underground scene of the 1980s, became a force in American popular culture. They turned their album *American Idiot* into a stage play in 2010 that ran on Broadway. In the previous chapter, I mentioned some films about punks. Since 2000, a new wave of documentaries and films about punk have been produced. The same media that demonized punks in the 1970s and 1980s now delight in discovering punk scenes in unexpected locales, such as in Myanmar (Burma).[2] But they often flatten the meaning and complexity of local punk scenes and ignore the connections to the larger punk imagined community. The mainstream culture now treats punk as celebrated cultural rebels rather than dangerous outsiders, one youth subculture among many. Punk continues to be an underground culture that spans the globe and exists outside of the mainstream culture.

For this concluding chapter, I briefly explore several aspects of punk in the twenty-first century. First, we will see how the structures punk built in the 1980s and 1990s easily translated to an online environment. Many of the ways that people began to use the internet to connect to each other were inspired by the already existing punk counterpublic, especially before the more commercialized internet of today. Second, I discuss how punk combined with elements of ethnic cultural identities to form subgenres, such as Celtic punk, Gypsy punk, Taqwacore, and Afro-punk. These are often found in diasporic communities. I conclude with a discussion of the punk scene in Myanmar/Burma in the mainstream media and how that differs from the punk media.

Cyberpunks

Cyberpunk is a popular science fiction genre that broke into the public imagination in the 1980s, popularized by writers like William Gibson and Bruce Sterling. The atmosphere they evoked in their works was influenced by an earlier wave of writers, such as Samuel Delany, J. G. Ballard, Philip K. Dick, William S. Burroughs, and Harlan Ellison. By the early 1980s, cyberpunk made it to the big screen. One of the most well-known cyberpunk films from the 1980s was the adaptation of Dick's classic *Do Androids Dream of Electric Sheep?*, renamed *Blade Runner*.[3] In 1980, Bruce Bethke wrote a short story called "Cyberpunk," which was first published in 1983. According to Bethke, the story was "about a bunch of teenage hackers." He coined the phrase because he was "actively trying to invent a new term that grokked the juxtaposition of punk attitudes and high technology . . . I wanted to give my story a snappy, one-word tittle that editors would remember."[4] He argued that William Gibson's work put the genre on the map.[5] Cyberpunk books and films tend to be set in the near future. Gibson's work explored computer hackers operating on the edges of society in an urban environment. The "outsider" nature of the hackers marked them as aligned with punks, who often enacted their communities in the margins of society. The technology in his books was futuristic, but it is not widely accessible for everyone in the stories. Gibson's famous quote "the future is already here—it's just not very evenly distributed" illustrated two realities, according to Tim Chatterton and Georgia Newmarch. First was that the technologies of tomorrow are here today and available to some—not all. It also indicates that the future will have deep inequalities unless they are addressed today.[6] The fact that Bethke settled on punk to describe the people rebelling against the dystopian inequalities of the future shows how the subculture was being understood by some in the early 1980s—as rebels criticizing society. A punk attitude from the fringes could be expected should inequalities continue to mark a highly technological society, these authors argued. Punks were already enacting a version of the cyberpunk model in how they organized their communities outside of the mainstream culture. Some turned to the emerging technology of the internet to help in that organization.

Science fiction can often be understood as predictive. But people often get the order of things incorrect, mistaking inspiration for clairvoyance. Take the example of the Apple iPad. When the product was revealed, many said that the popular sci-fi series *Star Trek: The Next Generation* had "predicted" the future.[7] However, it was more likely that Apple's designers were fans of the show and replicated the form with their new device, either purposefully or not. Looking back, one could also say that punk scenes anticipated the rise of a more fractured, subcultural society that the internet helped spread. Punks brought their ideas about organizing the production of music and community with them to an online environment. Some were trailblazers in embracing the internet and the possibilities it represented. Punks thought in terms of democratic cultural practices and influenced others to do the same. They were not the first counterculture to embrace the internet. Fred Turner connected the practices of the internet with the 1960s counterculture in his book *From Counterculture to Cyberculture*.[8] This shaped how people understood what was possible with the internet infrastructure. Many have hailed the internet as offering a more democratic mode of communication, especially people with familiarity with punk cultural practices. Sophie Lasken discussed the "democratizing power of the internet" in her article about singer and pianist Amanda Palmer, whose roots were in the underground music scene. Lasken noted how Palmer works to build strong connections between herself and her fanbase—critical for someone seeking to exist outside the mainstream music industry.[9]

Underground music had a major influence on Palmer's career trajectory. In her book *The Art of Asking*, she described the rise of her band, The Dresden Dolls, with drummer Brian Viglione (who had a background in the hardcore scene).[10] They went from being a local Boston band to a touring act via the traditional punk pathways of DIY around 2001. The pair would pack up Palmer's car and drive to gigs while handling all aspects of touring themselves.[11] They had access to the internet, which made organizing out-of-town shows more seamless. She noted that her "own email address was front and center on our website."[12] The band began to burn their own CDs to sell on the road. They had been able to record their demos for free thanks to a friend who worked in a studio. They invested in a CD burner to make discs to sell at shows for $5 each, very much like hardcore punk bands in the 1980s selling their cassettes dubbed at home.[13] While Palmer was reared on a steady diet of MTV, she was also introduced to more underground acts in high school, including a band she described as her favorite, the Legendary Pink Dots. The band is an Anglo-Dutch experimental rock band led by singer Edward Ka-Spel that has been around since the 1980s. She first saw them in Boston at the age of sixteen in a small club. She noted of the crowd that "I was standing in a room with three hundred people who seemed to have formed a real, connected comradeship by virtue of Loving One Thing and, by extension, one another." She recalled of meeting the band night that "I didn't feel like a fan meeting a rock star. I didn't feel like a groupie. I felt like a friend."[14] Her argument about the democratic possibilities of the internet grew directly out of her experiences with underground music and DIY punk attitudes. Some might argue that punks predicted the future. But Clodagh McGinley saw things the other way around. The podcaster and zine writer appeared on a 2020 episode of the podcast about Irish language and culture, *Motherfoclóir*, to discuss her bilingual zine (zín in the Irish). She argued that how we interact online was shaped by zine culture. Darach Ó Séaghdha concurred, recalling how punk and alternative music scenes employed zines in the 1980s and 1990s.[15]

Punks were well positioned to imagine the internet as a means of building a countermedia landscape in other ways. Punks were used to tape trading, where they shared the music they liked or made through the mail. A general tape trading culture emerged in the 1980s with a variety of cultures shared. Don Campau has a website dedicated to the history of cassette culture where he noted how some locate the origins of tape trading in punk culture.[16] Some punk subgenres developed directly out of this culture, such as grindcore, a high-powered mix of metal and hardcore. Shane Embury of Napalm Death discovered the first grindcore band Repulsion via tape trading in the 1980s.[17] You can see traces of this tape trading in punk zines from the 1980s. In a 1983 issue of *Flipside*, Donald M. Bailey from Winnipeg requested "punk and HC tapes, trade only." Tom Clark from Birmingham, Michigan, had a similar request. Bands took advantage of tape trading, such as The Pukes, who hailed from Greenbrae, California. For a blank tape and $3, you got eight songs, "lyric sheet incl."[18] Punks solicited bootlegs of live shows in the classified sections of punk zines, such as in a 1984 issue of *Flipside*. Steve Daycak requested live tapes by the Misfits and Sham 69, as well as "most other 'punk' Hardcore bands." Dan Waterman had a classified ad requesting to trade "TAPES. FLYERS. AND SKULLS WITH EVERYONE." A third ad from David requested tapes from the "Misfits, Mission of Burma, (recent) Meat Puppets, and others. I have a good selection to trade from," he said.[19]

Trading music continued into the digital era. By the early 2000s, sharing music on peer-to-peer networks on the internet was a well-established practice, with several online music sharing sites widely available. Most consider eMusic to be a pioneer in file sharing. That is not quite correct, however. eMusic bought out Internet Underground Music Archive (IUMA). According to Georgia Perry, this began in 1993 as an attempt to give "unsigned artists a place to share their music and connect with fans."[20] She interviewed founder Jon Luini in 2013. As a kid, Luini would bike to a local record shop, buy what he could afford, and swap mix tapes with friends. This led him to start a music file-sharing website. After starting the site, Perry said that within months, CNN was posting articles about the service. Luini also founded an online music magazine that included audio samples, *Addicted to Noise*. He compared himself favorably with Napster, as he felt his project was artist-centered, but "Napster and other music sharing sites were more focused on themselves."[21] His ultimate goal was to help musicians better connect with fans and make music their full-time careers. He acknowledged that some damage had been done to music over the years by corporations co-opting online spaces. But he felt that musicians and music consumers had greater power in their own hands through the internet. Overall, though, "I think that the internet in general has failed to live up to its potential."[22] Punks might have beat him to the punch, as some began sharing their music online as soon as they received access to the pre–World Wide Web internet. In 1990, Matt Kelly in San Francisco wrote in to *MRR* let others know about his BBS (bulletin board system), which he called Nihilism. He said that he "gave free advertising" to a variety of different punk labels. He requested that labels get in touch and let him know about releases from their bands.[23]

Another example of punks organizing online prior to the IUMA going live was "Underground Sounds," which was hosted on WWIV, a BBS. According to Mutantis XXX, "Underground Sounds" "deals with all aspects of the underground music scene."[24] It is unclear whether file sharing was an aspect of this. But punks were using online spaces to get the word out about their music. Since the 2000s, punks have expressed a variety of views on the new phenomenon of sharing music online and what that meant for punk. In a 2001 interview with the band Machinegun, guitarist and singer Chris Fields was asked about the Napster controversy. He said, "I think I'm going to have to side with Lars [Ulrich of Metallica, who came out against Napster] on that one. Being a starving musician, it doesn't make sense to give it away for free."[25] A punk named Sock wrote in to *MRR* in 2006 about his preference for the physical over the digital. He said that he had used Napster to download songs by bands such as Operation Ivy and A

Global Threat, but still preferred physical media to digital. He appreciated getting a physical copy of *MRR* and did not enjoy online blogs as much.[26] In a 2007 interview with Lance Hahn for *MRR*, Steve Battershill from the British anarcho-punk band Lost Cherrees said they reformed in 2003 because their songs were trading on Napster. He said, "I put a notice on some punk website that we were reforming and within a week had received 40 or so emails, mostly from the States."[27]

Zines easily translated to the online format early on. Punks were already used to communicating at vast distances. Most zines such as *MRR* had a letters section, reviews of sound recordings and zines, a classified section, and the all-important scene report. Through scene reports, bands could figure out whom to get in touch with when planning tours, where to play, and what cities they could include on a tour. Employing the internet for these same activities seemed like a natural step, as shown by the discussions about the internet found in zines. By the late 1980s, many in zines began to discuss computers and computing in general. In 1989, Jerod Pore reviewed a book called *Out of the Inner Circle: A Hacker's Guide to Computer Security*. Pore argued that "if one understands the nuances of intellectual machismo . . . then this becomes 'A Guide to Hacking Computer Security'."[28] He also recommended "The Internet Worm Program: An Analysis" for learning how to write a "worm" program, a type of computer virus.[29] In a letter in 1992, Bob wrote to *MRR* to encourage other punks to go online. He said, "in the computer world there's what's called the internet." He said that "it gives people who have access to it access to each other."[30] He described e-mail and BBSs for the uninitiated. "The point of this is that punks are on the internet." He gave the information for the *Punk List*, which he described as a "virtual MR&R-type zine, only get your messages within minutes from when they are sent."[31] He even noted that some universities, such as University of California at Berkeley, provided access to the general public for a fee.[32] Some punks contributed directly to the infrastructure of the internet. Tom Jennings, known for his role in the queercore movement, created Fidonet in the 1980s. The program connected BBSs into a larger network.[33]

Zines started going online in the early 1990s, partly out of necessity. In the September 1992 issue of *MRR*, Pore wrote in about the apparent end of the zine *Factsheet Five*, the "zine of zines, the central clearinghouse of information about small presses."[34] He said that it was only "sort of" gone. *V* was a new publication that planned to pick up the slack. Pore had also volunteered to carry on *Factsheet Five*'s mission of being the "zine of zines." *F5—Electronic* would be entirely online. He touted more ways of getting online access outside of a local college, such as Prodigy, Genie, and America Online, but he was unsure if they were "internet gateways." He also encouraged people to connect to Usenet, an application in use since the early 1980s for online discussions. He hosted rec.mag and moderated a newsgroup on Usenet.[35]

Not everyone agreed with Pore's optimistic views on the power of the internet. He got pushback from Oberc, a punk from Chicago, on his solution to the problem of *Factsheet Five* folding. Oberc argued that going online was not a real solution for many as "most of the people in small and medium sized presses do not have access to computer systems."[36] He noted that Hudson Luce, who had taken over *Factsheet Five*, should have refunded subscriptions and sent back zines mailed in for review once they folded as a physical zine.[37] In the August 1993 issue of *MRR*, Andy Gronberg compared his online activities as similar to a zine. However, he was disappointed that his Alternative BBS was not getting much traffic and asked other punks to connect.[38] These letters were all before the "Eternal September" in 1993,[39] where companies like America Online began to allow access to online communities for a wider cross-section of the public.[40] In the 1993 edition of *MRR*'s "Book Your Own Fuckin' Life"—an edition of the zine published periodically to collect resources for punk bands—a Finland BBS was listed in the miscellaneous section.[41] By the early 2000s, "Book Your Own Fuckin' Life" had gone online. Joao Da Silva of the Chilean hardcore band Redención 9-11 said that the website (and print version) were useful to his scene.[42] *MRR* continued to publish a physical issue until 2019. The last physical copy to hit newsstands and be mailed out was May 2019. It is still published online.[43]

In the mid-1990s, *Punk Planet* began publication. It was organized online. According to coeditor Will Dandy, it emerged out of conversations on "a nation-wide bulletin board system expressing discontent with policies of other zines out there."[44] The rise of the internet meant new means of organizing. "With the computer we are able to use resources and have writers that would never have been possible before."[45] As a result, writers in the magazine often discussed the internet in a largely positive way. In 1995, they published an article on organizing DIY culture online. Joe Nrrrd answered general questions about the internet and how punks could take what they were already doing online. Nrrrd said that one of his favorite part of zines was the classified ads. "That was pretty cool when I was fourteen and didn't have a computer and the key mode for communicating with strangers was a stamp and some spit."[46] But what had changed with the internet was "immediacy. You can do all the same things you did before, except quickly and simply." Zines could be more easily shared and distributed, for example.[47] They also went into details about how to connect to the internet.[48] The article mocked *MRR* columnist Ben Weasel, who had recently expressed his concerns about the internet. Weasel noted that television was "useless crap," but the internet "is actually much worse." He said that "on the surface [the internet] would seem to be a wonderful tool of communication. It's not and the potential for it being a great tool of communication doesn't exist because one can't truly communicate about any important issues when an entire segment of the population . . . is cut off from discussion."[49] He pointed out that not everyone had access to the internet, as they could not afford the infrastructure to get them online. He concluded that "it's the most class-based piece of technology to come along since, umm . . . Well, actually, ANYTHING!"[50] Not everyone agreed about the organizing power of the internet.

Punk Planet had other articles on digital music indicating a general embrace of the digital turn in music production. Mike Evans wrote a how-to article on streaming in May 2001. He provided links to streaming software from Microsoft and Apple as well as free alternatives like Shoutcast.[51] In a May 2000 article in *Punk Planet*, David Grad discussed the lawsuit between the Recording Industry Association of America (RIAA) and MP3.com, a website that hosted MP3s. The service allowed online storage of MP3s that could be accessed anywhere with an internet connection, Grad explained.[52] He quoted Laura Betterly, the president of a company called Visiosonic that made digital electronic gear, who speculated on the motivations of the major labels. "This has a lot more to do with trying to control the industry itself than the technology. . . . The whole Time Warner-EMI thing is an attempt to figure out how they can capitalize and keep control. I think they want to own the digital arena and the best way they can do that is take down the big players first and replace them with your [meaning services controlled by the major labels] guys."[53] Grad pointed to a lawsuit against Napster as further evidence of that tactic. Competitors to MP3.com or Napster were critical, such as David Pakman, who was president of Myplay. He believed that MP3.com head Michael Robertson was simply trying to manipulate his stock by violating the rights of intellectual property holders. Hilary Rosen of the RIAA believed that Pakman was rightfully angry at MP3.com for trying to get an unfair advantage. Robertson also argued that he was the most "artist-friendly of companies." But he also argued that the consumer had rights as well. Rosen admitted that "the horse has left the barn" with regard to file sharing. She argued that litigation was the primary way to sort out fair use from illegal use.[54]

Kyle Ryan wrote about the acquisition of eMusic by Universal Music Group in *Punk Planet* in 2001. Before the buyout, many independent labels had signed up to provide their catalogs to the service because it was "all indies" according to a spokesman.[55] The problem was not just with the major label buyout from the artists' point of view. Jenny Toomey founded a musicians' rights organization called the Future of Music Coalition. She argued that eMusic's deal with independent labels was already rotten. She said the "small labels [that] gave away their entire catalog for a couple of thousand dollars for an advance found themselves in a rotten position." She felt that "exclusivity very rarely is beneficial except for the person with exclusive rights."[56] As the digital option for popular music expanded, Darren Walters of the label Jade Tree saw the writing on the wall. When given the chance to work with eMusic, he refused to sell his label's music. He said, "many people sought out the cash without ever really thinking about possibilities such as this [a major buying eMusic]."[57] Toomey added that eMusic had clauses in their contracts with labels that kept their music on the website until advances were recouped. A stark dichotomy existed with regard to these new technologies. It hurt capitalization of smaller labels. But it also had the promise to change the status quo of the music industry—possibly in favor of the artist.[58]

The digital turn shaped the music industry in other ways. Intellectual property (IP) became another flash point. By the late 1990s, corporations started to think about their IP as something in need of greater protections. This ran counter to an important aspect of the punk aesthetic—the bricolage nature of punk art and the use of parody. Punks took freely from any number of sources without attribution. Circulating underground helped shield punks from lawsuits. But corporate IP could more easily find knock-offs and remixes of the works that they owned. *MRR* columnist and frontman for the band Furious George, George Tabb discussed his encounter with the publisher Houghton Mifflin, who owned the rights to the Curious George books.[59] Tabb and his lawyer drove to Boston to take a deposition from the publisher's representative. He was seeking to trademark the phrase "Furious George" but not any derivative image of the iconic monkey.[60] In a previous column, he noted that there were other uses of "Furious George" that the publisher did not sue over, such as a professional wrestler and the owner of the New York Yankees.[61] In 2006, *Punk Planet* reprinted an interview that the hosts of *Sound Opinions*, Jim DeRogatis and Greg Kot, conducted with

Stanford law professor Lawrence Lessig. He founded the Creative Commons and the Center for Internet and Society. According to DeRogatis, "At the heart of Lessig's philosophy is the simple fact that copyright, as it is now being defined in America, simply didn't exist until about a century ago, and its extensions are being advocated strictly out of greed by megacorporations such as Disney."[62] Disney had historically benefited from works in the public domain, DeRogatis noted.[63] They discussed Lessig's defense of Napster at the Supreme Court. Lessig was against copying copyrighted content without permission but took the Napster case for "an esoteric legal question." He cited the Sony Betamax case that found that new technologies should be legal as long as they are not used solely for illegal means. He noted that "it's a problem for Congress, not for the courts."[64] When asked about the RIAA's campaign against Napster and other peer-to-peer networks, Lessig argued that the very existence of these networks drove an "extremist" view of IP. The organization existed to represent the middleman in the industry, not artists or consumers. Lessig noted that "the publishers and the recording industry obviously have interests that are not necessarily the same interests as the artist."[65] Another copyright scholar, L. Ray Patterson, compared the relationship "as the cow to the cattle rancher."[66] Lessig concluded that "if they can't provide value to the artists then they have no reason to be here in business."[67] DeRogatis pushed Lessig on the issue of file sharing by comparing it to taping a complete broadcast of Pink Floyd's *The Wall* off the radio. Home taping was considered a threat to the industry before file sharing, he argued. But Lessig argued that there was a real difference based on the scope. Dubbing a copy of a tape took time and was limited, but putting a file up online made a recording available to hundreds of thousands of people. Even so, he believed the penalties that the RIAA was hoping to inflict were disproportional.[68]

Lessig was not the only person worried about the corrosive effects of overly broad interpretations of copyright laws. In the September 2005 issue of *Punk Planet*, artist Anne Elizabeth Moore discussed the perceived attacks on the doctrine of fair use. Her article began with a discussion the remix album by Danger Mouse. *The Grey Album* was a mash-up of the Beatles' *White Album* and Jay-Z's *Black Album*. Danger Mouse received a cease-and-desist letter from EMI for unauthorized use of the Beatles' work. Kembrew McLeod argued that the purpose of such cease and desist letters was " 'to scare people' . . . And it works," Moore argued.[69] Moore discussed the work of artist Chris Reilly, whose project challenged corporations to sue him for his use of corporate images in his artwork, although he asked them not to do so. McLeod noted that although Reilly's "Don't Sue Chris Reilly Campaign" was "snarky and self-promotional," it was also " 'in keeping with the long-term strategy of maintaining fair use."[70] An overly broad interpretation of copyright and a narrow one for fair use stifled artistic expression, Moore argued. She talked about how one of her own art projects included a criticism of Mattel's American Girl dolls. She was concerned enough about receiving a cease-and-desist from the company that she censored her work when it came time to display it. She said that "as intelligent, knowledgeable cultural producers, we may understand that, according to the letter of the law, we retain the right to parody, teach, and criticize the intellectual property of others. Yet we also understand that defending those rights takes more dedication, intelligence, money, and time than most of us have to work with."[71] Lessig also weighed in in the issue of the *Grey Album*. He was concerned that the technologies that allowed for a work of art like the *Grey Album* were written when very different technologies existed.[72]

The digital turn opened new opportunities and created new pitfalls for punks. Some were on the cutting edge of thinking about how the internet could be used to strengthen their cultural and communal ties. Others were wary of the new technology and the problems it could cause. The ways that punks used traditional types of media informed their foray into the internet and shaped how others thought about the internet as well. The internet lowered the barriers of entry into the world of punk rock. The punk underground grew online as new punks were introduced to underground genres of music after the alternative movement of the 1990s. A key reason Bethke settled on "punk" to describe his short story was because of how he saw punks as organizing in real life in the 1980s in a way that more people might in the future. Many punks saw that they could replicate what were doing in physical spaces in the digital world and more easily organize their scenes.

Postcolonial Punk?

During the late 1980s and 1990s, new subgenres of punk emerged, such as thrash, grindcore, emo, and riot girl. Another combined traditional folk music with punk rock. Folk punk embraced a variety of different folk idioms from various ethnic traditions. These ethnic punk bands often celebrated specific national, ethnic, or racial identity via traditional folk song styles, structures, or instrumentation. This was not just a band from a particular place. Take the Belfast band Stiff Little Fingers. Their lived experiences in a de facto war zone informed their lyrical content, as living in Belfast during the Troubles made violence an inescapable fact of life. Stiff Little Fingers' music was not particularly influenced by traditional Irish or British folk music but from rock music and their punk contemporaries. The band went on to become one of the early UK successes when their first album charted in 1979.[73] The bands that make up various categories of "ethnic punk" by way of contrast tend to lean into folk music traditions. They often do so to make a political or cultural point. These subgenres found popularity among diasporic communities or those operating in a postcolonial context. Here I discuss four of these genres: Celtic punk, gypsy punk, Taqwacore, and Afro-punk. These subgenres function as responses to oppression and objectification in the ethnic groups' history, making them something of a postcolonial expression of punk rock.

Probably the earliest and most well-known of these punk idioms was Celtic punk, a subset of punk rock and Irish folk. Celtic punk offers up an interesting set of historically situated problems. We can use the case of Celtic punk to think about the other three genres. Modern Irish identity was shaped by centuries of colonization of Ireland by the British and then the division of the island into the Republic of Ireland and Northern Ireland, which remained in the United Kingdom. Many consider music and storytelling to be a central element of the Irish identity. This was both a stereotype of the colonial period and a part of Irish culture. In their article about Irish rock music in the journal *Popular Music*, Noel McLaughlin and Martin McLoone argued that the link between the Irish and their music was "finally consolidated in the Victorian era at the height of the British imperial project."[74] Because of colonization, ideas about what it meant to be Irish were "imposed" on the Irish. Aspects of those ideas, the authors argued, "have now become internalized and today bear traces of a particular nationalist political and cultural history."[75] Irish rock artists of the 1990s that gained international acclaim, like Sinéad O'Connor and Dolores O'Riordan of the Cranberries, were often described using stereotypical language about the Irish by the mainstream rock press, such as O'Connor's "fiery Irish temper." Yet both artists leaned into traditional Irish styles of performing.[76] In the postcolonial Republic of Ireland, rebellious music fans in the 1930s through the 1950s found American popular culture a pleasurable alternative to "an overly essential national culture" that had strong conservative aspects. Music fans in Ireland also had to deal with the problem of the homogenizing effect of globalization. Rather than destroying traditional music, McLaughlin and McLoone argued that the dominant globalized music industry often leans into the local via a "marketing of 'difference'."[77] If clinging to the local presented problems but so did turning to a globalized culture, what was the solution? McLaughlin and McLoone argued that some embraced "forms of hybridity that grow out of the 'liminal spaces' provided at this intersection, offering a critical perspective on both."[78] If the national culture was too dogmatic and conservative, but the globalized or colonial perspective could be destructive or essentializing, why not inhabit the spaces in between to reveal that reality? The result was what McLaughlin and McLoone dubbed "hybrid texts." They discussed artists that highlighted "the ways in which these [artists] inhabit the spaces between 'Irishness' and the global culture of rock music."[79]

We can see this same dynamic at play with Celtic punk. The term "Celtic" included several different ethnic groups found in the United Kingdom, Ireland, and parts of France. The Welsh, the Scots, and the Bretons of Brittany in modern-day France, among others, are all Celtic peoples. They speak one of two branches of Celtic languages (Brittonic and Gaelic) and each have their own cultural traditions.[80] Before punk, there was a major folk revival in the 1960s and 1970s around the world. Irish artists like the Dubliners, the Chieftains, and Christy Moore were part of this international folk revival. The Dubliners were popular in Dublin and London, and the Chieftains had international success and continue to perform today, as does Christy Moore.[81] The Chieftains were considered the unofficial music ambassadors from the Republic of Ireland in the late 1980s.[82] Moore was honored as Ireland's greatest living musician in 2007.[83] In their article, McLaughlin and McLoone focused on how the Celtic folk revival became incorporated into rock in Ireland. The band Horslips made their debut in 1971 with a mix of traditional Irish and rock instruments. They took influence from the progressive rock genre and traditional Irish music. They incorporated Irish mythology into their lyrical content.[84] Many considered these Celtic rock bands a more authentic expression of Irish traditional music despite playing a hybrid type of music. They largely replaced what were known as show bands that many considered a cultural debasement. These bands were popular from the 1920s and 1930s, playing forms of American popular music in clubs and on the radio. McLaughlin and McLoone noted how these bands created the national infrastructure for Celtic rock to emerge later.[85]

Celtic punk took inspiration from bands like Horslips. Celtic punk combined punk with traditional Irish music. These bands often used folk instruments. This could include a tin whistle or flute, fiddle, uilleann pipes (a type of bagpipe), harp, concertina or accordion, mandolin, banjos, or bodhrán (a traditional drum). Normal rock music could be used, just played with a more "Celtic" sound. These bands will sometimes play traditional Irish songs or discuss aspects of Irish culture in their lyrics. Most consider the Pogues to be pioneers of Celtic punk. Banjo player Jem Finer recalled discovering punk while living in London in the 1970s. He shared a flat with singer Shane MacGowan. In an interview in the *New Statesman*, he told Colm McAuliffe, "He'd always play the Dubliners [the band] when he came in late at night [to a local pub]. One day he said he wanted to play these songs like punk. I thought this was a really good idea."[86] Finer called the Pogues "misunderstood." He argued that they had a variety of musical influences outside of traditional Irish folk, including "rockabilly, country, the Velvet Underground." Like other punks, he said, "we were making it all up on instruments we couldn't play."[87] In her book on Irish music *Bringing It All Back Home*, Nuala O'Connor said that in their music the "Irish ballad . . . collided with punk."[88] Most members of the bands were British, but several were the children of recent immigrants from Ireland, notably MacGowan, who was born in the United Kingdom but spent his early childhood in Ireland. They played up that cultural connection. According to O'Connor, "The Pogues disported themselves like archetypal Paddies: hard drinking, bad mannered, foul mouthed and unkempt."[89] Elvis Costello was a fan, saying their music was a "promise of a good time."[90] The authenticity of their Irishness has long been the subject of heated debate. In the discussion on the band on the *Motherfoclóir* podcast, Peadar Ó Caomhánaigh said the band was not well received when they first played on Irish television in the 1980s. They were later redeemed when they performed alongside the Dubliners on the popular program *The Late Show*.[91] In 2010, Ed Power penned what can only be described as a St. Patrick's Day screed against the Pogues and other "Plastic Paddies" (his words) of Celtic punk. He said that "their supposed 'Irishness' is a mish-mash of hairy, outmoded cliches, many of which they seem actively interested in perpetuating."[92] He lamented that the Pogues were often seen as an authentic voice of Ireland abroad when bands like "Thin Lizzy, Fatima Mansions and My Bloody Valentine" actually came from the Republic of Ireland. He also seemed to take a dim view of Eugene Hutz of the Gypsy punk band Gogol Bordello, mentioning his "rockabilly-Borat charm" and "comedy mustache."[93]

Critics of Celtic punk focus on the authenticity of a supposedly pure national identity. Authenticity is a troublesome concept in the best of times, and is even more fraught when national identity meets diasporic communities and popular culture. The criticism raised by Power ignored the realities of people who identified as Irish despite being born outside of Ireland. Paul Gilroy called the word "diaspora" ancient as it was originally found in a third-century BCE translated text of Hebrew scripture in reference to the status of the Jewish people—the original diasporic community. In their book of collected essays *Theorizing Diaspora*, Jana Evans Braziel and Anita Mannur define diaspora as "displaced communities of people who have been dislocated from their native homeland through the movements of migration, immigration, or exile."[94] The concept of a diaspora in the modern context has been connected to the concept of the nation-state. They noted that "nationhood and national identity" have been rethought; they argued that "critical analyses should also interrogate contemporary forms of movement, displacement, and dislocation" that helped create diasporic communities.[95] The people who find themselves in exile tend to "inhabit" multiple "national spaces" at once. As such, they speak to "critical discourses on race, ethnicity, nation, and identity."[96] With regards to the Irish diaspora, Piaras Mac Éinrí argued that since the 150th anniversary of the Great Famine in the 1990s, scholars have taken a renewed interest in migration from Ireland. The 1990s also saw "a new and remarkable emphasis on the ties between the Irish at home and those around the world. In part this was cultural—the new wave of Irish singers, musicians and cultural artists, from within the country but also from within the diaspora, who put Irish identity on the map and even made it cool."[97] During that time, there started to be a less geography-bound definition of Irish identity. Two Irish presidents, Mary Robinson and Mary McAleese, helped shape that understanding. Robinson gave diasporic communities a new legitimacy by visiting Irish communities around the world. McAleese continued that outreach. Since then, Mac Éinrí said, "there has been an increasing if initially grudging acceptance that the Irish identity of those within the diaspora is not simply a pale shadow of 'authentic' Irish identity in Ireland, but has something distinctive to contribute."[98] Celtic punk has become one such contribution.

The Pogues often wrote songs that spoke to the Irish diasporic experience, such as on the album *If I Should Fall from Grace from God*. One of their biggest hits (and Christmas favorite) "Fairytale of New York" told the story of a working-class couple in New York struggling with drugs and each other. It explored the connection between the Irish diaspora and the New York Police Department. Guitarist Philip Chevron wrote "Thousands Are Sailing," which discussed the fraught experiences of many Irish immigrants to the United States. The song mentions the coffin ships of the Great

Famine era and President John F. Kennedy, the first Irish American and Catholic president. The album also has one of the band's most political songs, "Streets of Sorrow/Birmingham Six." The two-part song spoke to the specific situation of Northern Ireland. The Troubles, the violence between those who wanted to remain in the United Kingdom and those who wished to join the Republic of Ireland, drove internal migration within the United Kingdom. The "Streets of Sorrow" part of the song spoke to the pain of leaving home because of the violence. The second, more controversial part of the song criticized the UK government for arbitrarily targeting Irish people in response to the IRA bombing campaign. The title refers to the Birmingham Six, who were wrongfully accused and convicted of bombing a pub in Birmingham, UK. They later had their sentences overturned and received compensation from the government. At the time the song was written, the high-profile case of the Guildford Four and Maguire Seven was the subject of public debate. The two groups had been convicted of a pub bombing in Guildford. One member of the Guildford Four, Gerry Conlon, became something of a cause célèbre by the time the song was written. Conlon's father had also been arrested and had died in prison. At the time of the song, Conlon and the rest were still in prison on what most considered false pretenses, though their convictions were eventually overturned.[99] The Pogues also covered traditional songs on the album, such as their version of "Rocky Road to Dublin" as part of a larger medley. The album cover evoked a traditional folk set-up. The band stands with their instruments against a neutral background. MacGowan was centered, leaning on a bodhrán.[100] Several members of the Pogues claimed membership in the Irish diaspora, including MacGowan and bassist Cait O'Riordan. Long-time guitarist Philip Chevron and Terry Woods were both from the Republic of Ireland. Chevron, who died in 2013 after a battle with cancer, had a long history in the Dublin punk scene.[101]

Other bands followed the Pogues and helped shape the folk punk genre more generally. Scottish band the Nyah Fearties also married folk and punk in the early 1980s. The band were influenced by reggae, dub, and even industrial music. In addition to tuning a guitar like a banjo, which they called a "ganjo," they incorporated sheets of metal and oil drums into their performances.[102] Roaring Jack formed in Sydney, Australia, in the mid-1980s. The singer of the band, Alistair Hulett, was from Scotland but immigrated to New Zealand in the late 1960s. He went to Australia, where he discovered punk by the late 1970s.[103] In the mid-1990s, Celtic punk bands appeared in the United States among the Irish diasporic communities.

The band Dropkick Murphys formed in 1996 in Massachusetts, combing elements of hardcore, Oi!, and traditional Irish music.[104] Their label, Hellcat, described them as "a combination of 1970s-era punk rock, Irish folk songs and 'old-fashion working class rock 'n' roll."[105] The band claimed strong working-class roots. Bass player and songwriter Ken Casey said, "in a way, I don't feel like a musician. I feel like we're carrying a torch for the working class."[106] They had a history of playing gigs in support of labor unions and worked with the Democratic political organization Punkvoter during the 2004 presidential election. Many working-class people in Massachusetts claim Irish heritage, the band included.[107] Flogging Molly got together in Los Angeles around the same time. Members of the band came from Ireland and the United States. Much like their contemporaries out of Massachusetts, they combined punk with Irish folk music. They were one of the earliest bands on the Hollywood-based label SideOneDummy Records.[108] The genre has proven popular outside of the Irish diaspora. In 1992, Orthodox Celts formed in Serbia and continues to be popular there. Though the members seemed to have no direct ties to Ireland, they embraced traditional Irish music.[109] In 2011, Selfish Murphy formed in Romania, and again, there seem to be no direct ties with Ireland.[110]

Others took influence from Celtic punk bands and combined other folk traditions with punk. Gypsy punk combined elements of Romani music with punk rock. In the late 1990s, a refugee from the Chernobyl disaster in the 1980s Eugene Hütz started Gogol Bordello while living in New York City.[111] He promoted the band as "gypsy punk cabaret." In their mission statement they laid out their collective goals. It said that "we chose to work with Gypsy cabaret and punk traditions. It is what we know and feel."[112] It was an interesting choice to use the word "Gypsy," as many in the Romani community consider this term a slur. Moving to New York was a key event in helping him merge those musical traditions. But he first encountered Romani music and his connection to the culture while living in internal exile in western Ukraine after Chernobyl. His mother had family there, who he learned were Romani. He was inspired by the DIY mindset of the community there, which was born out of necessity. The make-up of the band was international, with members from Russia and Israel.[113] Later members came from Latin America, Jamaica, and China.[114] In addition to promoting a kind of musical multiculturalism, Hütz regularly used his platform to highlight the discrimination the Romani still face in Europe.[115] Their song "Break the Spell" from their fifth album, *Trans-Continental Hustle*, specifically discussed discrimination against Romani. Even though Hütz embraced his Romani heritage and sought to highlight the plight of many Romani communities in Europe, not everyone appreciated this project. In the film about Hütz's journey to better understand Romani culture, *The Pied Piper of Hützovina*, some of the Romani musicians he met expressed distaste for the Gogol Bordello tracks he played for them.[116] Much like the Pogues, the band faced rejection by those who thought of themselves as gatekeepers of a larger tradition.

Other Gypsy punk bands have emerged since Gogol Bordello. These bands tend to lean into and embrace multiculturalism. Denver-based DeVotchKa included band members who were either immigrants or the children of immigrants, including some with Romani ancestry.[117] In some cases, they have no direct connections to Romani culture. Balkan Beat Box had origins in New York City and Tel Aviv, Israel. They combined Balkan brass band, hip-hop, dub, and traditional Middle Eastern music.[118] One thing that set Gypsy punk apart from Celtic punk was that the Romani people have no homeland, even as they share a cultural heritage. Alan Ashton-Smith argued that "while Roma Worldwide identify as a single group, they have no home country."[119] He continued, "this means they cannot be literally postcolonial."[120] Hence they have generally been ignored by those who work in postcolonial studies.[121] But a real sense of unity persisted among Romani people and among those who persecuted them. In the 1970s, some Romani people formed several organizations intended to fight discrimination. Ashton-Smith described the founding of the World Romani Congress that was started in 1971. They spun off other organizations to fight racism, such as the European Romani Rights Center in 1978. Ashton-Smith said that "these activities can be taken as reactions against the centuries of misrepresentation that the Roma endured."[122] Gypsy punk could be seen as part of this larger postcolonial project to bring awareness to the racism still faced by many Romani.

Two other ethnic punk genres appeared in the 2000s: Taqwacore and Afro-punk. These developed in the United States and spoke to specific American realities, one during the first two decades of the new century and the other for centuries. Michael Muhammad Knight wrote his novel *The Taqwacores* to square his flagging faith in Islam and his love of punk rock. Born into a Catholic family, Knight converted to Islam as a teenager after reading *The Autobiography of Malcolm X*. He took up a study of Arabic and began attending a mosque in Rochester, New York. He traveled to Pakistan while in high school to attend the International Islamic University in Islamabad. His experiences there caused him to question his faith. After writing the book (in true punk fashion), he made it into a zine and sold copies at the 2003 Islamic Society of North America convention. Alternative Tentacles and then Soft Skull Press picked it up for publication. Writing the book helped Knight reconnect with his faith as he figured out an alternative practice of Islam that worked for him.[123] The title of the book was a reference the Islamic concept of piety (*taqwa*) and hardcore punk. The narrative follows Yusuf Ali, a Pakistani American engineering student, who moves into an Islamic punk house, which introduces him to punk and helps him deal with his religious insecurities. Similar to the queer punks who often felt out of place in both the nonpunk LGBQT+ community and in the punk communities, the Islamic punks in the book sought a space of their own that incorporated both elements of their lives into one. One of the women wears a burqa decorated with punk patches, for example. The punks are depicted as religious but constantly challenging tradition. In one scene, a woman leads the group in prayer, which is traditionally conducted by men.[124] The book combined a critique of the anti-Muslim sentiment common in the United States after September 11, 2001 with a critique of more conservative Islamic practices. Because of a sense of being out of place in the United States and with the more conservative elements of Islam, the characters struggle to reconcile their punk rock and Islamic identities.

Knight's book inspired some young Muslims to create a new genre of punk. A 2008 article in the *New York Times* included some of the young men and women he inspired. Hannan Arzay, a fifteen-year old Moroccan immigrant in East Islip, New York, faced discrimination from her non-Muslim neighbors and the teachers at her Islamic school. The school van was regularly pelted with eggs and coffee cups, and once a bottle broke a window. Her Q'uran instructor once "threw chalk at her for requesting literal translations of the holy texts." She said that the copy of *The Taqwacores* that her uncle gave her "saved my faith."[125] A documentary was made of a tour of Taqwacore bands as well as a narrative film based on the book. The documentary *Taqwacore: The Birth of Punk Islam* (see figure 5.1) followed a tour with the Kominas and Secret Trial Five. In one memorable scene that could have come straight from Knight's book, the bands were booked to play at the Islamic Society of North America's convention. The all-female Secret Trial Five and the Kominas managed to cause quite a controversy. The organizers demanded that Secret Trial Five stop their set as women were prohibited from singing at the convention. The Kominas took the stage and led the hijab-clad young women in the front row in chants of "stop the hate." After the police were called in to shut them down, the band led the

Figure 5.1. Basim Usmani of The Kominas. (Eye Steel Film/Creative Commons CC BY 2.0)

crowd in a chant of "pigs are *haram* [forbidden] in Islam." The bands were then ejected from the conference.[126]

These young Muslims expressed deep concerns about living in Western countries as Islamophobia was at a fever pitch. But they also sought to square their faith with their non-Islamic cultural practices. The bricolage nature of punk gave them a means of doing so. According to scholar Hisham D. Aidi, Basim Usmani and Shahjehan Khan of the Kominas (both immigrants from Pakistani) returned to Lahore in 2007. There they started a punk ska band named Noble Drew. They named the band for Noble Drew Ali, the founder of the unorthodox branch of Islam the Moorish Science Temple of America. Usmani explained his choice of the band name, saying, "Noble Drew changed my view of Islam." He called Drew "anti-hegemonic" and said that he "created his own Islamic culture" that "reached back to rescue the Islam beat out of African slaves."[127] It was that American syncretism he hoped to share with people in Pakistan via his music and his own unortho-dox religious practice.[128] They were not the first young Pakistani immigrants to do so. In 1980 three Pakistani young men and one "token white man" formed the punk band Alien Kulture. They hailed from south London and wanted to form a band in response to the racist violence aimed at South

Asians at the time. They wrote songs that "broadly originated from their experiences and observations about being a second generation Asian in the UK."[129] Here they differed from the Taqwacore bands. Alien Kulture focused more on the racism they faced, rather than Islamophobia. In one song, "Asian Youth," they lament the lack of unity among South Asian young people living in the United Kingdom.

The Kominas made religious discrimination the focal point of their songs for the same reasons. Their song "Sharia Law in the USA" played with the irrational fear some conservatives expressed of Sharia law being made the law of the land in the United States. Taking the point of view of the imagined Islamist bent on making America an Islamic republic, the song becomes a dual critique of fearful American conservatives and figures like Osama Bin Laden. Wendy Fangyu Hsu argued that the transnational nature of the on- and offline community built around Taqwacore by bands such as the Kominas were "linked to, if not a consequence of, the feeling of lack of national belonging and social comfort experienced by individuals of South Asian descent living in the United States."[130] She said that September 11 "brought this collective state of melancholia into relief." She argued that "the band deploys the punk sound and do-it-yourself social-networking to re-territorialize and re-embed itself into a world partitioned by ideology, politics, and migration."[131] Doing so "decenters the Anglo-American domination of punk" by creating "an alternative community, a new home away from its physical home."[132] They built up an "audiotopia" of sorts.[133] Josh Kun defined an audiotopia as using music to build a shared sense of community and alternative ways of understanding the world. He said, "music functions like a possible utopia for the listener, that music is experienced not only as sound that goes into our ears and vibrates through our bones but as a space that we can enter into, encounter, move around in, inhabit, be safe in, and learn from."[134] I would argue that rather than transnational, the Kominas' activities were translocal and democratic. They were enacted locally in a shared community but were also shared across various borders—national, religious, and otherwise. Their activities included a high degree of egalitarianism. I would agree that the Kominas were seeking to create an audiotopia that was built on intersecting networks of punks and young Muslims.

Afro-punk also made a splash in the 2000s. It was less a genre and more a response to the whiteness of many punk spaces. Black American identity emerged out of the realities of enslavement and then segregation. Those caught up in New World enslavement came from different ethnic groups and religions. The newly enslaved spoke different languages, which hindered organizing against enslavement at first. In the coming centuries, a shared culture emerged in response to this brutality. Eugene Genovese argued that "the question of nationality—of identity—has stalked Afro-American history from its colonial beginnings, when the expression 'a nation within a nation' was already being heard."[135] He argued that "I refer to the 'black nation' and argue that the slaves, as an objective social class, laid the foundations for a separate black national culture while enormously enriching American culture as a whole."[136] Genovese projected the project of Black national identity backward in time influenced by Black Nationalism, a nationalist movement that followed the civil rights movement. In his biography of Amiri Baraka, Komozi Woodard noted that "during the 1970s the politics of black cultural nationalism emerged from its local roots to become a national phenomenon. The Modern Black Convention Movement hastened black nationality formation by helping to create a black national political community."[137] Baraka rose to leadership in the Modern Black Convention movement. That grew out of the Black Arts movement and sought to empower and train young Black people for leadership roles in their community and American life.[138] A shared history and culture helped create a Black American identity. Black punks had common experiences with other punks, but they also had a common experience with other Black Americans. As such, the concept of a shared set of experiences informing one's identity brings Afro-punk under the same umbrella as Celtic punk, Gypsy punk, and Taqwacore.

Afro-punk became a cultural movement that spawned a series of festivals to showcase an eclectic mix of Black artists, including but not limited to punk and metal bands. The festival was inspired by a 2003 documentary by James Spooner, *Afro-Punk*.[139] Born in Apple Valley, California, Spooner's family moved to Manhattan by the time he entered high school. According to Devon Maloney in *Village Voice*, the biracial Spooner was one of the few Black punks around, which led to an identity crisis on his part. He told Maloney, "I wanted to figure out what it meant to be a black person who moves outside of the black stereotypes."[140] Through his work on *Afro-Punk* he came to believe that he had "a very valid black experience." He interviewed around seventy Black punks for the documentary. Many of them shared "a sense of double alienation, as a minority within a minority, in a subculture that was supposedly built on more progressive ideology than the mainstream."[141] The film helped highlight the whitewashing of rock music more generally, according to Maloney. The film gave birth to the Afropunk Festival, which started in New York City, with other large cities following suit. High-profile artists like Janelle Monáe and Erykah Badu brought in large audiences and introduced people to less well-known bands, such as the metal band Unlocking the Truth.[142] The New York festival was originally free, but as word spread, commercialization set in. Brian Josephs wondered if the Afropunk Festival had "sold out."[143] Spooner felt alienated from the community he helped build as it became more commercial. He ended his connections with the festival in 2008.[144]

The documentary was discussed in the usual punk zines. Carolyn Keddy reviewed the film in the September 2003 issue of *MRR*. After pointing out that punks loved to complain, she noted that the film was just that—punks complaining. She said that the film revealed that "Black punks have the same insecurities as white punks."[145] She did find it funny that people struggled to name Black punk bands. She said wryly, "I am always shocked when punks don't know anything about music."[146] Keddy seemed uninterested in examining the subject matter of race in punk spaces in any depth.[147] George B. Sanchez interviewed Spooner in the July 2004 issue of *Punk Planet*. He had a more nuanced discussion on the issues. In the introduction, Spooner said that punks talk a good game on antiracism in their songs, but many were far too close to the mainstream views on race. He said, "not until our subculture truly becomes a counter culture will this discussion really progress."[148] Spooner noted how difficult it was to get white audiences to engage meaningfully with the subject matter. He told Sanchez that during Q&As for the film, "the questions that white folks ask are really safe."[149] He showed the film in Minneapolis. It was screened in a punk space that was in a Black neighborhood. He found the white punks there to be "out of touch with people of color." There had been only one Black person in the audience aside from those who came with Spooner.[150] The interview struck a chord with Reuben Marks, who wrote to *Punk Planet* in issue 64. He had discovered punk as a teenager and been part of the DC punk scene. He liked lots of punk and New Wave bands because they spoke to his general sense of alienation. His attitude toward music was to "look for something that I like and [ask] does it say something that I can relate to."[151] He said that "my problem is with the music industry in general where some record labels and night club owners have concluded that Black Americans and people of color cannot play anything other than funk, rap, soul, R&B, gospel, or jazz."[152] He said, "I know this is not true." He hoped that racist attitudes go away one day.[153]

In July 2005 issue of *Punk Planet*, Brian Peterson interviewed one of the bands in the *Afro-Punk* documentary, New York–based hardcore band

Cipher. Singer and activist Moe Mitchell recalled how immigrating from Trinidad informed his experiences living in Long Island. He lived a more comfortable life after immigrating. As for the rich white kids he met in Long Island, "it seemed like they were living in oblivion." He said he felt more "alive in Trinidad . . . than I felt in Long Island where I had cable TV. I began to question early on the true value of all this stuff in America."[154] As for his political organizing, he focused on the Black and Latino working-class communities in Long Island. Mitchell discovered hardcore in the mid-1990s. He wanted Cipher's music to express the complexities he had encountered as an activist to the hardcore audience.[155] He said he found a "demystification of the music industry" in the punk scene. But he also felt that punks "would like to think it's very different from broader society, but there's racism in the hardcore scene, there's sexism in the hardcore scene, there are class issues, too. As the country becomes more and more depoliticized, so will the scene."[156] He wanted radical change to US society that dismantled white privilege and changed the nature of consumer culture. He said, "the sheer opulence of American consumerist culture is out of control. The earth cannot—and will not—continue to feed the American appetite for natural resources."[157] The same realities that drew Mitchell to social activism also drew him to punk rock. Even while noting how punk scenes often have aspects of the same prejudices found in wider society, it also offered a space for injecting criticism into the discussion via music. As we saw with riot girl and queercore in the 1990s, punks sometimes used the language and structures of punk to get across wider messages and shape their understanding of their place in the world.

I wish to draw a distinction here between these postcolonial, diasporic forms of punk rock and punk practices in a country that is not in Western Europe or North America. Punk continues to be a globalized community with a strong emphasis on local activity. In these contexts, there are not necessarily "ethnic" punk subgenres, as the goal is to be part of the punk community, not differentiate themselves by playing a punked-out version of traditional music. In December 2016, *MRR* had an issue dedicated to punk rock in China. Local knowledge has always been key to how the zine operated, and this issue was no exception. Nevin Domer lived in Beijing and coordinated the issue. Domer had helped put together a 2012 *MRR* radio show featuring bands from China's DIY music scene.[158] In his overview of the Beijing scene, Dave O'Dell discussed the spread of punk in the mid-1990s. Even as the country began to open to Western culture as early as the mid-1980s, censorship initially made some kinds of Western music harder to access. Black market cassettes called *dakoudai* made metal and grunge popular in China by the 1990s. Nirvana led to punk rock for some Beijing music fans. Underbaby and Catcher in the Rye were among the earliest bands formed in the early 1990s during the cassette culture period. As we saw in Eastern Europe during the Cold War, these bands were "unlicensed" and unable to legally play. They eventually managed to put together some shows and make some recordings. According to O'Dell, most considered Underbaby's "All the Same" to be the first punk single that "gave the burgeoning punk scene a new vocabulary to speak with."[159] Other bands at this time were primarily playing metal or covering Nirvana.[160]

The first places that allowed punks to play were often bars near universities. O'Dell noted that they hosted poetry slams and open mic nights despite running afoul of China's licensing laws for live music. Cost became a problem for many punks as the venues lost money and began charging an exorbitant cover of 20 yuan (US$3) that many could not afford. O'Dell later formed a band with Underbaby's singer and began to put together events for the growing scene. They managed to get some venues hosting punks to lower prices, which helped with the growth of the scene.[161] Nevin Domer and Leo discussed the scene as of 2005. Bands like Demerit and Gum Bleed had toured internationally and wrote songs primarily in English. Other bands were influenced by the British wave of punk rock, such as Joyside and Bedstars, while Quickshot was influenced by American hardcore and riot girl. Musicians band hopped as in other punk scenes, such as when the Gum Bleed drummer went to play for the Diders. Domer and Leo called the Diders "the best live band in Beijing" with "wild stage antics [that] make them as much a danger to themselves as to their audience."[162] Some of the bands in the scene included foreigners, such as the band Dress Code, who played a mix of thrash, grind, and hardcore. Members hailed from not only China but Morocco, Australia, and the United States.[163] This China edition of *MRR* included reprints of Chinese scene reports from April 1998 and December 1997.[164]

In the 2000s, more mainstream media outlets discovered that punk existed in what they considered unexpected locations. Online magazine *The Diplomat* ran two articles that focused on punks across Asian countries. In 2013, Jonathan DeHart covered punk scenes from Indonesia to China. He argued that "punk may have become watered down in its places of origin," but in the regions he covered "it has taken root as a relevant and very alive form of dissent."[165] Punks in Myanmar were reacting to social and political conditions similar to punks in New York in the 1970s. Punk was considered a threat by many of the governments in question. He noted how even as places like Myanmar had begun to open in other regards, punks were still being subjected to state repression.[166] Olaf Schuelke ran a 2014 photo essay on Myanmar punks in *The Diplomat*. The pictures were largely of young men from the punk scene, which he characterized as illegal. In one shot, he juxtaposed two monks in robes and two punks with spiked hair and patched jean jackets. In another, three young boys with jackets covered in spikes are centered, with the smallest sporting a Mohawk and holding his middle finger next to his face. Schuelke argued that "the punks of Myanmar exist on the fringes of the country's once closed society. Many continue to rebel against political injustice."[167] DeHart downplayed other points in punk history where it was considered a real threat to public order in both the West and the communist world. As we saw, that continued to some degree into the 1990s. Schuelke focused on specific images that the audience would recognize as punk and sought to contrast that with a more traditional understanding of Myanmar for that audience.

Photographer Sandra Hoyn also covered the Myanmar punk scene. She zeroed in on twenty-six-year-old punk Kyaw Kyaw, who was in the band. The Rebel Riot. He addressed the changes in society happening at the time. He said that the newly elected government was "mostly made up of members of the former military junta. The change to democracy is just a change in words not a real change."[168] Kyaw Kyaw and other punks in the city of Yangon did more than just organize shows and hang out. They founded an organization called Food not Bombs where they spent Mondays feeding the homeless. Hoyn showed a wider lens on Myanmar punks as she narrowed in on a single member of the scene. In one of her images, Kyaw Kyaw was shown doing what most would expect of punks, such as playing guitar and singing, dying a friend's hair, and putting a cigarette out on his tongue. In others, Hoyn framed him as part of Myanmar society. In one image, he was eating dinner with his mother at home. In several others, he hands out food to homeless people in Yangon. One shows him meditating at a temple while a nun looks on in the background.[169] Hoyn's work examined how punks like Kyaw Kyaw signaled his cultural allegiance to a globalized punk identity, his local scene, and the larger community in which he lives. The Rebel Riot's music did not pull from traditional Burmese music but from hardcore punk. But he was still Burmese. His cultural identities overlapped.

The mainstream media came to the Myanmar punk party late, and they often projected a depoliticized image of punks in foreign locales. The narratives they tell were of young people rebelling against oppression by dropping out of their society and embracing a Western cultural practice. Except for Hoyn's photoessay on Kyaw Kyaw, their punk practices were positioned as apolitical and rejecting other aspects of their identities. Coverage of punk in Myanmar goes back much further in the punk press. In September 2006 in *MRR*, Gunter from Germany highlighted punk scenes outside of Western Europe and the Americas. He said that the internet had facilitated an online community called "World Wide Punk" that he had been participating in for three years. He gave the Myanmar scene a paragraph in his global scene review. He noted that there were a "few independent rock bands, but you can't easily get in contact with them."[170] The few who were in bands "were connected to the opposition against the military regime, although the kids who can afford to play in such bands are the children of the small wealthy class."[171] Myanmar received coverage for the political situation in *MRR*. In November 2008, a report was reprinted from the Associated Press on the release of Burmese writer and political prisoner Win Tin who had been imprisoned for nineteen years.[172]

The September 2017 issue *MRR* covered the Myanmar punk scene. In the introduction to an interview with Burmese punk band No U Turn, Mika Reckinnen noted that punk has a long history in East and Southeast Asia. In the late 1970s, Japan and the Philippines had punk scenes, with other countries around the region having scenes by the 1980s. Myanmar's first punk bands started in the 1990s. Reckinnen argued that the country was "more like the dystopia in Orwell's *1984* than anything else."[173] He said that one of the first releases by Burmese punks in the West came in 2000 in France, a split seven-inch with The Ants and Ghost Rider. Reckinnen mentioned mainstream media interest in the Burmese punk scene that only saw punk as an image. He argued that these reports "failed to focus on the political content—like Food not Bombs or the spreading of anarchist thought in the country—but instead wrote about the look of these punks."[174] He noted that "other bands in Yangon didn't get the same attention, in some part because they do not look like punk clichés."[175] The international attention on their scene increased participation according to the members of No U Turn. Vocalist Ye Ngwe Soe said more bands were forming in Yangon and Mandalay for the past three years thanks to this coverage. Guitarist Eaiddhi believed it was easier for these new bands. The cost of starting a studio had dropped, and there were more places to practice. He also said that "when we started in 2002, it was difficult to reach out to people. We gave away demos to people at concerts or in downtown or at universities."[176] The newer bands had access to the internet, which helped spread the word. "It is faster now to get attention and fans," he concluded.[177]

French punk Lük Haas might be one of the most critical figures in documenting just how widespread punk rock became in the 1990s and 2000s. He penned an *MRR* guest column in September 1998 about "out-of-the-way scenes." His label, Tian An Men 89, was working on a collaboration with Profane Existence Far East for a compilation, and he included Myanmar in his request for bands that could be included on the compilation.[178] A 2012 interview noted how Haas had been to more than 120 countries. Haas said that by the time he started his label in 1993, he had been traveling for eight years to less well-known scenes starting with Czechoslovakia in 1986. He argued that by that time while *MRR* and other zines had facilitated a "world punk scene" that created an "informal unity network through the exchanges of music, letters, scene reports, and touring bands,"[179] but that network was primarily focused on Europe, the Americas, Australia, New Zealand, and Japan. His label had bands from over forty countries at the time of the interview, including from areas of not known for punk rock.[180] Figures like Haas show just how important physical connections remain to the functioning of translocal punk. Even as the internet has made those connections a bit smoother, the importance of face-to-face interactions to cement punk ties still dominates. Sadly an online search showed that the label seems to no longer be active. The last record produced by Tian An Men was from 2015. Hopefully other intrepid punk travelers have taken up Haas's mantle and traveled far and wide to bring more far-flung punks together in a democratic underground imagined community that centers local action.

Punk in the age of the internet continues to thrive as an underground set of practices carried out in person. More than just a pose, being a punk means active participation in a local scene. This includes (but is not limited to) making music, creating zines, going to and facilitating shows, and spending time with like-minded compatriots. These practices are all local, and generally carried out face to face. But punk practices also include participation in the networks built by punks over the decades. Sharing music across borders and writing to internationally circulating zines like *MRR* helps burnish punk credentials. More than that, it furthers the goal of creating a noncommercial, translocal space for creativity, activism, and community. Punks today participate in a set of cultural practices forged in the late Cold War as an alternative to mainstream, commercial rock culture. It connects them with each other and with those in the past who did much the same. It shows no signs of fading anytime soon.

Conclusions

Will the "Real" Punk Rockers
Please Stand Up?

In recent years, the old debate about who was a "real" punk has appeared in the broader discourse. Many of the people making the argument that they are "real" punks seem to have never spent time in punk scenes. Of course, we saw how active underground punk scenes still exist. Although it no longer comes out as a physical copy, *MRR* still publishes on a regular basis online. Reddit has an active punk forum. Blogs that focus on local scenes abound. In the July 2018 issue of *MRR*, Erik Egenes interviewed the Bogatá hardcore band Muro. They argued that the reason punk was still around was because of the structures punks built over the years. They said that punk persevered "as something else than just a cosplay nostalgic retro fashion."[1] The band created an organization called the Rat Trap Collective, which grew out of a punk house founded in 2012. It became a location for music, art shows, and forms of activism.[2] Many punks continued to write politically charged music opposing right-wing politics in American society. Opposition to racism animated the Portland, Oregon, band Death Ridge Boys. In Mike English's interview with the band in the May 2018 issue of *MRR*, he described them as "long standing members of the D.I.Y. community."[3] Their album *The Right Side of History* was released in 2017. It included songs about the 2016 Standing Rock protests that opposed the building of an oil pipeline near the Standing Rock Indian Reservation in the Dakotas and the police shooting of twelve-year old Tamir Rice. The band expressed concerns with the rise of right-wing politics fueled by their experiences with relatives who embraced the far right.[4] These punks feel a sense of alienation from the mainstream culture and rejected inclusion within it. Punk for them was more than just a genre of loud and fast music. It was

195

a means of organizing community, sharing information, and trying to make social change. For them, punk continues to provide a space for an alternative to commercial culture. Scene participants see punk as a constructive and democratic space for making music, building community, and having fun.

Others have attempted to claim that they are punk without seeming to have strong connections to punk scenes. They merely see it as a dead subculture they can recontextualize for their own purposes. White supremacist groups have attempted to claim the countercultural space that punk represents, which has been a long-standing problem in punk. Some claim to be opposing a kind of authoritarian liberalism that they believe has made white Americans a beleaguered minority. This notion has been picked up by more mainstream conservative groups that have moved further right during the Trump presidency. They were building on a longer term process of white middle-class Americans identifying as social outcasts. As Grace Elizabeth Hale argued, the white middle class "romanticized outsiders," which led them to see themselves "as different and alienated, too." This became "an essential characteristic of white middle-class subjectivity."[5] Being seen as a rebel against the ill-defined oppressive mainstream culture became something to embrace, a direct contradiction to the Nixon-era embrace of the "silent majority." Key locations of that subjectivity were found among conservative Christians, especially in the Evangelical movement. Hale argued that Randall Terry's pro-life organization Operation Rescue developed an outsider's rhetoric. They used tactics deployed by the anti–civil rights antibusing campaigns in the 1970s. Ironically, the roots of these tactics were from the civil rights movement. They both cited Dr. Martin Luther King Jr. to justify their positions and actions.[6] This embrace of an identity as an outsider became part and parcel of our political landscape. In a blog post during the 2015 election, conservative commentator Megan Barth argued that candidates for the Republican presidential nomination like Carly Fiorina, Ben Carson, and Donald Trump were outsiders like Ronald Reagan.[7] That same year on the political blog *The Hill*, Shermichael Singleton argued that many Americans were turning to populist figures like Donald Trump and Bernie Sanders "out of frustration" with the failures of the mainstream parties.[8]

In 2016, Donald Trump was elected US president with the support of this "alienated" white middle class. He also received support from white supremacist groups. These groups saw his campaign rhetoric on immigration and cultural issues as mirroring their own. White nationalist David Duke endorsed Trump during the 2016 election.[9] The official newspaper of the KKK also endorsed Trump.[10] Trump had a galvanizing effect on what has become known as the alt-right, a motley collection of online groups that embraced traditional right-wing, racist ideologies that organized online. They often saw themselves as countercultural. Writing for *Al Jazeera*, Patrick Strickland argued that the alt-right was a key demographic in Trump's 2016 electoral victory. Not long after his election, one of the major public faces of the alt-right movement, Richard Spencer, shouted, "Hail Trump, hail our people, hail victory!" at the National Policy Institute Conference as the audience cheered and gave Nazi-like salutes.[11] Strickland interviewed Matthew Lyons, who researches American far-right movements. Lyons dissected the various groups that make-up this movement. In addition to white nationalists and supremacists, it includes misogynists from the "Manosphere" who promote an extreme form of traditional gender norms.[12] Thanks to Trump's victory, this populist, white nationalist language moved further into our mainstream political discourse. Recently, comedian and political commentator John Oliver walked his audience through the connections between white nationalist talking points and those used by *Fox News* commentator Tucker Carlson. The replacement theory states that white Americans are being pushed from the center of American life and will be marginalized and oppressed themselves. This (untrue) theory lies at the heart of modern white supremacist discourse.[13] The spread of this conspiracy theory has led to an uptick in racist violence. In 2019 in *The Atlantic*, Adam Serwer tied Trump's rhetoric and the Republican defense of it to several mass shootings.[14] Antigovernment militia groups, long connected with white supremacy, participated in the January 6 insurrection at the US Capitol building that attempted to overturn the 2020 election that Trump lost.[15]

Many see embracing white supremacist talking points as taking an outsider position. This contrasted with earlier attempts to lay claim to the mainstream via the "silent majority" rhetoric, famously used by Richard Nixon's presidential campaign in 1968. In recent years, many movement conservatives have begun to argue that they are the real "counterculture." In the *National Review* in 2015, Shelby Steele, a senior fellow at the Hoover Institution, a conservative think-tank at Stanford University, recalled speaking at a charity event where he mentioned the concept of American exceptionalism. It elicited a round of boos from some in the crowd and then cheers in support of the idea. He argued that liberalism (as in progressive political positions rather than classical liberalism) had won the culture wars. This caused the dissociation of universal values of "two or three millennia of profound cultural evolution in the West" from the concept of American exceptionalism. American exceptionalism became little more than "garden-variety white supremacy" in the minds of progressives. He called the reaction from the booing liberals a sad by-product of progressive cultural conditioning. He compared it with whites accepting segregation during the Jim Crow era when he grew up. They were not actively trying to hurt him and other African Americans, but they had been culturally conditioned to accept segregation as necessary. Because of the victory of cultural liberalism "conservatives . . . feel evicted from their culture, who are made to feel like outsiders."[16] In *The Federalist*, Greg Jones agreed with this assessment. He defined rebellion as "opposing the existing power structure at every turn." He believed that a progressive establishment was "equally as authoritarian . . . [as] the system the decade [the sixties] attempted to overthrow."[17] It was a "fanatical progressivism [that] permeates nearly every facet of American life."[18] Jones pointed to figures popular on the right like Ben Shapiro and Jordan Peterson as being some of the few voices willing to stand against this "progressive authoritarianism."[19] Jones presented little in the way of evidence to prove that this "new" authoritarianism existed, but it seems to be an article of faith among many conservatives.

Some conservatives evoked punk rock specifically to claim the mantle of counterculture in American life. In *Forbes*, David Alm wrote about Sabo, an "alt-right street artist." He noted the similarity of the name "Sabo" to Jean-Michel Basquiat's graffiti tag "SAMO." Although Alm believed that Sabo's work was derivative, he admitted some similarities between punks and the GOP. He argued that both wanted to tear down the status quo. But Alm argued that punks were tearing down "social structures and norms centuries in the making" that did open new culture spaces.[20] But the GOP merely wish to tear down much of the progress that made America more democratic and inclusive in recent years.[21] Many of the younger white supremacists or white nationalists associated with the alt-right invoked punk and other underground cultures of the 1980s and 1990s. Reggie Ugwu explored the electronic subgenre known as "fashwave" in 2016. He connected it with the racist wing of Oi! and bands aligned with Rock Against Communism but noted that fashwave "doesn't sound like those genres."[22] Much like the rise of a global, racist neo-Nazi skinhead movement was fueled in part by those other genres, the rise of the alt-right was in part fueled by fashwave. Ugwu called it the "de-facto soundtrack to a new era of white nationalism."[23] Others in the alt-right imagine themselves as true punks. Michelle Goldberg covered the controversy over Steve Bannon's inclusion in the Conservative Political Action Conference in 2017. She discussed the ejection of white nationalist Richard Spencer from the conference. James O'Mailia, a student from Penn State, begged Spencer to come speak at his school as he was being escorted out. O'Mailia described himself as a member of the alt-right and called it "the new punk rock."[24] He rejected the characterization of his group as racist, despite his attempt to bring an actual white supremacist to his campus.[25] The extreme ideology embraced by members of the alt-right have come to dominate elements of the Republican Party in the age of Trump, including some anarchic and chaotic elements that some might see as being similar to punk culture. The constructive and democratic elements of punk culture just do not exist on the extreme right. Although it can certainly be communal, it is a community built on hierarchy and order rather than more democratic connections and interactions. More important, these far-right groups seek to impose and reinforce existing racial hierarchies and gender roles in society, something that many punks have actively opposed. Slapping the label "punk" or "countercultural" on something does not make it a fact.

Many actual punks objected to punk being claimed by supporters of the former president. Part of that objection rested on how Trump appealed to right-wing, racist ideas such as "law and order" during his two presidential campaigns. Jamie Thomson discussed how punk often ran afoul of the forces of law and order that Trump embraced. In 1984, punks were one of the groups targeted for the urban cleansing that happened before that year's Olympics in Los Angeles. Although punks sometimes struggled to find locations to play, they eventually found permanent spaces, such as 924 Gilman in Berkeley. These locations were often nonprofit, all-ages, democratic, and connected to left-wing politics. Thomson discussed how punks in Jakarta, Indonesia, faced similar struggles with the police. The folk punk band Marjinal opened their house as an art collective to create space for their scene. Thomson met the band on tour in Japan, which they had undertaken to raise money for their punk venue back home.[26] Thomson also argued that there have always been strong connections between punk and the antifascist movement or Antifa, as it has been called more recently. Mark Bray argued that the modern antifa movement grew out of punks defending themselves and their scenes against white supremacists. He said that "the fascist/anti-fascist struggle was essentially a fight for control of the punk scene [during the 1980s], and that was true across much of North America and in parts of Europe in this era."[27] He noted how the "stereotype about dirty anarchists and punks" had some grounding in truth.[28] Many punks directly rejected racism, even as the punk scene overall struggled with its overwhelming whiteness. On the blog BlogXSplitter, Noel the TrollXSplitter noted that right-wing elements have always been part of the larger punk scene, but on the margins and never without objections from others. He said that bands like Agnostic Front had some racist songs and received pushback as a result. He was not aware of many bands currently doing that even if some right-wing people lurked in punk scenes.[29] Right wingers might have always been part of the punk scene, but extreme positions on the right were met with resistance from other punks. Punks active in scenes today do not like being equated with any specific political ideology, especially those associated with racism. Punk is a cultural practice, not a political party. Many conservatives seek to embrace only certain aspects of punk, meaning its rebellion against the establishment. But they fail to see it as a set of democratic, constructive practices that seek to construct noncommercial cultural spaces. The fact that some try to claim a punk identity without having been punk speaks volumes to how incorporated punk has become to US culture. It also shows how the mainstream culture keeps misunderstanding punk rock.

Other aspects of punk culture have shaped mainstream culture in recent years, such as DIY. This is especially true with popular culture production. As noted, *Maximum Rocknroll* carries on as a zine, although now it's fully online. Many who cut their teeth in punk rock as teenagers continue to promote punk and other kinds of independent music. Many punk labels founded in the 1980s and 1990s continue to put out music. Dischord and Alternative Tentacles might be the best known examples of punk labels continuing to thrive. They are not the only ones. Kent McClard continues to operate the Ebullition label out of Goleta, California. Their first seven-inch release was the band Downcast in 1990, released with McClard's *No Answers* zine. As of this writing, the label's most recent release was in May 2020 by Portland band Visions.[30] Jack Rabid, of the New York band Even Worse and punk zine *The Big Takeover*, carried his love of music into a full-color, glossy music magazine focused on all forms of independent music (see figure c.1). Despite the more "professional" look, *TBT* still retains the same enthusiasm of the earlier zine. Rabid also hosts a weekly radio show that airs on Real Punk Radio. Each show can also be streamed on *The Big Takeover* website.[31] These are excellent examples of durable institutions that punks built over the years to offer a real alternative to corporate entertainment and cultural production.

The DIY punk spirit has shaped popular culture in other ways. In the May 2018 issue of *MRR*, Grace Ambrose covered the Bay Area Girls Rock Camp, a summer camp where girls learn to play in bands. She interviewed the five volunteers who ran the camp. Ambrose said that although the girls end up playing a variety of genres of music, it "does have some connection to punk and DIY communities."[32] Chelsey Del Castillo, program and site coordinator, argued that "Rock Camp is punk as fuck . . . I'm purely using what I've learned from punk and DIY to inform how I work."[33] Development coordinator Sep Mashiahof argued that "Rock Camp informs punk and punk informs it."[34] Ambrose interviewed one of the bands that came out of the camp, Little Debbie and the Crusaders. They combined influences such as

Figure C.1. Issue 88 of *The Big Takeover*. (Used by permission of Jack Rabid)

Bikini Kill, Sleater-Kinney, and the Dead Kennedys with early 2000s pop artists like Brandy and Rihanna. One of their songs was a cover of a Brandy song.[35] They embraced punk and political activism based in part on their experiences in punk spaces. Guitarist and vocalist Liv Collom recalled being groped at a show and how that made her afraid to come to punk shows for a while. "But Little Debbie helped me get through that rough patch," she said.[36] An organization like the Bay Area Girls Rock Camp might not be directly built as a punk space, but it certainly embodies the DIY punk rock spirit. The girls who attend the camp get to learn how making music can be a powerful way to communicate and connect with others.

The punk space in the popular imagination has recently been strongly associated with young women. An article by Hannah Ewens in *The Guardian* argued that the genre of pop punk is currently being reinvented by Gen Z, especially young women. This includes artists like Willow Smith and Olivia Rodrigo, both pop musicians. Ewens argued that previously, pop punk had been the domain of white men "whining about high school, his mediocre home town, or a faceless girl."[37] Now, "a diverse group of women are emerging who have kept the genre's sense of belligerence and fun, but are developing it to create something youthful that also has a quality those older bands eschewed—emotional maturity."[38] As a result, "pop punk has become the defining sound of 2021."[39] The Linda Lindas signed to Epitaph Records; they also opened for Alice Bag and Bikini Kill.[40] The streaming service Peacock recently released a sit-com called *We Are Lady Parts*. Set in the United Kingdom, it follows five young British Muslim women in a punk band called Lady Parts. The show, written by a Muslim woman, upends some notions many have about Muslims in the West. For example, the main character seeks out a traditional marriage arrangement at the beginning of the show, which her parents support but do not push on her.[41] These engagements with punk in the mainstream culture still sometimes miss the mark, but they tend to be far more informed than how punk was depicted in the past. At the very least, they do not seem bent on making punk into a moral threat to mainstream society. Underground punk coexists with these more mainstream depictions of punk. But it also shapes who many of us think about the role culture should play in our lives.

What conclusions can we draw for the history of punk rock? It grew out of a longer struggle with the commercialization of popular culture and the development of youth subcultures in the postwar era. Punks sought to criticize mainstream culture and youth subcultures that came before them. They also drew on the invented traditions of both. Punk was shaped by Cold War globalization as the United States and Soviet Union competed for hearts and minds of young people around the world. As those young people came to see institutions in the West and communist world (private and public institutions) as suspect, they endeavored to build their own translocal communities based on a shared set of cultural practices. They took the first-wave punk music that was subcultural, but part of the mainstream recording industry, and made them underground and countercultural. Punk became more than just a genre of music as a result. Punks built durable cultural institutions that often (but not exclusively) sought to avoid commercialization. Today there is an even greater incorporation and acceptance of punk as part of the mainstream culture, at least in the West. Many punks resist this incorporation. They continue to build their own cultural spaces and maintain long-standing underground institutions. The durability of these underground cultural institutions are remarkable and inspiring. The continued existence of the punk underground reveal that humans will build what they need in life, even in (or perhaps especially in) times of adversity. If we look at modern popular culture and despair that it inculcates a high level of social passivity, punk and other subcultures stand in sharp contrast to that. The history of punk rock is one of the cracks in the facade of modernity. The cracks illuminate a better way to make culture that is meaningful and creates community. It helps us remember that creating culture is not just a means of creating wealth for a chosen few but instead makes us more fully human. As shown in figure c.2, punk continues to a means of forging community translocally.

Figure C.2. Estamos en todas partes punks!! (Blmurch/Creative Commons CC BY 2.0)

Notes

Introduction

1. Howard Zinn, *The People's History of the United States, 1492–Present* (New York: Harper Collins, 2003).

2. Nikole Hannah-Jones, "The 1619 Project," *New York Times*, August 14, 2019.

3. Dewar MacLeod, " 'Kids of the Black Hole': Youth Culture in Postsuburbia," PhD diss., City University of New York, 1998, 3.

4. Dewar MacLeod, *Kids of the Black Hole: Punk Rock in Postsuburban California* (Norman: University of Oklahoma Press, 2010).

5. Mary Montgomery Wolf, " 'We Accept You, One of Us?': Punk Rock, Community, and Individualism in an Uncertain Era, 1974–1985," PhD diss., University of North Carolina at Chapel Hill, 2007, 1.

6. Wolf, " 'We Accept You, One of Us?,' " 2.

7. Brock Ruggles, "Not So Quiet on the Western Front: Punk Politics during the Conservative Ascendancy in the United States, 1980–2000," PhD diss., Arizona State University, 2008, 4.

8. Jeff Patrick Hayton, "Culture from the Slums: Punk Rock, Authenticity, and Alternative Culture in East and West Germany," PhD diss., University of Illinois at Urbana-Champaign, 2013, 4–5.

9. Daniel Sinker, "Ian MacKaye," in *We Owe You Nothing: Punk Planet the Collected Interviews*, ed. Daniel Sinker (Chicago: Punk Planet Press, 2008), 11.

10. Josh Kun, *Audiotopia: Music, Race, and America* (Berkeley: University of California Press, 2005), 3.

Chapter 1

1. Terry Pratchett, *The Globe: The Science of Discworld II* (New York: Random House, 2002), 152.

2. Evan Eisenberg, *The Recording Angel: Music, Records, and Culture form Aristotle to Zappa* (New Haven, CT: Yale University Press, 2005), 57–70.

3. Bad Brains, "Banned in DC," track 5, *Bad Brains*, Reach Out Records, 1982. Bikini Kill, "Rebel Girl," track 10, *Pussy Whipped*, Kill Rock Stars, 1993.

4. Charles C. Mann, *1493: Uncovering the New World Columbus Created* (New York: Vintage Books, 2001); Alfred W. Crosby, *Ecological Imperialism: The Biological Expansion of Europe, 900–1900* (Cambridge: Cambridge University Press, 1986).

5. Sidney W. Mintz, *Sweetness and Power: The Place of Sugar in Modern History*, New York: Penguin Books, 1985.

6. Alison Weir, *Henry VIII: The King and His Court* (New York: Ballantine Books, 2001).

7. Daniel Goffman, *The Ottoman Empire and Early Modern Europe* (Cambridge: Cambridge University Press, 2002).

8. Jerry Brotton, *The Sultan and the Queen: The Untold Story of Elizabeth and Islam* (New York: Viking, 2016).

9. Benedict Anderson, *Imagined Communities: Reflections on the Origin of and Spread of Nationalism* (London: Verso, 1983).

10. Alfred Crosby, *The Columbian Exchange: Biological and Culture Consequences of 1492* (Santa Barbara, CA: Praeger, 2003), esp. chap. 1.

11. Mintz, *Sweetness and Power*, 43–44.

12. E. P. Thompson, *The Making of the English Working Class*, New York: Vintage Books, 1966.

13. Thompson, *The Making of the English Working Class*, 46.

14. Eric Hobsbawm, *The Age of Revolution, 1789–1848* (New York: Vintage Books, 1962).

15. Anderson, *Imagined Communities*, 51.

16. C. L. R. James, *The Black Jacobins: Toussaint L'Ouverture and the San Domingo Revolution* (New York: Vintage Books, 1963).

17. Hartmut Pogge von Strandmann, "1848–1849: A European Revolution?," in *The Revolutions in Europe 1848–1849: From Reform to Reaction* (Oxford: Oxford University Press, 2000), 1–8.

18. Dirk Hoerder, *Migrations and Belongings: 1870–1945* (Cambridge, MA: Harvard University Press, 2014).

19. Max Weber, *The Protestant Ethic and the Spirit of Capitalism* (New York: Norton, 2008).

20. Guy Debord, *The Society of the Spectacle* (Detroit: Black & Red, 1983).

21. Karl Polanyi, *The Great Transformation: Origins of Our Times* (New York: Farrar & Rinehart, 1944).

22. William Leach, *Land of Desire: Merchants, Power, and the Rise of a New American Culture* (New York: Vintage, 1993), xiii.

23. Victoria de Grazia, *Irresistible Empire: America's Advance through 20th-Century Europe* (Cambridge, MA: Belknap Press, 2005), esp. chap. 7, 336–75.

24. The text of the debate can be found at "The Kitchen Debate," Teaching American History, https://teachingamericanhistory.org/library/document/the-kitchen-debate/ (accessed January 11, 2020).

25. Penny M. Von Eschen, *Satchmo Blows Up the World: Jazz Ambassadors Play the Cold War* (Cambridge, MA: Harvard University Press, 2006).

26. Judd Stitziel, "Shopping, Sewing, Networking, Complaining: Consumer Culture and the Relationship between State and Society in the GDR," in *Socialist Modern: East German Everyday Culture and Politics*, ed. Katherine Pence and Paul Betts (Ann Arbor: University of Michigan Press, 2008), 253–86.

27. David Suisman, *Selling Sounds: The Commercial Revolution in American Music*, Cambridge, MA: Harvard University Press, 2009.

28. Eisenberg, *The Recording Angel*.

29. Anderson, *Imagined Communities*; Andrew Baruch Wachtel, *Making a Nation, Breaking a Nation: Cultural Politics in Yugoslavia* (Stanford, CA: Stanford University Press, 1998).

30. Suisman, *Selling Sounds*, 21.

31. Suisman, *Selling Sounds*, 4–5.

32. Jon Savage, *Teenage: The Prehistory of Youth Culture, 1875–1945* (New York: Penguin Books, 2007), 53.

33. Savage, *Teenage*, 30. On the concerns over disciplining leisure time, see John F. Kasson, *Amusing the Million: Coney Island at the Turn of the Century* (New York: Hill & Wang, 1978), 4.

34. Kasson, *Amusing the Million*, 18.

35. Quoted in Kasson, *Amusing the Million*, 23.

36. Lizabeth Cohen, *Making a New Deal: Industrial Workers in Chicago, 1919–1939* (Cambridge, MA: Harvard University Press, 1990), 102.

37. Cohen, *Making a New Deal*, 100.

38. Cohen, *Making a New Deal*, 144.

39. Cohen, *Making a New Deal*, 147.

40. Kasson, *Amusing the Million*, 108.

41. Antonio Gramsci, *An Antonio Gramsci Reader: Selected Writings 1916–1935*, ed. David Forgacs (New York: Schocken Books, 1988), 58.

42. David Forgacs, comments in *An Antonio Gramsci Reader*, 53.

43. Gramsci, *An Antonio Gramsci Reader*, 194.

44. Theodor Adorno and Max Horkheimer, "The Culture Industry: Enlightenment as Mass Deception," in *Dialectics of Enlightenment* (Stanford, CA: Stanford University Press, 2002), 94.

45. Adorno and Horkheimer, "The Culture Industry," 95.

46. Adorno and Horkheimer, "The Culture Industry," 111.

47. Adorno and Horkheimer, "The Culture Industry," 115–16.

48. Adorno and Horkheimer, "The Culture Industry," 122.

49. Adorno and Horkheimer, "The Culture Industry," 134–35.

50. Adorno and Horkheimer, "The Culture Industry," 136.

51. Walter Benjamin, *The Work of Art in the Age of Mechanical Reproduction* (New York: Schocken, 2005).

52. Benjamin, *The Work of Art in the Age of Mechanical Reproduction*, 4.

53. Benjamin, *The Work of Art in the Age of Mechanical Reproduction*, 5.

54. Benjamin, *The Work of Art in the Age of Mechanical Reproduction*, 6.

55. Benjamin, *The Work of Art in the Age of Mechanical Reproduction*, 11–12.

56. Walter Lippman, *Public Opinion* (New York: Harcourt, Brace, 1922), 249.

57. Adam Curtis, *Century of the Self*, BBC 2, 2002.

58. Edward Bernays, *Propaganda* (New York: Routledge, 1928).

59. Noam Chomsky and Edward Herman, *Manufacturing Consent: The Political Economy of the Mass Media* (New York: Pantheon Books, 1988).

60. Greil Marcus, *Lipstick Traces: A Secret History of the Twentieth Century* (Cambridge, MA: Harvard University Press, 1989), 192.

61. Marcus, *Lipstick Traces*, 251.

62. Marcus, *Lipstick Traces*, 239.

63. Marcus, *Lipstick Traces*, 164.

64. Debord, *Society of the Spectacle*.

65. Sam Cooper, *The Situationist International in Britain: Modernism, Surrealism, and the Avant-Gardes* (London: Routledge, 2017), 109–42. For McLaren's involvement, see Paul Gorman, *The Life and Times of Malcolm McLaren: The Biography* (London: Constable, 2020), 95.

66. Marcus, *Lipstick Traces*, 133.

67. Kasson, *Amusing the Million*, 8.

68. Kasson, *Amusing the Million*, 9.

69. Cohen, *Making a New Deal*, 106.

70. Cohen, *Making a New Deal*, 104–5.

71. Cohen, *Making a New Deal*, 106.

72. Cohen, *Making a New Deal*, 133.

73. Cohen, *Making a New Deal*, 135.

74. Cohen, *Making a New Deal*, 145.

75. Savage, *Teenage*, 13.

76. Savage, *Teenage*, 14.

77. Savage, *Teenage*, 13.

78. Savage, *Teenage*, 15.

79. Savage, *Teenage*, 36.

80. Savage, *Teenage*, 47.

81. Savage, *Teenage*, 48.

82. Savage, *Teenage*, 66–67.

83. Savage, *Teenage*, 68.

84. Savage, *Teenage*, 72.

85. Savage, *Teenage*, 19.

86. David Greenblatt, *The Ball Is Round: A Global History of Soccer* (New York: Riverhead Books, 2006), 27.

87. Savage, *Teenage*, 19–20.

88. Savage, *Teenage*, 23.

89. Savage, *Teenage*, 27.

90. Savage, *Teenage*, 60.

91. Savage, *Teenage*, 61.

92. Savage, *Teenage*, 136.

93. Savage, *Teenage*, 161–62.

94. Savage, *Teenage*, 168.

95. Savage, *Teenage*, 183.

96. Savage, *Teenage*, 200.

97. Cohen, *Making a New Deal*, 144.

98. Savage, *Teenage*, 201.

99. Savage, *Teenage*, 205.

100. Thomas Frank, *The Conquest of Cool: Business Culture, Counterculture, and the Rise of Hip Consumerism* (Chicago: University of Chicago Press, 1997).

101. Quoted in Savage, *Teenage*, 206.

102. Savage, *Teenage*, 258–59.

103. Savage, *Teenage*, 257.

104. Savage, *Teenage*, 305.

105. Savage, *Teenage*, 313.

106. Savage, *Teenage*, 313.

107. Savage, *Teenage*, 313.

108. Savage, *Teenage*, 313–14. On invented tradition, see Eric Hobsbawm and Terrence Ranger (eds.), *The Invention of Tradition* (Cambridge, MA: Harvard University Press, 1983).

109. Savage, *Teenage*, 318.

110. Savage, *Teenage*, 317.

111. Savage, *Teenage*, 320.

112. Savage, *Teenage*, 326–28.

113. Savage, *Teenage*, 363.

114. Savage, *Teenage*, 364.

115. Savage, *Teenage*, 376 and 386.

116. Savage, *Teenage*, 397–401.

117. Savage, *Teenage*, 416.

118. Savage, *Teenage*, 417.

119. Savage, *Teenage*, 365.

120. Savage, *Teenage*, 448.

121. Savage, *Teenage*, 445–46.

122. Savage, *Teenage*, 446–47.

123. Savage, *Teenage*, 453.

124. Savage, *Teenage*, 455–56.

125. Savage, *Teenage*, 464.

126. Von Eschen, *Satchmo Blows Up the World*.

127. Nicklaus Thomas-Symonds, *Attlee: A Life in Politics* (London: Tauris, 2010), 18.

128. British Nationality Act 1948, 1948, c. 56, https://www.legislation.gov.uk/ukpga/Geo6/11-12/56/section/33/enacted.

129. Norman Mailer, *The White Negro* (San Francisco: City Lights Books, 1957), n.p.

130. Mailer, *The White Negro*.

131. Raj Chandarlapaty, *The Beat Generation and Counterculture: Paul Bowles, William S. Burroughs, Jack Kerouac* (New York: Peter Lang, 2009), 4.

132. Chandarlapaty, *The Beat Generation and Counterculture*, 5; emphasis original.

133. Amiri Baraka (LeRoi Jones), *Blues People: Negro Music in White America* (New York: Harper Perennial, 2002), viii.

134. Baraka, *Blues People*, viii.

135. Julian Lord, *Teddy Boys: A Concise History* (London: Milo Books, 2012); Mitch Mitchell, "A Brief History of the Teddy Boys," *RS21*, February 19, 2019, https://www.rs21.org.uk/2019/02/19/a-brief-history-of-the-teddy-boys/.

136. Dick Hebdige, "The Meaning of Mod," in *Resistance through Rituals: Youth Subcultures in Post-War Britain*, ed. Stuart Hall and Tony Jefferson (London: Routledge, 1993), 71.

137. Dick Hebdige, "Reggae, Rastas, and Rudies," in *Resistance through Rituals: Youth Subcultures in Post-War Britain*, ed. Stuart Hall and Tony Jefferson (London: Routledge, 1993), 124.

138. Hebdige, "Reggae, Rastas, and Rudies," 124.

139. Hebdige, "Reggae, Rastas, and Rudies," 125.

140. Hebdige, "Reggae, Rastas, and Rudies," 125–26.

141. Alexis Petridis, "Misunderstood or Hateful? Oi!'s Rise and Fall," *The Guardian*, March, 18, 2010, https://www.theguardian.com/music/2010/mar/18/oi-cockney-rejects-garry-bushell-interview.

142. James Von Geldern, "Stilyaga," *Seventeen Moments in Soviet History*, http://soviethistory.msu.edu/1954-2/stilyaga/ (accessed February 22, 2021); Kevin Kelly, "Jazz on Bones: X-Ray Sound Recordings," *KK*, August 28, 2006, https://kk.org/streetuse/jazz-on-bones-xray-sound-recor-1/. Artemy Troitsky, *Back in the USSR: The True Story of Rock in Russia* (London: Omnibus Press, 1987).

143. Uta G. Poiger, *Jazz, Rock, and Rebels: Cold War Politics and American Culture in a Divided Germany* (Berkeley: University of California Press, 2000), 1.

144. David Burner, *Making Peace with the 60s* (Princeton, NJ: Princeton University Press, 1996), 151.

145. Maia Szalavitz, "The Legacy of the CIA's Secret LSD Experiments on America," *Time*, March 23, 2012, https://healthland.time.com/2012/03/23/the-legacy-of-the-cias-secret-lsd-experiments-on-america/; on the Merry Pranksters, see Tom Wolfe, *The Electric Kool-Aid Acid Test* (New York: Farrar Straus Giroux, 1968).

146. Danny Goldberg, "All the Human Be-In Was Saying 50 Years Ago, Was Give Peace a Chance," *The Nation*, January 13, 2017, https://www.thenation.com/article/archive/all-the-human-be-in-was-saying-50-years-ago-was-give-peace-a-chance/.

147. Gorman, *The Life and Time of Malcolm McLaren*, 139–40.

148. John McMillian, *Smoking Typewriters: The Sixties Underground Press and the Rise of Alternative Media in America* (Oxford: Oxford University Press, 2011), 4–5.

149. Dagmar Herzog, *Sex after Fascism: Memory and Morality in Twentieth Century Germany* (Princeton, NJ: Princeton University Press, 2003), 141–85; Cosey Fanni Tutti, *Art, Sex, Music* (London: Faber & Faber, 2017), 56–57.

150. "Mexico's 1968 Massacre: What Really Happened?," *All Things Considered*, December 1, 2008, https://www.npr.org/templates/story/story.php?storyId=97546687.

151. Eric Zolov, *Refried Elvis: The Rise of the Mexican Counterculture* (Berkeley: University of California Press, 1999).

152. Gerd-Rainer Horn, *The Spirit of '68: Rebellion in Western Europe and North America, 1956–1976* (Oxford: Oxford University Press, 2007), 104–11.

153. Michael J. Kramer, *The Republic of Rock: Music and Citizenship in the Sixties Counterculture* (Oxford: Oxford University Press, 2013), 195–98.

154. Poiger, *Jazz, Rock, and Rebels*, 218–19.

155. Reebee Garofalo, *Rockin' Out: Popular Music in the USA* (Boston: Allyn and Bacon, 1997), 219.

156. Steven Lee Beeber, *The Heebie-Jeebies at CBGB's: A Secret History of Jewish Punk* (Chicago: Chicago Review Press, 2006), 77–86.

157. Peter Doggett, *There's a Riot Going on: Revolutionaries Rock Stars, and the Rise and Fall of the '60s* (Edinburgh: Canongate, 2007).

158. Robert Greenfield, *The Last Sultan: The Life and Times of Ahmet Ertegun* (New York: Simon & Schuster, 2011), 191–95.

159. Kieran Williams, *The Prague Spring and Its Aftermath: Czechoslovak Politics, 1968–1970* (Cambridge: Cambridge University Press, 2011).

160. Joseph Yanosik, "The Plastic People of the Universe," *Perfect Sound Forever*, March 1996, http://www.furious.com/perfect/pulnoc.html.

161. Karl Ackermann, "Invisible Man: Willis Conover and the Jazz Hour," *All About Jazz*, April 30, 2019, https://www.allaboutjazz.com/invisible-man-willis-conover-and-the-jazz-hour-by-karl-ackermann.php.

162. Kramer, *The Republic of Rock*, 141–44.

Chapter 2

1. Marcus, *Lipstick Traces*, 5.

2. Marcus, *Lipstick Traces*, 2.

3. Marcus, *Lipstick Traces*, 200.

4. Marcus, *Lipstick Traces*, 251.

5. Jed Perl, *New Art City* (New York: Knopf, 2005), 434.

6. John A. Walker, "Cross-Overs, Art into Pop, Pop into Art," in *Sound & Vision*, ed. Luca Beatrice (Bologna: Damiani, 2007), 23–24.

7. Kelly M. Cresap, *Pop Trickster Fool: Warhol Performs Naivete* (Urbana: University of Illinois Press, 2004), 121.

8. Gorman, *The Life and Times of Malcolm McLaren*, 95.

9. Gorman, *The Life and Times of Malcolm McLaren*, 97–98.

10. Gorman, *The Life and Times of Malcolm McLaren*, 133–34.

11. Gorman, *The Life and Times of Malcolm McLaren*, 155.

12. Gorman, *The Life and Times of Malcolm McLaren*, 146–47.

13. Gorman, *The Life and Times of Malcolm McLaren*, 178.

14. Gorman, *The Life and Times of Malcolm McLaren*, 191–95.

15. Tutti, *Art, Sex, Music*, 50–51.

16. Tutti, *Art, Sex, Music*, 59. Although Tutti used he/him pronouns for P-Orridge at the time, in my own text I default to "they" because this was what they used later in life.

17. Tutti, *Art, Sex, Music*, 61.

18. Tutti, *Art, Sex, Music*, 89–90.

19. "Throbbing Gristle," in *Industrial Culture Handbook*, ed. V. Vale and Andrea Juno (San Francisco: RE/Search 1983), 11.

20. "Throbbing Gristle," 14.

21. "Fluxus Portal for the Internet," *Fluxus X Portal*, 2006, http://www.fluxus.org/; Hannah Higgins, *Fluxus Experience* (Berkeley: University of California Press, 2002); Ken Friedman (ed.), *The Fluxus Reader* (West Sussex, UK: Academy Editions, 1998).

22. "Overview: Who Were (Are) the Diggers?," *Digger Archives*, https://www.diggers.org/overview.htm (accessed March 26, 2021).

23. Adam Block, "Tomata du Plenty," *Portfolio*, January 25, 1989.

24. J. P. Robinson, "The Rotten Etymology of Punk," *Medium*, August 20, 2018, https://jprobinson.medium.com/the-rotten-etymology-of-punk-86db2fcc16f8.

25. Dave Marsh, "? and the Mysterians," *Creem*, May 1971, n.p.

26. Jim DeRogatis, *Let It Blurt: The Life and Times of Lester Bangs America's Greatest Rock Critic* (New York: Broadway Books, 2000), 119.

27. Lester Bangs, "MC5: Kick Out the Jams," *Rolling Stone*, April 5, 1969, n.p.

28. Lester Bangs, "James Taylor Marked for Death (What We Need Is a Lot Less Jesus and a Whole Lot More Troggs)," *Who Put the Bomp!*, no. 2, 1971, 62–63.

29. Greg Shaw, "Love that Dirty Water: The Standells," *Who Put the Bomp!*, no. 12, 1974, 6.

30. John Rockwell, "Rock Concert Give by Elliot Murphy," *New York Times*, February 19, 1974, 24.

31. William Safire, " 'Punk's Horror Show': Punk Is Sweeping the Country," *New York Times*, June 30, 1977, 19.

32. Mick Farren, "Introduction," in *Bomp!: Saving the World One Record at a Time*, ed. Mick Farren and Suzy Shaw (Los Angeles: American Modern Books, 2007), 7.

33. Greg Shaw, "Who Put the Bomp!," *Bomp!*, 2007, 91; Robert Coulson, "Fandom as a Way of Life," in *Science Fiction Fandom*, ed. Joe Sanders (Westport, CT: Greenwood Press, 1994), 11.

34. Iggy Pop, "Iggy Pop's Keynote Speech," *BBC Music John Peel Lecture*, 2014, https://www.bbc.co.uk/programmes/articles/1DBxXYBDJLt2xZgxjzCkLRg/bbc-music-john-peel-lecture-iggy-pops-keynote-speech-transcript.

35. See https://www.residents.com/. There is a documentary about the band: Don Hardy, *Theory of Obscurity: A Film about the Residents* (KTF Films, 2015).

36. Mick Wall, *Lou Reed: The Life* (London: Orion House, 2013), 18–20.

37. Wall, *Lou Reed*, 27.

38. Legs McNeil and Gillian McCain, *Please Kill Me: The Uncensored Oral History of Punk* (New York: Grove Press, 1996), 27–31.

39. McNeil and McCain, *Please Kill Me*, 39–40.

40. Thomas J. Sugrue, *The Origins of the Urban Crisis: Race and Inequality in Postwar Detroit* (Princeton, NJ: Princeton University Press, 1996), 3.

41. Sugrue, *The Origins of the Urban Crisis*, 5.

42. Sarah Schulman, *The Gentrification of the Mind: Witness to a Lost Imagination* (Berkeley: University of California Press, 2013), 32.

43. Jörg Hoppe, Heiko Lange, and Klaus Maeck, *B-Movie: Lust & Sound in West Berlin 1979–1989* (DEF Media, 2015).

44. Georgy Katsiaficas, *The Subversion of Politics: European Autonomous Social Movements and the Decolonization of Everyday Life* (Oakland, CA: AK Press, 2006), 88–89.

45. Katsiaficas, *The Subversion of Politics*, 89.

46. Katsiaficas, *The Subversion of Politics*, 88–89.

47. Katsiaficas, *The Subversion of Politics*, 90.

48. "MC5 Timeline," *MC5 Gateway*, 2000–2018, http://makemyday.free.fr/mc5.htm; Clinton Heylin, *From the Velvets to the Voidoids: A Pre-Punk History for a Post-Punk World* (New York: Penguin Books, 1993), 32–36; McNeil and McCain, *Please Kill Me*, 46.

49. Heylin, *From the Velvets to the Voidoids*, 33.

50. Heylin, *From the Velvets to Voidoids*, 36.

51. Heylin, *From the Velvets to the Voidoids*, 38.

52. Heylin, *From the Velvets to the Voidoids*, 38.

53. Heylin, *From the Velvets to the Voidoids*, 38.

54. Heylin, *From the Velvets to the Voidoids*, 37.

55. Heylin, *From the Velvets to the Voidoids*, 37.

56. Brendan Mullen and Marc Spitz, *We Got the Neutron Bomb: The Untold Story of LA Punk* (New York: Three Rivers Press, 2001), 19.

57. Stuart Lenig, *The Twisted Tale of Glam Rock* (Santa Barbara, CA: Praeger, 2010).

58. Ken Barnes, "The Glitter Era: Teenage Rampage," *Bomp!*, March 1978.

59. Mary Campbell, "David Bowie Is the Newest Rock Star Imported from England," *Nashua Telegraph*, November 4, 1972, 14.

60. Phillip Auslander, "Watch That Man, David Bowie: Hammersmith Odeon London, July 3, 1973," in *Performance and Popular Music: History, Place, and Time*, ed. Ian Inglis (London: Routledge, 2006), 72.

61. Gorman, *The Live and Times of Malcolm McLaren*, 234–45.

62. Suzi Quatro, *Unzipped* (London: Hodder & Stoughton, 2007), 81–82.

63. Mullen and Spitz, *We Got the Neutron Bomb*, 11–12.

64. Mullen and Spitz, *We Got the Neutron Bomb*, 16–17.

65. Quoted in Mullen and Spitz, *We Got the Neutron Bomb*, 14.

66. Mullen and Spitz, *We Got the Neutron Bomb*, 17.

67. Kevin Kerslake, *Joan Jett: Bad Reputation* (Magnolia Pictures, 2018).

68. Mullen and Spitz, *We Got the Neutron Bomb*, 45. For more on Krome's relationship with the band, see Lene Cortina, "Kari Krome—The First Runaway," *Punk Girl Diaries*, July 22, 2020, https://punkgirldiaries.com/kari-krome-the-first-runaway/.

69. Mullen and Spitz, *We Got the Neutron Bomb*, 46.

70. Mullen and Spitz, *We Got the Neutron Bomb*, 49.

71. Marc Maron, "Episode 953—Joan Jett," *WTF with Marc Maron*, September 24, 2018, http://www.wtfpod.com/podcast/episode-953-joan-jett.

72. Mullen and Spitz, *We Got the Neutron Bomb*, 51.

73. Kerslake, *Joan Jett: Bad Reputation*.

74. Nina Antonia, *Johnny Thunders: In Cold Blood* (London: Cherry Red Books, 2000), 22.

75. Antonia, *Johnny Thunders*, 11.

76. Antonia, *Johnny Thunders*, 31; Gorman, *The Life and Times of Malcolm McLaren*, 193.

77. Gorman, *The Life and Times of Malcolm McLaren*, 236–346.

78. Mark Christopher Covino and Jeff Howlett, *A Band Called Death* (Drafthouse Films, 2012).

79. For some information on Afro-punk, see Rawiya Kameir, "The True Story of How Afropunk Turned a Message Board into a Movement," *The Fader*, August 21, 2015, http://www.thefader.com/2015/08/21/james-spooner-afropunk, and the Afropunk website, https://afropunk.com/.

80. McCain and McNeil, *Please Kill Me*, 3–24.

81. McCain and McNeil, *Please Kill Me*, 42–50.

82. Quoted in McCain and McNeil, *Please Kill Me*, 63.

83. Quoted in McCain and McNeil, *Please Kill Me*, 66.

84. Quoted in McCain and McNeil, *Please Kill Me*,67.

85. Quoted McCain and McNeil, *Please Kill Me*, 79–80.

86. "Suicide—Chronology," *From the Archives*, November 4, 2020, https://www.fromthearchives.org/av_mr/chronology.html.

87. Beeber, *The Heebie-Jeebies at CBGB's*, 43.

88. Beeber, *The Heebie-Jeebies at CBGB's*, 43.

89. Beeber, *The Heebie-Jeebies at CBGB's*, 43–44.

90. Ian Port, "Suicide City: The Punk Explosion Rages on in Rarely Screened Films," *Village Voice*, July 12, 2017, https://www.villagevoice.com/2017/07/12/suicide-city/.

91. Port, "Suicide City: The Punk Explosion Rages on in Rarely Screened Films," *Village Voice*, July 12, 2017, https://www.villagevoice.com/2017/07/12/suicide-city/.

92. "Ford to City: Drop Dead," *New York Daily News*, October 30, 1975.

93. Beeber, *The Heebie-Jeebies at CBGB's*, 45.

94. Nina Antonia, *Too Much, Too Soon: The Makeup & Breakup of the New York Dolls* (London: Omnibus Press, 1998), 15.

95. Antonia, *Too Much, Too Soon*, 28.

96. Antonia, *Too Much, Too Soon*, 34.

97. Antonia, *Too Much, Too Soon*, 41.

98. Antonia, *Too Much, Too Soon*, 50.

99. Antonia, *Too Much, Too Soon*, 53–54. On getting a contract with Mercury, see Antonia, *Too Much, Too Soon*, 77.

100. Antonia, *Too Much, Too Soon*, 57.

101. Antonia, *Too Much, Too Soon*, 77.

102. Quoted in McCain and McNeil, *Please Kill Me*, 163.

103. Quoted in McCain and McNeil, *Please Kill Me*, 165.

104. Quoted in McCain and McNeil, *Please Kill Me*, 165.

105. Quoted in McCain and McNeil, *Please Kill Me*, 169.

106. McCain and McNeil, *Please Kill Me*, 169–70.

107. Quoted in McCain and McNeil, *Please Kill Me*, 171–73.

108. Beeber, *The Heebie-Jeebies at CBGB's*, 85.

109. Yvonne Sewall Ruskin, *High on Rebellion: Inside the Underground at Max's Kansas City* (New York: Thunder's Mouth Press, 1998), 1–2.

110. Patti Smith, *Just Kids* (New York: Harper Collins, 2010), 116–18.

111. Randy Kennedy, "Revisiting Max's, Sanctuary for the Hip," *New York Times*, September 1, 2010, https://www.nytimes.com/2010/09/05/arts/design/05maxs.html.

112. Phil Marcade, *Punk Avenue: Inside the New York City Underground 1972–1982* (New York: Three Rooms Press, 2017).

113. Jeffrey S. Debies-Carl, *Punk Rock and the Politics of Place: Building a Better Tomorrow* (London: Routledge, 2014), 5.

114. Marcade, *Punk Avenue*, 53–54.

115. Marcade, *Punk Avenue*, 59.

116. Marcade, *Punk Avenue*, 59–0.

117. Marcade, *Punk Avenue*, 59–60.

118. Jame Porter, "Neon Leon Alive and Well!," *Roctober*, no. 40, 2005, https://web.archive.org/web/20101230031903/http://www.roctober.com/roctober/neonleon.html.

119. Marcade, *Punk Avenue*, 66.

120. "Patti Smith—Biography," *Arista Records*, June 1996, http://www.aristarec.com/psmith/smithbio.html.

121. Austin Scaggs, "Q&A: Michael Stipe," *Rolling Stone*, October 6, 2004, http://www.rollingstone.com/artists/rem/articles/story/6539431/qa_michael_stipe.

122. "Talent Talk," *Billboard*, October 22, 1977, 54.

123. Marky Ramone, *Punk Rock Blitzkrieg* (New York: Touchstone, 2015), 82.

124. Ben Sisario, "Marty Thau, Manager in Early New York Punk Scene, Dies at 75," *New York Times*, February 23, 2014, https://www.nytimes.com/2014/02/24/arts/music/marty-thau-manager-in-early-new-york-punk-scene-dies-at-75.html.

125. Quoted in Monte Melnick and Frank Meyer, *On the Road with the Ramones* (London: Sanctuary Publishing, 2003), 59–60.

126. Melnick and Meyer, *On the Road with the Ramones*, 62–63.

127. Simon Reynolds, *Rip it Up and Start Again: Postpunk 1978–1984* (London: Penguin Books, 2005), 159; Andy Greene, "Flashback: Talking Heads Perform 'Psycho Killer' at CBGB in 1975," *Rolling Stone*, July 11, 2013, https://www.rollingstone.com/music/music-news/flashback-talking-heads-perform-psycho-killer-at-cbgb-in-1975-174455/.

128. For an example of the Sire advertising approach, see Rev. Keith A. Gordon, "Fossils: Sire Records' Don't Call it Punk," *That Devil Music*, August 13, 2016, http://www.thatdevilmusic.com/2016/08/fossils-sire-records-dont-call-it-punk.html.

129. Patti Smith, *Live in London at the Roundhouse in May 1976* (Smilin' Ears, 1977), a bootleg album of that performance.

130. Marcade, *Punk Avenue*, 43–47.

131. Marcade, *Punk Avenue*, 51.

132. Marcade, *Punk Avenue*, 51.

133. Marcade, *Punk Avenue*, 52.

134. Gorman, *The Life and Times of Malcolm McLaren*, 276.

135. *Max's Kansas City: New York New Wave* (CBS, 1978).

136. Ivan Kral and Amos Poe, *The Blank Generation* (Poe Productions, 1976).

137. Don Letts, *The Punk Rock Movie* (Punk Rock Films, 1978); Derek Jarman, *Jubilee* (Megalovision, 1978).

138. Zagria, "Jayne County (1947–) Part III: London and Berlin," *A Gender Variance Who's Who*, September 28, 2015, https://zagria.blogspot.com/2015/09/jayne-county-1947-part-iii-london-and.html#.YJWlkV0pBhE.

139. Frances Stonor Saunders, *The Cultural Cold War: The CIA and the World of Arts and Letters* (New York: New Press, 2013); Von Eschen, *Satchmo Blows Up the World*.

140. Tim Mohr, *Burning Down the Haus: Punk Rock, Revolution, and the Fall of the Berlin Wall* (Chapel Hill, NC: Algonquin Books, 2019).

141. Mohr, *Burning Down the Haus*, 134.

142. Mohr, *Burning Down the Haus*, 134–35.

143. Quoted in Melnick and Meyer, *On the Road with the Ramones*, 63.

144. Quoted in Melnick and Meyer, *On the Road with the Ramones*, 77.

145. Mick Wall, *John Peel: A Tribute to the Much-Loved DJ and Broadcaster* (London: Orion, 2004), 9.

146. Marcus Gray, *The Clash: Return of the Last Gang in Town* (Winnona, MN: Hal Leonard, 2004), 26–27.

147. Gorman, *The Life and Times of Malcolm McLaren*, 188.

148. Gorman, *The Life and Times of Malcolm McLaren*, 206.

149. Gorman, *The Life and Times of Malcolm McLaren*, 260.

150. Gorman, *The Life and Times of Malcolm McLaren*, 279–81.

151. Gorman, *The Life and Times of Malcolm McLaren*, 261–62.

152. Gorman, *The Life and Times of Malcolm McLaren*, 262–63.

153. Gorman, *The Life and Times of Malcolm McLaren*, 266.

154. Gray, *The Clash*, 48–49.

155. Gorman, *The Life and Times of Malcolm McLaren*, 357.

156. Jon Savage, *England's Dreaming: Anarchy, Sex Pistols, Punk Rock, and Beyond* (New York: St. Martin's Griffin, 2001), 71–72.

157. Quoted in Savage, *England's Dreaming*, 75–77.

158. Savage, *England's Dreaming*, 80.

159. Savage, *England's Dreaming*, 116.

160. Savage, *England's Dreaming*, 122.

161. Quoted in Gorman, *The Life and Times of Malcolm McLaren*, 294–95.

162. Quoted in Gorman, *The Life and Times of Malcolm McLaren*, 300.

163. Gorman, *The Life and Times of Malcolm McLaren*, 303–4.

164. Gorman, *The Life and Times of Malcolm McLaren*, 293; Savage, *England's Dreaming*, 108.

165. Quoted in Gorman, *The Life and Times of Malcolm McLaren*, 333.

166. "From the Archive: 18, October 1976: Controversial Art Plunges in to the Rust Hilt at the ICA," *The Guardian*, October 18, 2014, https://www.theguardian.com/music/2014/oct/18/genesis-p-orridge-ica-exhibition-1976.

167. Gorman, *The Life and Times of Malcolm McLaren*, 313–14.

168. Gorman, *The Life and Times of Malcolm McLaren*, 316.

169. Gorman, *The Life and Times of Malcolm McLaren*, 317.

170. Gorman, *The Life and Times of Malcolm McLaren*, 320–21.

171. Gorman, *The Life and Times of Malcolm McLaren*, 327.

172. Gorman, *The Life and Times of Malcolm McLaren*, 323.

173. Gorman, *The Life and Times of Malcolm McLaren*, 323.

174. Gorman, *The Life and Times of Malcolm McLaren*, 323.

175. Savage, *England's Dreaming*, 267.

176. Savage, *England's Dreaming*, 267.

177. Gorman, *The Life and Times of Malcolm McLaren*, 338–41. See also Savage, *England's Dreaming*, 261–66.

178. Gorman, *The Life and Times of Malcolm McLaren*, 342.

179. Gorman, *The Life and Times of Malcolm McLaren*, 357–58.

180. Gorman, *The Life and Times of Malcolm McLaren*, 375.

181. Gorman, *The Life and Times of Malcolm McLaren*, 359–62.

182. Savage, *England's Dreaming*, 433.

183. Savage, *England's Dreaming*, 435.

184. Savage, *England's Dreaming*, 445.

185. "1977: Elvis Costello Banned from Saturday Night Live Over 'Radio, Radio,'" *Groovy History*, December 17, 2020, https://groovyhistory.com/elvis-costello-saturday-night-live-radio-radio.

186. Savage, *England's Dreaming*, 445. For information on some of the bands that played at this now defunct club, see "The Great Southeast Music Hall," *Chamblee54*, May 16, 2011, https://chamblee54.wordpress.com/2011/05/16/the-great-southeast-music-hall/.

187. "NBC News Report of Sex Pistols Tour in U.S.A.," *YouTube*, April 25, 2007, https://www.youtube.com/watch?v=MoO591pGkjA&t=371s.

188. Savage, *England's Dreaming*, 446.

189. Savage, *England's Dreaming*, 446–47.

190. Savage, *England's Dreaming*, 446–47.

191. Savage, *England's Dreaming*, 452.

192. Savage, *England's Dreaming*, 455.

193. Savage, *England's Dreaming*, 457–60.

194. Savage, *England's Dreaming*, 463–64.

195. Savage, *England's Dreaming*, 475–76.

196. Savage, *England's Dreaming*, 507–8.

197. Savage, *England's Dreaming*, 527–29.

198. Gorman, *The Life and Times of Malcolm McLaren*, 260.

199. Gorman, *The Life and Times of Malcolm McLaren*, 299.

200. Gorman, *The Life and Times of Malcolm McLaren*, 315.

201. Gorman, *The Life and Times of Malcolm McLaren*, 314–15.

202. John Robb, *Punk Rock: An Oral History* (Oakland, CA: PM Press, 2012), 243. On the release of their first album, see Robb, *Punk Rock*, 295–96.

203. Robb, *Punk Rock*, 298–300. For the LA punks crashing the in-store, see Mullen and Spitz, *We Got the Neutron Bomb*, 72–75.

204. "Stiff Records: If It Ain't Stiff, It Ain't Worth a Debt," *Independent*, September 22, 2011, https://www.independent.co.uk/arts-entertainment/music/features/stiff-records-if-it-ain-t-stiff-it-ain-t-worth-a-debt-415988.html.

205. Gray, *The Clash*, 122. See also Gareth Murphy, *Cowboys and Indies: The Epic History of the Record Industry* (New York: Thomas Dunne Books, 2014).

206. Suisman, *Selling Sounds*.

207. Gray, *The Clash*, 29.

208. Gray, *The Clash*, 65–66.

209. Gray, *The Clash*, 81–83.

210. Gray, *The Clash*, 89.

211. Gray, *The Clash*, 102.

212. Gray, *The Clash*, 124–25.

213. Gray, *The Clash*, 143.

214. Compare Robb, *Punk Rock*, 216, and Savage, *England's Dreaming*, 220.

215. Clinton Heylin, *Public Image Limited: Rise/Fall* (London: Omnibus Press, 1989), 8–9.

216. Gray, *The Clash*, 216–18 and see "Bullets-In," *Sniffin' Glue*, June, 1977, No. 10, 2. The entire run of the zine is collected in Mark Perry, *Sniffin' Glue: The Essential Punk Accessory* (Lanham, MD: Sanctuary, 2000).

217. For more on the Bromley Contingent, see Mary Marmelek, "The Bromley Contingent: Shocking the Moral Majority in the UK," *Please Kill Me*, May 14, 2018, https://pleasekillme.com/bromley-contingent-early-punk-attitude/; "The Bromley Contingent," *Mital-U Punk*, https://mital-u.ch/punkwave/the-bromley-contingent/?lang=en (accessed April 22, 2021). Soo Catwoman maintains a website, http://www.soocatwoman.com/.

218. John Lydon, *Rotten: No Irish, No Blacks, No Dogs* (London: Hodder & Stoughton, 1993), 75, 117–18.

219. Donn Letts, *Culture Clash: Dread Meets Punk Rockers* (London: SAF, 2007), 149.

220. Caroline Coon, *1988: The New Wave Punk Rock Explosion* (London: Omnibus Press, 1982), 106.

221. Leah Schnelbach, "Neil Gaiman's Inner Workings Are Explored in New Documentary Dream Dangerously," *Tor*, August 12, 2016, https://www.tor.com/2016/08/12/neil-gaiman-documentary-dream-dangerously-review/.

222. Neil Gaiman, "How to Talk to Girls at Parties," *Fragile Things* (New York: William Morrow, 2006), 255–70.

223. Josh Weiss, "Cinamon Hadley, Who Inspired Death in Neil Gaiman's Sandman, Has Died," *SyFy Wire*, February 12, 2020, https://www.syfy.com/syfywire/cinamon-hadley-who-inspired-death-in-neil-gaimans-sandman-has-died.

224. Erin Janosik, "Dreamboys: A Punk Band with Peter Capaldi and Craig Ferguson," *BBC America*, 2013, https://www.bbcamerica.com/anglophenia/2013/08/dreamboys-a-punk-band-with-peter-capaldi-and-craig-ferguson/.

225. August Bernadicou and Chris Coats, "Jayne County: The Electric Chairs, Actress, Performer," *LGBTQ History Project*, September 17, 2020, https://www.lgbtqhp.org/jayne-county.

226. Bernadicou and Coats, "Jayne County."

227. Lily Wakefield, "Trans Electronic Music Pioneer Wendy Carlos Appeared on the BBC Dressed as a Cis Man. This Is Why," *Pink News*, February 9, 2021, https://www.pinknews.co.uk/2021/02/09/wendy-carlos-transgender-trans-electronic-music-robert-moog-synthesizer-bbc/.

228. Gray, *The Clash*, 165.

229. Savage, *England's Dreaming*, 183.

230. Savage, *England's Dreaming*, 183.

231. Savage, *England's Dreaming*, 183.

232. Quoted in Mullen and Spitz, *We Got the Neutron Bomb*, 59–60.

233. Mullen and Spitz, *We Got the Neutron Bomb*, 58.

234. Mullen and Spitz, *We Got the Neutron Bomb*, 58.

235. Mullen and Spitz, *We Got the Neutron Bomb*, 60–61.

236. Quoted in Mullen and Spitz, *We Got the Neutron Bomb*, 65.

237. Quoted in Mullen and Spitz, *We Got the Neutron Bomb*, 76.

238. Mullen and Spitz, *We Got the Neutron Bomb*, 79–80.

239. Mullen and Spitz, *We Got the Neutron Bomb*, 83.

240. Mullen and Spitz, *We Got the Neutron Bomb*, 85.

241. Mullen and Spitz, *We Got the Neutron Bomb*, 85.

242. Mullen and Spitz, *We Got the Neutron Bomb*, 123.

243. Quoted in Mullen and Spitz, *We Got the Neutron Bomb*, 123.

244. Mullen and Spitz, *We Got the Neutron Bomb*, 125.

245. Mullen and Spitz, *We Got the Neutron Bomb*, 126.

246. Quoted in Mullen and Spitz, *We Got the Neutron Bomb*, 126–27.

247. Mullen and Spitz, *We Got the Neutron Bomb*, 129–30.

248. Mohr, *Burning Down the Haus*, 9–11.

249. Sabrina Ramet, "Shake, Rattle and Self-Management," in *Kazaam! Splat! Ploof!: The American Impact on European Popular Culture Since 1945*, ed. Gordana P. Crnković and Sabrina Ramet (Lanham, MD: Rowan & Littlefield, 2003), 178.

250. "BalkansNet—Rock," *Balkans Pages*, http://balkansnet.org/rock.html (accessed April 27, 2021).

251. "Igor Vidmar," *Uzurlikzurli e-zine*, http://members.iinet.net.au/~predrag/vidmar.html (accessed April 27, 2021).

252. See Pankrti's website for a discography, "Pankrti: Discography," *Pankriti*, http://pankrti.tripod.com/eng/discography.html (accessed April 27, 2021).

253. "Igor Vidmar."

Chapter 3

1. Alan O'Connor, *Punk Record Labels and the Struggle for Autonomy: The Emergence of DIY* (Lanham, MD: Lexington Books, 2008), x.

2. O'Connor, *Punk Record Labels and the Struggle for Autonomy*, xi.

3. O'Connor, *Punk Record Labels and the Struggle for Autonomy*, 1.

4. O'Connor, *Punk Record Labels and the Struggle for Autonomy*, 2.

5. Steve Albini, "The Problem with Music," *The Baffler*, no. 5 (December 1993).

6. Mullen and Spitz, *We Got the Neutron Bomb*, 131.

7. Mullen and Spitz, *We Got the Neutron Bomb*, 74.

8. Mullen and Spitz, *We Got the Neutron Bomb*, 161.

9. Mullen and Spitz, *We Got the Neutron Bomb*, 162.

10. Roman Kozak, "Rock'n'Rolling' 'Saturday Night' Fights?; Siouxsie Battles Symbols," *Billboard*, November 14, 1981, 15; Roman Kozak "The Night John Belushi Booked the Punk Band Fear on Saturday Night Live, and They Got Banned from the Show," *Open Culture*, May 5, 2016, http://www.openculture.com/2016/05/the-night-john-belushi-booked-the-punk-band-fear-on-snl.html.

11. Mullen and Spitz, *We Got the Neutron Bomb*, 192–93.

12. Mullen and Spitz, *We Got the Neutron Bomb*, 173–74.

13. Mullen and Spitz, *We Got the Neutron Bomb*, 222.

14. Mullen and Spitz, *We Got the Neutron Bomb*, 222.

15. Lou Adler, *Ladies and Gentlemen, the Fabulous Stains* (Paramount, 2008).

16. Tomi, David, and Gregor, "Yugoslavia," *Maximum Rocknroll*, no. 11, January/February 1984, 55.

17. David Hesmondhalgh, "Post-Punk's Attempt to Democratize the Music Industry: The Success and Failure of Rough Trade," *Popular Music*, vol. 16, no. 3 (October 1997): 255–74, http://www.jstor.com/stable/853045.

18. Michael Azerrad, *Our Band Could Be Your Life: Scenes form the American Indie Underground 1981–1991* (Boston: Little Brown and Company, 2001), 4.

19. O'Connor, *Punk Record Labels and the Struggle for Autonomy*, 1.

20. O'Connor, *Punk Record Labels and the Struggle for Autonomy*, 1–2.

21. O'Connor, *Punk Record Labels and the Struggle for Autonomy*, 4. Pierre Bourdieu, *The Rules of Art: Genesis and Structure of the Literary Field*, trans. Susan Emanuel (Stanford, CA: Stanford University Press, 1996); Pierre Bourdieu, *The Field of Cultural Production* (New York: Columbia University Press, 1993).

22. O'Connor, *Punk Record Labels and the Struggle for Autonomy*, 5–6.

23. Daniel Dylan Wray, "$5 Gigs, Not $10m Deals: The Story of US Punk Label Dischord Records," *The Guardian*, November 20, 2020, https://www.theguardian.com/music/2020/nov/20/40-years-of-dischord-records.

24. Wray, "$5 Gigs, Not $10m Deals."

25. Wray, "$5 Gigs, Not $10m Deals."

26. Wray, "$5 Gigs, Not $10m Deals."

27. Wray, "$5 Gigs, Not $10m Deals."

28. O'Connor, *Punk Record Labels and the Struggle for Autonomy*, 8.

29. O'Connor, *Punk Record Labels and the Struggle for Autonomy*, 9.

30. O'Connor, *Punk Record Labels and the Struggle for Autonomy*, 19.

31. O'Connor, *Punk Record Labels and the Struggle for Autonomy*, 19.

32. O'Connor, *Punk Record Labels and the Struggle for Autonomy*, 22.

33. O'Connor, *Punk Record Labels and the Struggle for Autonomy*, 25.

34. Terry Burrows with Daniel Miller, *Mute: A Visual Document from 1978 →Tomorrow* (London: Thames & Hudson, 2007), 24.

35. Burrows with Miller, *Mute*, 24.

36. Burrows with Miller, *Mute*, 24.

37. Dave Thompson, *Depeche Mode: Some Great Reward* (London: Sidgwick & Jackson, 1995), 22–23.

38. Jack Rabid, "Dance with Me Some More: Frontier Records' Lisa Fancher Celebrates the Legendary Label's 40th Anniversary!," *The Big Takeover*, no. 87 (2020), 96.

39. Rabid, "Dance with Me Some More," 98.

40. "About K," *K Records*, 2017, https://krecs.com/pages/about; Mark Baumgarten, *Love Rock Revolution: K Records and the Rise of Independent Music* (Seattle: Sasquatch Books, 2012).

41. Baumgarten, *Love, Rock, Revolution*, 43.

42. Tony Nitwit, "Holland: Scene Report," *Maximum Rocknroll*, no. 5 (March–April 1983), 45–48; Fabio, "Brazil: Scene Report," *Maximum Rocknroll*, no. 5 (March–April 1983), 35–37.

43. See Pankrti's website for their discography, "Pankrti: Discography," *Pankrti*, http://pankrti.tripod.com/discography.html (accessed September 16, 2020).

44. ŠKUC, https://www.skuc.org/domov/ (accessed September 16, 2020); ŠKUC Association, Republic of Slovenia Ministry of Culture, https://www.culture.si/en/%C5%A0KUC_Association (accessed September 16, 2020).

45. "Italy," *Maximum Rocknroll*, no. 10 (December 1983), 48–49.

46. O'Connor, *Punk Record Labels and the Struggle for Autonomy*, 27.

47. O'Connor, *Punk Record Labels and the Struggle for Autonomy*, 35.

48. Ruth Schwartz, "Warning! This Label May Be Hazardous to Your Health," *Maximum Rocknroll*, no. 2 (1982), 42–43.

49. Jack Rabid, "Rabid's Ramblings," *Maximum Rocknroll*, no. 10 (December 1983), 6–7; emphasis in original.

50. "Letters," *Maximum Rocknroll*, no. 11 (January/February 1984), 5–6.

51. There were two different spellings for this club, Guildersleeves in *MRR* by Wendel and Gildersleeves by Rabid in *TBT.*

52. Jack Rabid, "Part III The State of Thins [*sic*]. Shows (editorial content)," *The Big Takeover*, no. 14 (June 1983), 2–3.

53. Rabid, "Part III The State of Thins [*sic*]. Shows (editorial content)," 3.

54. Rabid, "Part III The State of Thins [*sic*]. Shows (editorial content)," 3.

55. Rabid, "Part III The State of Thins [*sic*]. Shows (editorial content)," 3.

56. Rabid, "Part III The State of Thins [*sic*]. Shows (editorial content)," 3.

57. Rabid, "Part III The State of Thins [*sic*]. Shows (editorial content)," 3.

58. Dewar MacLeod, " 'Social Distortion': The Rise of Suburban Punk Rock in Los Angeles," in *America under Construction: Boundaries and Identities in Popular Culture*, ed. Kristi Long and Matthew Nadelhaft (New York: Garland, 1997), 136.

59. Robert Mason and Iwan Morgan (eds.), *The Liberal Consensus Reconsidered: American Politics and Society in the Postwar Era* (Oxford: Oxford University Press, 2017).

60. Kevin Mattson, *We're Not Here to Entertain: Punk Rock, Ronald Reagan, and the Real Culture War of 1980s America* (Oxford: Oxford University Press, 2020).

61. Mark Berdin, "I Don't Want to Fight," *Maximum Rocknroll*, vol. 1, no. 2 (1982), 36–39.

62. Dave Insurgent, "Letters," *Maximum Rocknroll*, vol. 1, no. 3 (November–December 1982), 4.

63. Ben Nadler, *Punk in NYC's Lower East Side 1981–1991* (Portland: Microcosm Publishing, 2014), 14–15.

64. Nadler, *Punk in NYC's Lower East Side*, 4–5.

65. "UK," *Maximum Rocknroll*, no. 12 (March 1984), 48. For an overview of the tape and to hear it, see Richard Metzger, "Anarcho-Punk'D: Crass's Infamous 'Thatchergate' Tape," *Dangerous Minds*, January 24, 2012, https://dangerousminds.net/comments/anarcho_punkd_crasss_infamous_thatchergate_tape.

66. Sara Diamond, "The New Right's Intelligence Connections," *Maximum Rocknroll*, no. 28 (September 1985), 61–65.

67. Tim Yohannan and Jeff Bale, "A Discussion with Mykel Board of Art, Artless, and Seidboard World Enterprises," *Maximum Rocknroll*, no. 8 (September 1983), 30.

68. Mohr, *Burning Down the Haus*.

69. Mohr, *Burning Down the Haus*, 9.

70. Mohr, *Burning Down the Haus*, 23.

71. Mohr, *Burning Down the Haus*, 31.

72. Mohr, *Burning Down the Haus*, 74.

73. Mohr, *Burning Down the Haus*, 58–59.

74. Mohr, *Burning Down the Haus*, 53.

75. Mohr, *Burning Down the Haus*, 53.

76. Mohr, *Burning Down the Haus*, 57.

77. Mohr, *Burning Down the Haus*, 123.

78. Mohr, *Burning Down the Haus*, 129.

79. Mohr, *Burning Down the Haus*, 134.

80. Mohr, *Burning Down the Haus*, 194.

81. Mohr, *Burning Down the Haus*, 210.

82. Dario Cortese, "Yugoslavia," *Maximum Rocknroll* (July–August 1983), 48.

83. Cortese, "Yugoslavia," 48.

84. Alexei Monroe, *Interrogation Machine: Laibach and NSK* (Cambridge, MA: MIT Press, 2005), 155.

85. Monroe, *Interrogation Machine*, 24.

86. Monroe, *Interrogation Machine*, 159.

87. Monroe, *Interrogation Machine*, 164.

88. "1985–1990: The Story So far," *Laibach*, 2020, https://www.laibach.org/bio/.

89. Monroe, *Interrogation Machine*, 206.

90. Monroe, *Interrogation Machine*, 206.

91. John R. Lampe, *Yugoslavia as History: Twice There was a Country* (Cambridge: Cambridge University Press, 1996), 232.

92. "It Is on These Principles . . . ," *Maximum Rocknroll*, no. 1 (1982), 3.

93. "It Is on These Principles . . . ," 3.

94. "Letters," *Maximum Rocknroll*, no. 1 (1982), 6.

95. Maria, "Punk Propaganda Protest or Proselytism," *Maximum Rocknroll*, vol. 1, no. 1 (1982), 30–31.

96. Joe Losurdo and Kristina Tillman, *You Weren't There: A History of Chicago Punk 1977–1984* (Regressive Films, 2007). Strike Under, *Immediate Action*, Wax Trax! Records, 1981.

97. Susan Dynner, *Punk's Not Dead* (Punk's Not Dead Productions, 2007).

98. Lauraine LeBlanc, *Pretty in Punk: Girl's Gender Resistance in a Boys' Subculture* (New Brunswick, NJ: Rutgers University Press, 1999), 36–39, 45.

99. LeBlanc, *Pretty in Punk*, 50.

100. LeBlanc, *Pretty in Punk*, 49–50.

101. LeBlanc, *Pretty in Punk*, 8.

102. LeBlanc, *Pretty in Punk*, 8.

103. LeBlanc, *Pretty in Punk*, 51.

104. LeBlanc, *Pretty in Punk*, 51.

105. Quoted in Mullen and Spitz, *We Got the Neutron Bomb*, 194.

106. Mullen and Spitz, *We Got the Neutron Bomb*, 197,

107. Mullen and Spitz, *We Got the Neutron Bomb*, 199.

108. Mullen and Spitz, *We Got the Neutron Bomb*, 199.

109. Mullen and Spitz, *We Got the Neutron Bomb*, 199.

110. Mullen and Spitz, *We Got the Neutron Bomb*, 229.

111. Quoted in Mullen and Spitz, *We Got the Neutron Bomb*, 226.

112. Mullen and Spitz, *We Got the Neutron Bomb*, 224.

113. Mullen and Spitz, *We Got the Neutron Bomb*, 224.

114. Wray, "$5 Gigs, Not $10m Deals."

115. Ian Glasper, *Burning Britain: The History of UK Punk 1980–1984* (London: PM Press, 2014), 224–25.

116. Glasper, *Burning Britain*, 17.

117. Glasper, *Burning Britain*, 332.

118. Elijah Wald, *Escaping the Delta: Robert Johnson and the Invention of the Blues* (New York: Amistad, 2004) and *How the Beatles Destroyed Rock 'n' Roll: An Alternative History of American Popular Music* (Oxford: Oxford University Press, 2009).

119. Baraka, *Blues People*, 222.

120. Jeff Chang, *Can't Stop, Won't Stop: A History of the Hip-Hop Generation* (New York: Picador, 2005), 92.

121. Chang, *Can't Stop, Won't Stop*, 151.

122. Quoted in Gray, *The Clash*, 371–73.

123. Paul Sng, *Poly Styrene: I Am a Cliché* (Skyart, 2021).

124. Alice Bag, *Violence Girl: East LA Rage to Hollywood Stage: A Chicana Punk Story* (Port Townsend, WA: Feral House, 2011).

125. James Spooner, "Foreword," in *White Riot: Punk Rock and the Politics of Race*, ed. Stephen Duncombe and Maxwell Tremblay (London: Verso, 2011), xiii.

126. Stephen Duncombe, "One White Riot?," in *White Riot: Punk Rock and the Politics of Race*, ed. Stephen Duncombe and Maxwell Tremblay (London: Verso, 2011), 5.

127. Duncombe, "One White Riot?," 5.

128. Duncombe, "One White Riot?," 5–6.

129. Edward Said, *Orientalism* (New York: Pantheon Books, 1978).

130. W. E. B. Du Bois, *The Souls of Black Folk* (Oxford: Oxford University Press, 2007), 8.

131. Greil Marcus, *Ranters & Crowd Pleasers: Punk in Pop Music, 1977–92* (New York: Doubleday, 1993), 184.

132. Marcus, *Ranters & Crowd Pleasers*, 182.

133. Quoted in Marcus, *Ranters & Crowd Pleasers*, 184.

134. On the controversy over Powell, see Nicholas Hillman, "A 'Chorus of Execration'? Enoch Powell's 'Rivers of Blood' 40 Years On," *Patterns of Prejudice*, vol. 42, no. 1 (February 2008): 83–104.

135. "40 Years since the Birth of Rock Against Racism: Rebel Music Broke Down that Fear," *Unite against Fascism*, October 7, 2016, http://uaf.org.uk/2016/10/40-years-since-the-birth-of-rock-against-racism-rebel-music-that-broke-down-fear/.

136. "40 Years since the Birth of Rock Against Racism."

137. "40 Years since the Birth of Rock Against Racism."

138. Glasper, *Burning Britain*, 159.

139. *Rebel Music*, no. 1 (June 1981).

140. Jah Ovjam, "RAR Badges and a Protest Walk . . . ," *New Crimes*, vol. 4 (1980): 10.

141. Ovjam, "RAR Badges and a Protest Walk . . . ," 10–11.

142. Garry Johnson, *The Story of Oi!: A View from the Dead-End of the Street* (Manchester: Babylon Books, 1988), 8.

143. Johnson, *The Story of Oi!*, 17–18. The term "herbert" comes up several times in relation to some of the working-class Oi! bands. A primer on this slang can be found "What Is the Meaning of the Term 'Herbert' in British Slang," *StackExchange*, August 12, 2011, https://english.stackexchange.com/questions/37663/what-is-the-meaning-of-the-term-herbert-in-british-slang.

144. Glasper, *Burning Britain*, 310–11.

145. Glasper, *Burning Britain*, 321.

146. Robert Forbes and Eddie Stampton, *The White Nationalist Skinhead Movement: UK & USA 1979–1993* (Port Townsend, WA: Feral House, 2015), 10.

147. Forbes and Stampton, *The White Nationalist Skinhead Movement*, 10.

148. Forbes and Stampton, *The White Nationalist Skinhead Movement*, 10.

149. John Hamblett and Phil McNeil, "NF Prints Punk Zine," *New Musical Express*, June 17, 1978; reprinted in Forbes and Stampton, *The White Nationalist Skinhead Movement*, 11–12.

150. Forbes and Stampton, *The White Nationalist Skinhead Movement*, 14–15.

151. Forbes and Stampton, *The White Nationalist Skinhead Movement*, 17.

152. "Rock Against Communism," *The ADL*, https://www.adl.org/education/references/hate-symbols/rock-against-communism (accessed May 15, 2021).

153. @ndy, "A Brief History of Neo-Nazi Music in Australia," *Slackbastard*, December 2, 2010, https://slackbastard.anarchobase.com/?p=22224; Geoffrey Wright, *Romper Stomper* (Film Victoria, 1992).

154. Steve Knopper, "Nazi Punks F**K Off: How Black Flag, Bad Brains, and More Took Back Their Scene from White Supremacists," *GQ* (January 16, 2018), https://www.gq.com/story/punks-and-nazis-oral-history.

155. Mohr, *Burning Down the Haus*, 262–63.

156. Mohr, *Burning Down the Haus*, 265–67.

157. Wray, "$5 Gigs, Not $10m Deals."

158. Knopper, "Nazi Punks F**K Off."

159. Knopper, "Nazi Punks F**K Off."

160. Mic Crenshaw, Celina Flores, and Erin Yanke, "Episode 2: The Murder of Mulugeta Seraw," *It Did Happen Here*, November 20, 2020, https://kboo.fm/media/84478-episode-two-murder-mulugeta-seraw.

161. Mic Crenshaw, Celina Flores, and Erin Yanke, "Episode 5: They Thought We Were Everywhere: Portland Anti-racist Action," *It Did Happen Here*, December 11, 2020, https://kboo.fm/media/99661-episode-five-they-thought-we-were-everywhere-portland-anti-racist-action.

162. Mic Crenshaw, Celina Flores, and Erin Yanke, "Episode 4: The Minneapolis Baldies & the ARA," *It Did Happen Here*, December 4, 2020, https://kboo.fm/media/99472-episode-four-minneapolis-baldies-and-anti-racist-action. See especially the show notes.

163. Nadler, *Punk in NYC's Lower East Side*, 2.

164. Nadler, *Punk in NYC's Lower East Side*, 9.

165. Nadler, *Punk in NYC's Lower East Side*, 9.

166. Nadler, *Punk in NYC's Lower East Side*, 11.

167. Nadler, *Punk in NYC's Lower East Side*, 17.

168. Nadler, *Punk in NYC's Lower East Side*, 17–18.

169. Nadler, *Punk in NYC's Lower East Side*, 19.

170. Nadler, *Punk in NYC's Lower East Side*, 19.

171. Nadler, *Punk in NYC's Lower East Side*, 20–21.

172. Claude Chastagner, "The Parents' Music Resource Center: From Information to Censorship," *Popular Music*, vol. 18, no. 2 (May 1999): 179–92, https://www.jstor.org/stable/853600.

173. Michael Silverberg, "The Obscenity Trial that made HR Giger an Icon for Punk Rock and Free Speech," *Quartz*, May 20, 2014, https://qz.com/210900/the-obscenity-trial-that-made-h-r-giger-an-icon-for-punk-rock-and-free-speech/.

174. Poiger, *Jazz, Rock, and Rebels*, 136.

175. Tim Peacock, "The Filth and The Fury! How Sex Pistols Sparked a Media Outrage," *Discover Music*, December 1, 2019, https://www.udiscovermusic.com/stories/sex-pistols-media-outrage/.

176. Alexis Petridis, "The Slits' Viv Albertine on Punk, Violence, and Doomed Domesticity," *The Guardian*, June 1, 2014, https://www.theguardian.com/music/2014/jun/01/the-slits-viv-albertine-punk-violence-domesticity.

177. Paul Cobley, " 'Leave the Capitol,' " in *Punk Rock: So What? The Cultural Legacy of Punk*, ed. Roger Sabin (London: Routledge, 1999), 172.

178. Cobley, " 'Leave the Capitol,' " 172.

179. Cobley, " 'Leave the Capitol,' " 179.

180. Adrian Goldberg and Jim Frank, "A Time When Gigs Were Violent," *BBC*, September 10, 2015, https://www.bbc.com/news/magazine-34184563.

181. Mullen and Spitz, *We Got the Neutron Bomb*, 188–91; MacLeod, *Kids of the Black Hole*, 107–30.

182. Black Flag, "Police Story," track 7, *Damaged*, SST, 1981.

183. Lorenz Benet, "Taking Control of a Punk Who Happens to Be Your kid," *Chicago Tribune*, March 10, 1986, https://www.chicagotribune.com/news/ct-xpm-1986-03-10-8601180210-story.html.

184. The exact air dates are unclear. hipsville, "Punk Rock," and "Phil Donahue Punk Show, Part 1–4," *YouTube*, January 6, 2011, https://www.youtube.com/watch?v=UGOQUahAmxg; *Quincy M.E.*, season 8, episode 8, "Next Stop, Nowhere," directed by Ray Danton, December 1, 1982, NBC.

185. bostoncrew82, "Donahue—NYC Hardcore 27.10.86," *YouTube*, January 1, 2015, https://www.youtube.com/watch?v=XdQVQjTsrcs.

186. mazinz2, "(High Quality) New York Hardcore—1986 on Regis Philbin Morning Show ABC—NYHC," *YouTube*, January 22, 2011, https://www.youtube.com/watch?v=_XDQLmkegEc.

187. tmullens, "OK City 5 Alive News Story about Punk Rock in Oklahoma with the Reactors—1980," *YouTube*, February 25, 2015, https://www.youtube.com/watch?v=NspubfVkwk8.

188. BlankTV, "Black Flag—Local News Feature on Punk Violence—(1980)," *YouTube*, May 4, 2007, https://www.youtube.com/watch?v=VFTTE6zbFYU.

189. Blank TV, "Black Flag—News Report on Punk (Early 80s)."

190. Dantemadison, "We Destroy the Family: Punks vs. Parents (1982)," *YouTube*, August 25, 2008, https://www.youtube.com/watch?v=s-1HJnz4Zgk.

Chapter 4

1. The spelling of riot girl varies in the sources, so I default to using "riot girl" in my analysis, though the sources have a variety of spellings.

2. Grace Elizabeth Hale, *Cool Town: How Athens, Georgia, Launched Alternative Music and Changed American Culture* (Chapel Hill: University of North Carolina Press, 2020), 12.

3. Sheffield Doc/Fest, "I Get Knocked Down Trailer," *YouTube*, May 17, 2021, https://www.youtube.com/watch?v=dsAVHNPpUtQ.

4. Robin Vote, "War on Women," *Maximum Rocknroll*, no. 31 (December 1985), 35–40.

5. "Letters," *Maximum Rocknroll*, no. 32 (January 1986), 10–12.

6. "Letters," *Maximum Rocknroll*, no. 33 (February 1986), 10–13.

7. "Letters," *Maximum Rocknroll*, no. 34 (March 1986), 6.

8. Iain Chambers, *Urban Rhythms: Pop Music and Popular Culture* (New York: St. Martin's Press, 1985), 179.

9. LeBlanc, *Pretty in Punk*, 51.

10. LeBlanc, *Pretty in Punk*, 51.

11. LeBlanc, *Pretty in Punk*, 53.

12. LeBlanc, *Pretty in Punk*, 64.

13. LeBlanc, *Pretty in Punk*, 132.

14. LeBlanc, *Pretty in Punk*, 132.

15. Kathleen Hanna, "My Herstory," *Le Tigre*, http://www.letigreworld.com/sweepstakes/html_site/fact/khfacts.html (accessed June 1, 2021).

16. Carrie Brownstein, *Hunger Makes Me a Modern Girl: A Memoir* (New York: Riverhead Books, 2015), 8.

17. Brownstein, *Hunger Makes Me a Modern Girl*, 8–9.

18. Janice Radway, "Girl Zine Networks, Underground Itineraries, and Riot Grrrl History: Making Sense of the Struggle for New Social Forms in the 1990s and Beyond," *Journal of American Studies*, 50 (2016): 8, https://doi.org/10.1017/S0021875815002625.

19. P. Ness, "Scene Reports: NYC," *Maximum Rocknroll*, no. 119 (April 1993), 54–57.

20. Baumgarten, *Love Rock Revolution*, 168–69.

21. Baumgarten, *Love Rock Revolution*, 172.

22. Baumgarten, *Love Rock Revolution*, 173.

23. Radway, "Girl Zine Networks," 8.

24. Emily White, "Revolution Girl Style Now," in *Rock She Wrote: Women Write about Rock, Pop, and Rap*, ed. Evelyn McDonnell and Ann Powers (New York: Delta, 1995), 404.

25. Baumgarten, *Love Rock Revolution*, 49.

26. Baumgarten, *Love Rock Revolution*, 49.

27. White, "Revolution Girl Style Now," 406.

28. "Girls & Women, Pissed Off?," *Maximum Rocknroll*, no. 100 (September 1991), 2.

29. Christy Colcord, "Girls Women Chicks Babes Fucktoys Sluts Bitches Whores Holes . . . ," *Maximum Rocknroll*, no. 103 (December 1991), 126.

30. Leslie, "Girls Women Chicks Babes Fucktoys Sluts Bitches Whores Holes . . . ," *Maximum Rocknroll*, no. 103 (December 1991), 127.

31. "What Would Motivate You . . . ," *Maximum Rocknroll*, no. 105 (February 1992), 2.

32. "Letters," *Maximum Rocknroll*, no. 106 (February 1992), 10–11.

33. "Letters," *Maximum Rocknroll*, no. 108 (May 1992), 12.

34. "Letters," *Maximum Rocknroll*, no. 106 (February 1992), 10–11.

35. Jeff Bale, "Column: Or Is the Winner . . . ," *Maximum Rocknroll*, no. 107 (April 1992), 13.

36. "Sour Mash," *Maximum Rocknroll*, no. 117 (February 1993), 96.

37. "Sour Mash," 96–97.

38. "Letters," *Maximum Rocknroll*, no. 121 (June 1993), 17.

39. Mykel Board, "Column: You're Wrong," *Maximum Rocknroll*, no. 117 (February 1993), 26–27.

40. "Letters," *Maximum Rocknroll* (April 1993), 10–11.

41. "Classified: Riot Boy Zine," *Maximum Rocknroll*, no. 117 (February 1993), 169.

42. Sinker, *We Owe You Nothing*, 64.

43. Sinker, *We Owe You Nothing*, 62.

44. Sinker, *We Owe You Nothing*, xii.

45. "Letters," *Maximum Rocknroll*, no. 114 (November 1992), 12.

46. "Letters," *Maximum Rocknroll*, no. 121 (June 1993), 198. The review of *Eureka* can be found Sarah Zimmerman, "Between the Lions: Eureka," *Maximum Rocknroll*, no. 119 (April 1993), 153.

47. Karin Gembus, "Columns," *Maximum Rocknroll*, no. 114 (November 1992), 30–31.

48. White, "Revolution Girl Style Now," 402.

49. Mimi Thi Nguyen, "Preface," in Michelle Cruz Gonzales, *The Spitboy Rule: Tales of a Xicana in a Female Punk Band* (Oakland, CA: PM Press, 2016), 14.

50. Nguyen, "Preface," 14.

51. Michelle Cruz Gonzales, *The Spitboy Rule: Tales of a Xicana in a Female Punk Band* (Oakland, CA: PM Press, 2016) 95.

52. Gonzales, *The Spitboy Rule*, 28.

53. Gonzales, *The Spitboy Rule*, 28–29.

54. Gonzales, *The Spitboy Rule*, 32.

55. Gonzales, *The Spitboy Rule*, 104.

56. Gonzales, *The Spitboy Rule*, 103–4.

57. Jose Palafox, "Columns," *Maximum Rocknroll*, no. 197 (October 1999), 26.

58. Quoted in Sinker, *We Owe You Nothing*, 69.

59. Jayne Brown and Tavia Nyong'o, "Queer as Punk: A Guide to LGBQTIA+ Punk," *NPR Music*, June 15, 2020, https://www.npr.org/2020/06/15/876087623/queer-as-punk-a-guide-to-lgbtqia-punk.

60. You can hear a discussion of the Pogues and this song at Darach Ó Séaghdha, "Raft of the Medusa: The Pogues and London Irish Identities," *Motherfoclóir*, February 28, 2020, https://www.headstuff.org/motherfocloir/120-raft-of-the-medusa-the-pogues-and-london-irish-identities/.

61. Kathleen Chapman and Michael du Plessis, "Queercore: The Distinct Identities of Subculture," *College Literature* 24, no. 1 (February 1997): 46, https://www.jstor.org/stable/25099625.

62. Chapman and du Plessis, "Queercore," 46.

63. Chapman and du Plessis, "Queercore," 46.

64. Chapman and du Plessis, "Queercore," 49.

65. Chapman and du Plessis, "Queercore," 50.

66. Chapman and du Plessis, "Queercore," 52.

67. Jon Ginoli, *Deflowered: My Life in Pansy Division* (San Francisco: Cleis Press, 2009), 14.

68. Ginoli, *Deflowered*, 14.

69. Sam Sunderland, *Perfect Youth: The Birth of Canadian Punk* (Toronto: ECW, 2012), 97.

70. Sunderland, *Perfect Youth*, 95–96.

71. Sunderland, *Perfect Youth*, 101.

72. Sunderland, *Perfect Youth*, 101.

73. Sunderland, *Perfect Youth*, 101.

74. Sunderland, *Perfect Youth*, 102–3.

75. Quoted in Sunderland, *Perfect Youth*, 104.

76. Sunderland, *Perfect Youth*, 107.

77. Ginoli, *Deflowered*, 18–19.

78. Adam Rathe, "Queer to the Core," *Out*, May 2012, 56.

79. Rathe, "Queer to the Core," 56.

80. Ginoli, *Deflowered*, 13.

81. Ginoli, *Deflowered*, 21.

82. Ginoli, *Deflowered*, 21.

83. Hal Niedzviecki, "Punk-Lad Love, Dyke-Core, and the Evolution of Queer Zine Culture in Canada," *Broken Pencil*, May 30, 2012, https://brokenpencil.com/features/punk-lad-love-dyke-core-and-the-evolution-of-queer-zine-culture-in-canada/.

84. Rathe, "Queer to the Core," 57.

85. Rathe, "Queer to the Core," 57.

86. Rathe, "Queer to the Core," 57.

87. Rathe, "Queer to the Core," 57.

88. Niedzviecki, "Punk-Lad Love, Dyke-Core."

89. Bill Hsu, "SPEW: The Queer Punk Convention," *Postmodern Culture*, vol. 2, no. 1 (September 1991): 1.

90. Hsu, "SPEW," 1.

91. Hsu, "SPEW," 3.

92. Rathe, "Queer to the Core," 58.

93. Rathe, "Queer to the Core," 60.

94. Rathe, "Queer to the Core," 59.

95. Rathe, "Queer to the Core," 59.

96. Rathe, "Queer to the Core," 59. For information about Homocore Chicago, see "Joanna Brown and Mark Freitas," *Never the Same*, August 2011, https://never-the-same.org/interviews/brown-frietas-homocore/.

97. Ginoli, *Deflowered*, 25.

98. Ginoli, *Deflowered*, 27.

99. Ginoli, *Deflowered*, 28.

100. Rathe, "Queer to the Core," 59.

101. Peter Margasak, "Rock 'n' Roll: They're Queer, They're Here, Get into It," *Chicago Reader*, August 1, 1995, https://www.chicagoreader.com/chicago/rock-n-roll-theyre-queer-theyre-here-get-into-it/Content?oid=888336.

102. Margasak, "Rock 'n' Roll."

103. Rathe, "Queer to the Core," 59.

104. Brown and Nyong'o, "Queer as Punk."

105. Rathe, "Queer to the Core," 95.

106. Rathe, "Queer to the Core," 95.

107. Rathe, "Queer to the Core," 95.

108. Ari Perezdiez, "G.L.O.S.S.," *Maximum Rocknroll*, no. 384 (May 2015), 34.

109. Perezdiez, "G.L.O.S.S.," 35.

110. Perezdiez, "G.L.O.S.S.," 35.

111. Perezdiez, "G.L.O.S.S.," 35–36.

112. Rene, "Reaching Nirvana," *Propaganda*, no. 18 (Spring 1992), 32–33.

113. Brad Morrell, *Nirvana and the Sound of Seattle* (London: Omnibus Press, 1993), 4.

114. Gina Arnold, *Route 666: On the Road to Nirvana* (New York: St. Martin's Press, 1993), 4–5.

115. Arnold, *Route 666*, 5.

116. Arnold, *Route 666*, 4–5.

117. Arnold, *Route 666*, 8.

118. Arnold, *Route 666*, 11.

119. Hale, *Cool Town*, 196.

120. Hale, *Cool Town*, 206.

121. Hale, *Cool Town*, 213.

122. Craig Marks and Rob Tannenbaum, *I Want My MTV: The Uncensored Story of the Music Video Revolution* (New York: Dutton, 2011), 353.

123. Marks and Tannenbaum, *I Want My MTV*, 354.

124. Marks and Tannenbaum, *I Want My MTV*, 354.

125. Quoted in Marks and Tannenbaum, *I Want My MTV*, 355.

126. Stuart Kallen, *The History of Alternative Rock* (Detroit: Lucent Books, 2012), 6.

127. Kallen, *The History of Alternative Rock*, 6.

128. Eric Weisbard, *Spin Alternative Record Guide* (New York: Vintage Books, 1995), vii–viii.

129. Weisbard, *Spin Alternative Record Guide*, vii–viii.

130. Weisbard, *Spin Alternative Record Guide*, xi.

131. Azerrad, *Our Band Could Be Your Life*, 160–61.

132. Azerrad, *Our Band Could Be Your Life*, 164.

133. Azerrad, *Our Band Could Be Your Life*, 170.

134. Azerrad, *Our Band Could Be Your Life*, 170–71.

135. Azerrad, *Our Band Could Be Your Life*, 170–71.

136. Azerrad, *Our Band Could Be Your Life*, 172.

137. Azerrad, *Our Band Could Be Your Life*, 172.

138. Azerrad, *Our Band Could Be Your Life*, 172.

139. Azerrad, *Our Band Could Be Your Life*, 180.

140. Azerrad, *Our Band Could Be Your Life*, 181–83.

141. Azerrad, *Our Band Could Be Your Life*, 184.

142. Azerrad, *Our Band Could Be Your Life*, 190.

143. Azerrad, *Our Band Could Be Your Life*, 191.

144. Azerrad, *Our Band Could Be Your Life*, 193.

145. Azerrad, *Our Band Could Be Your Life*, 193.

146. Azerrad, *Our Band Could Be Your Life*, 193.

147. Azerrad, *Our Band Could Be Your Life*, 192–93.

148. "Note to Advertisers," *Maximum Rocknroll*, no. 129 (February 1994), 3.

149. "Note to Advertisers," *Maximum Rocknroll*, no. 130 (March 1994), 3.

150. Tim Yohannan, *Maximum Rocknroll*, no. 131 (April 1994), 6.

151. Tim Yohannan, *Maximum Rocknroll*, no. 133 (June 1994), 6.

152. Brian Zero, "Corporate Rock, Punk?," *Maximum Rocknroll*, no. 133 (June 1994), 92.

153. Zero, "Corporate Rock, Punk?," 93.

154. Zero, "Corporate Rock, Punk?," 93.

155. Zero, "Corporate Rock, Punk?," 98.

156. Zero, "Corporate Rock, Punk?," 98.

157. "Letters," *Maximumrocknroll*, no. 135 (August 1994), 18.

158. "Letters," *Maximumrocknroll*, no. 135 (August 1994), 18–19.

159. "Letters," *Maximumrocknroll*, no. 137 (October 1994), 16.

160. "Letters," 16.

161. "Letters," 16.

162. "Letters," 16.

163. Sinker, *We Owe You Nothing*, xii.

164. Sinker, *We Owe You Nothing*, xi–xii.

165. "Punk Planet," *Punk Planet*, no. 1 (May/June 1994), 2.

166. Will Dandy, "Columns," *Punk Planet*, no. 1 (May/June 1994), 4.

167. Dandy, "Columns," 4.

168. Dandy, "Columns," 4.

169. "Mail," *Punk Planet*, no. 3 (September/October 1994), 5.

170. "Mail," 5.

171. Ebullition Records ad, *Maximum Rocknroll*, no. 130 (March 1994), 44.

172. Kent McClard, "Column," *Maximum Rocknroll*, no. 132 (May 1994), 30–31.

173. Kent McClard, *HeartattaCk*, no. 1 (March 1994), 2.

174. "Words on Paper," *HeartattaCk*, no. 1 (March 1994), 7.

175. "Words on Paper," 7.

176. Kent McClard, "Editorial," *HeartattaCk*, no. 2 (June 1994), 2–3.

177. Timojhen Mark, "Between the Lions: Punk Planet," *Maximum Rocknroll*, no. 135 (August 1994), 154.

178. Tim Yohannan, "Columns," *Maximum Rocknroll*, no. 137 (October 1994), 42.

179. Yohannan, "Columns," 41–42.

180. Dr. Nørd, "Columns," *Maximum Rocknroll*, no. 149 (January 1995), 33–34.

181. Quoted in Matt Average, "Zine of the Month," *Maximum Rocknroll*, no. 142 (March 1995), 156–57.

182. "Words on Paper," *HeartattaCk*, no. 2 (June 1994), 6.

183. "Words on Paper," 6.

184. "Words on Paper," 6.

185. "Words on Paper," 6.

186. "Words on Paper," 6.

187. "Words on Paper," 6.

188. "Mail," *Punk Planet*, no. 4 (November/December 1994), 6.

189. Alex Sayf Cummings, *Democracy of Sound: Music Piracy and the Remaking of American Copyright in the Twentieth Century* (Oxford: Oxford University Press, 2013), 5.

190. Daniel Sinker, "Column," *Punk Planet*, no. 4 (November/December 1994), 17.

191. Sinker, "Column," 17.

192. Sinker, "Column," 18.

193. Sinker, "Column," 17–18.

194. Will Dandy, "Rancid," *Punk Planet*, no. 2 (July/August 1994), 31–32.

195. Dan Sinker, "Never Mind the Rumors It's Epitaph Records," *Punk Planet*, no. 4 (November/December 1994), 28.

196. Sinker, "Never Mind the Rumors," 29.

197. Sinker, "Never Mind the Rumors" 29.

198. Sinker, "Never Mind the Rumors," 30.

199. Zach Long, "Lollapalooza's Rise from Touring Festival to Chicago Mainstay," *TimeOut*, May 31, 2016, https://www.timeout.com/chicago/music/lollapaloozas-rise-from-touring-festival-to-chicago-mainstay.

200. "Lollapalooza," *Jane's Addiction*, https://janesaddiction.org/lollapalooza/ (accessed June 16, 2021).

201. Ray Waddell, "Venue Views: Warped Wrap," *Billboard*, September 14, 2002, 25.

202. See http://vanswarpedtour.com/ and https://www.lollapalooza.com/.

203. "Letters," *Maximum Rocknroll*, no. 112 (September 1992), 10.

204. "Letters," 10.

205. Graham Russell, "Lydia Lunch Interview," *Maximum Rocknroll*, no. 127 (December 1993), 83.

206. Bruce Boehrs, "Columns," *Maximum Rocknroll*, no. 149 (October 1995), 40.

207. Ray Lujan, "Column," *Maximum Rocknroll*, no. 161 (October 1996), 44.

208. Lujan, "Column," 44.

209. Scott Yahtzee, "Record Reviews," *Punk Planet*, no. 20 (September/October 1997), 138.

210. Jim Connell, "Fanzine Review," *Punk Planet*, no. 18 (May/June 1997), 136.

211. Daniel Sinker, "Extreme Exploitation: The Selling of the Vans Warped Tour," *Punk Planet*, no. 34 (November/December 1999), 74.

212. Sinker, "Extreme Exploitation," 74.

213. Sinker, "Extreme Exploitation," 75.

214. "V/A—'Teriyaki Asthma' EP: Record Tape Reviews," *Maximum Rocknroll*, no. 77 (October 1989), 110.

215. *Maximum Rocknroll*, no. 87 (August 1990), 79–83, 90.

216. Grungeboy, "Scene Reports: Southern California," *Maximum Rocknroll*, no. 98 (July 1991), 60.

217. "Top 15," *Maximum Rocknroll*, no. 103 (December 1991), 3. The name of the live recording was not listed in either case, but presumably this was their first promotional DGC release, a cassette of a live performance on Halloween 1991 released that year.

218. Jeff Bale, "Column," *Maximum Rocknroll*, no. 103 (December 1991), 32.

219. Tim Yohannan, "Bill Graham Croaks!!!!," *Maximum Rocknroll*, no. 103 (December 1991), 46.

220. "Letters," *Maximum Rocknroll*, no. 105 (February 1992), 18.

221. Ben Weasel, "Column," *Maximum Rocknroll*, no. 106 (March 1992), 33.

222. "Letters," *Maximum Rocknroll*, no. 114 (November 1992), 13–14.

223. "Letters," *Maximum Rocknroll*, no. 117 (February 1993), 17.

224. "The Velvet Underground," *Rock & Roll Hall of Fame*, https://www.rockhall.com/inductees/velvet-underground (accessed June 19, 2021).

225. "Northern California," *Maximum Rocknroll*, no. 76 (September 1989), 61.

226. Kent McClard, "Columns," *Maximum Rocknroll*, no. 127 (December 1993), 31.

227. Eyesore Video Channel, "Fox Undercover News Report on Punk (Los Angeles, 1995)," *YouTube*, May 21, 2017, https://www.youtube.com/watch?v=5sMnuMCNkRU&t=1475s.

228. JohnB3k, "Jenny Jones: Hay PUNK Lose The FUNK," *YouTube*, April 30, 2017, https://www.youtube.com/watch?v=asS5BtvF55Y.

229. Chris Ziegler, "Death in Texas," *Punk Planet*, no. 36 (March/April 2000), 70–71.

230. Ziegler, "Death in Texas," 72–73.

231. Ziegler, "Death in Texas," 76–77.

232. Ziegler, "Death in Texas," 79.

233. Ziegler, "Death in Texas," 80.

234. Charles Landy, "Punk Rocker Slain in Amarillo, Texas: The Murder of Brian Deneke," *Maximum Rocknroll*, no. 203 (April 2000), 105–7.

235. "Letters," *Maximum Rocknroll*, no. 227 (April 2002), 11. On Camp's violation of probation, see "Probation Violator Gets 8-Year Term," *Houston Chronicle*, September 8, 2001, 30.

236. Mykel Board, "Column," *Maximum Rocknroll*, no. 290 (July 2007), 17.

237. Jameson Brooks, *Bomb City* (3rd Identity Films, 2017).

238. Abel Prieto, "Discursos y crímenes de odio," *Granma* (June 2019), 3.

239. Lara Leveritt, *Devil's Knot: The True Story of the West Memphis Three* (London: Simon & Schuster, 2002), 14–15.

240. Leveritt, *Devil's Knot*, 43, 45.

241. Leveritt, *Devil's Knot*, 40.

242. Leveritt, *Devil's Knot*, 43.

243. "The Story," *Free West Memphis 3*, 2016, https://www.westmemphis3.org/the-story/ (accessed July 3, 2021).

244. Mike Taylor, "Columns," *Maximum Rocknroll*, no. 246 (November 2003), 19.

245. "Circle Jerks," *Mosh Yankee*, no. 3 (2003), 5.

246. Bryan Mehr, "Henry Rollins," *SLUG Mag*, no. 169 (January 2003), 24–25.

247. Jillian Rayfield, "West Memphis Three Released from Prison in Plea Deal," *Talking Points Memo*, August 19, 2011, https://talkingpointsmemo.com/muckraker/west-memphis-three-released-from-prison-in-plea-deal.

248. Michael Moynihan and Didrik Søderlind, *Lords of Chaos: The Bloody Rise of the Satanic Metal Underground* (Port Townsend, WA: Feral House, 2003).

249. See C. Shepard, *A Columbine Site*, 1999–2019, http://www.acolumbine site.com/.

250. "Newtown Gunman Adam Lanza Had 'Obsession' with Columbine," *BBC News*, November 26, 2013, https://www.bbc.com/news/world-us-canada-25097127.

251. Adam Cohen, "A Curse of Cliques," *Time*, April 25, 1999, http://content.time.com/time/printout/0,8816,23521,00.html.

252. Ted Rall, "Columns," *Maximum Rocknroll*, no. 198 (November 1999), 26.

253. Leah Ryan, "Columns," *Punk Planet*, no. 34 (November/December 1999), 22–23.

254. Jeff Fox, "I Hate a Parade," *Razorcake*, no. 24 (February/March 2005), 24.

255. Ask a Mortician, "Why Do We Get Columbine So Wrong?," *YouTube*, April 20, 2019, https://www.youtube.com/watch?v=EG0PtwYJU0M (accessed June 23, 2021).

256. Peter Langman, *Why Kids Kill: Inside the Minds of School Shooters* (New York: Palgrave Macmillan, 2009), 13.

257. Dave Cullen, "The Depressive and the Psychopath," *Slate*, April 20, 2004, https://slate.com/news-and-politics/2004/04/at-last-we-know-why-the-columbine-killers-did-it.html.

258. Dave Cullen, *Columbine* (New York: Twelve, 2009).

259. Nicole Hemmer, "The Fairness Doctrine Sounds a Lot Better Than It Actually Was," *CNN*, January 27, 2021, https://www.cnn.com/2021/01/27/opinions/fairness-doctrine-wont-solve-disinformation-hemmer/index.html.

260. Eric Lipton, "Disturbed Shooters Weren't True Goths," *Chicago Tribune*, April 25, 1999, https://www.chicagotribune.com/news/ct-xpm-1999-04-25-9904250292-story.html.

261. The date on this article seems incorrect, as it was listed as being half a month before the shooting, which happened on April 20, 1999. MTV News Staff, "Columbine Students Debunk 'Goth' Ties to Shooters as Community Moves On," *MTV*, March 31, 1999, http://www.mtv.com/news/1427258/columbine-students-debunk-goth-ties-to-shooters-as-community-moves-on/.

262. Rachel Rodriguez and Christina Zdanowicz, "Nothing the Same after Columbine, Says Students, Teachers," *CNN*, April 21, 2009, http://www.cnn.com/2009/US/04/20/columbine.irpt/index.html.

263. Casey Ress, "Fanzine Reviews," *Maximum Rocknroll*, no. 196 (September 1999), 148–49.

264. Josh Medsker, "NYHC: A Play by Barry Levine," *Maximum Rocknroll*, no. 201 (February 2000), 102.

265. Carolyn Keddy, "Are There Really Any Punks in Salt Lake City," *Maximum Rocknroll*, no. 195 (August 1999), 109.

266. Sarah Jacobson, "Plastic Film," *Punk Planet*, no. 32 (July/August 1999), 134–35.

Chapter 5

1. Madeline Brand, "Sex Pistols' Steve Jones, Just Saying No," *NPR Music*, March 13, 2006, https://www.npr.org/templates/story/story.php?storyId=5259850.

2. Olaf Schuelke, "The Punks of Myanmar," *Diplomat*, May 12, 2014, https://thediplomat.com/2014/05/the-punks-of-myanmar/.

3. Philip K. Dick, *Do Androids Dream of Electric Sheep?* (New York: Doubleday, 1968); Ridley Scott, *Blade Runner* (Warner Bros., 1982).

4. Bruce Bethke, "Foreword to Cyberpunk: A Short Story," *Infinity Plus*, http://www.infinityplus.co.uk/stories/cpunk.htm (accessed July 5, 2021).

5. Bethke, "Foreword."

6. Tim Chatterton and Georgia Newmarch, "The Future Is Already Here—It's Just Not Very Evenly Distributed," *ACM Interactions*, vol. 24 (April 2017): 42.

7. Chris Foresman, "How Star Trek Artists Imagined the iPad . . . Nearly 30 Years Ago," *Ars Technica*, September 10, 2016, https://arstechnica.com/gadgets/2016/09/how-star-trek-artists-imagined-the-ipad-23-years-ago/.

8. Fred Turner, *From Counterculture to Cyberculture: Stewart Brand, the Whole Earth Network, and the Rise of Digital Utopianism* (Chicago: University of Chicago Press, 2008).

9. Sophie Lasken, "We Are the Media: Amanda Palmer and the Online Revolution," *Eyecandy*, March 21, 2013, https://eyecandyjournal.wordpress.com/2013/03/21/we-are-the-media-amanda-palmer-and-the-online-revolution/.

10. Amanda Palmer, *The Art of Asking, or How I Learned to Stop Worrying and Let People Help* (New York: Grand Central, 2014), 85.

11. Palmer, *The Art of Asking*, 90.

12. Palmer, *The Art of Asking*, 91.

13. Palmer, *The Art of Asking*, 97.

14. Palmer, *The Art of Asking*, 94.

15. Darach Ó Séaghdha, "Quarantine Sessions 4: At Swim Two Tongues," *Motherfoclóir*, no. 126, May 22, 2020, https://www.headstuff.org/motherfocloir/126-quarantine-sessions-4-at-swim-two-tongues/.

16. Don Campau, "A Brief History of Cassette Culture," *Living Archive of Underground Music*, August 29, 2009, http://livingarchive.doncampau.com/about/a-brief-history-of-cassette-culture.

17. Dave Everley, "The Story of Grindcore: 'This Isn't Metal, It Isn't Punk, I Don't Know What the F**k These Guys are Doing,'" *Metal Hammer*, January

30, 2020, https://www.loudersound.com/features/grindcore-this-isnt-metal-it-isnt-punk-i-dont-know-what-the-fk-these-guys-are-doing.

18. Unclassified ads, *Flipside*, no. 41 (1983), 64–65.

19. Unclassified ads, *Flipside*, no. 44 (1984), 69.

20. Georgia Perry, "Santa Cruz's Internet Music Pioneer," *SantaCruz.com*, August 20, 2013, https://www.santacruz.com/news/santa_cruzs_internet_music_pioneer.html

21. Perry, "Santa Cruz's Internet Music Pioneer."

22. Perry, "Santa Cruz's Internet Music Pioneer."

23. "Letters," *Maximum Rocknroll*, no. 85 (June 1990), 14.

24. "Letters," *Maximum Rocknroll*, no. 107 (April 1992), 37.

25. Bobby Manic, "Machinegun," *Maximum Rocknroll*, no. 215 (April 2001), 86.

26. "Letters," *Maximum Rocknroll*, no. 277 (June 2006), 12.

27. Lance Hahn, "You're You, I'm Me, The Story of Lost Cherrees: Part Two," *Maximum Rocknroll*, no. 287 (August 2007), 96.

28. Jerod Pore, "Book Reviews," *Maximum Rocknroll*, no. 73 (June 1989), 118.

29. Pore, "Book Reviews," 117–18.

30. "Letters," *Maximum Rocknroll*, no. 111 (August 1992), 10.

31. "Letters," *Maximum Rocknroll*, no. 111 (August 1992), 10.

32. "Letters," *Maximum Rocknroll*, no. 111 (August 1992), 10.

33. Pauline Borsook, "The Anarchist," *Wired*, April 1, 1996, https://www.wired.com/1996/04/jennings/.

34. "Letters," *Maximum Rocknroll*, no. 112 (September 1992), 17.

35. "Letters," *Maximum Rocknroll*, no. 112 (September 1992), 17.

36. "Letters," *Maximum Rocknroll*, no. 115 (December 1992), 15.

37. "Letters," *Maximum Rocknroll*, no. 115 (December 1992), 15.

38. "Letters," *Maximum Rocknroll*, no. 123 (August 1993), 14.

39. This was the date the internet opened up to a much broader audience via web portals such as America Online. It also begins the process of commercialization of the internet that typifies the modern experience of the internet.

40. Jason Koebler, "It's September, Forever," *Vice*, September 30, 2015, https://www.vice.com/en/article/nze8nb/its-september-forever.

41. "Miscellaneous," *MRR*, "Book Your Own Fuckin' Life 2" (1993), 71.

42. Joao Da Silva, "Chile: Scene Report," *Maximum Rocknroll*, no. 220 (September 2001), 65.

43. *Maximum Rocknroll*, no. 432 (May 2019). The website has a partial archive of past issues, https://maximumrocknroll.com/.

44. Will Dandy, "Columns," *Punk Planet*, no. 1 (May/June 1994), 4.

45. Dandy, "Columns," 4.

46. Joe Nrrrd, "DIY: The Real Cyberpunk," *Punk Planet*, no. 9 (September/October 1995), 70.

47. Nrrrd, "DIY: The Real Cyberpunk," 70.

48. Nrrrd, "DIY: The Real Cyberpunk," 70–74.

49. Ben Weasel, "Column," *Maximum Rocknroll*, no. 147 (August 1995), 27.

50. Weasel, "Column," 27.

51. Mike Evans, "DIY>Audio Streaming," *Punk Planet*, no. 43 (May/June 2001), 91.

52. David Grad, "RIAA vs. MP3.com: The Struggle for Music Distribution Monopolies in Cyberspace," *Punk Planet*, no. 37 (May/June 2000), 92.

53. Grad, "RIAA vs. MP3.com," 94.

54. Grad, "RIAA vs. MP3.com," 94.

55. Kyle Ryan, "Next Stop: Unknown: Universal's Acquisition of Emusic," *Punk Planet*, no. 44 (July/August 2001), 83.

56. Ryan, "Next Stop: Unknown," 84.

57. Ryan, "Next Stop: Unknown," 84.

58. Ryan, "Next Stop: Unknown," 84.

59. Chris Nelson, "'98's Best: Furious George Not Monkeying Around about Trademark Battle," *MTV*, December 21, 1998, http://www.mtv.com/news/510291/98s-best-furious-george-not-monkeying-around-about-trademark-battle/.

60. George Tabb, "Column," *Maximum Rocknroll*, no. 208 (September 2000), 54.

61. George Tabb, "Column," *Maximum Rocknroll*, no. 207 (August 2000), 22.

62. Jim DeRogatis and Greg Kot, "Lawrence Lessig," *Punk Planet*, no. 74 (July/August 2006), 50.

63. DeRogatis and Kot, "Lawrence Lessig," 50.

64. DeRogatis and Kot, "Lawrence Lessig," 54.

65. DeRogatis and Kot, "Lawrence Lessig," 54.

66. Quoted in DeRogatis and Kot, "Lawrence Lessig," 54.

67. DeRogatis and Kot, "Lawrence Lessig," 54.

68. DeRogatis and Kot, "Lawrence Lessig," 54–55.

69. Anne Elizabeth Moore, "Playing Fair," *Punk Planet*, no. 69 (September/October 2005), 88.

70. Moore, "Playing Fair," 90.

71. Moore, "Playing Fair," 91.

72. DeRogatis and Kot, "Lawrence Lessig," 52.

73. "History," *Stiff Little Fingers*, 2020, https://www.slf.rocks/about-slf.

74. Noel McLaughlin and Martin McLoone, "Hybridity and National Musics: The Case of Irish Rock Music," *Popular Music*, vol. 19, no. 2 (April 2000): 181, https://www.jstor.org/stable/853667.

75. McLaughlin and McLoone, "Hybridity and National Musics," 181.

76. McLaughlin and McLoone, "Hybridity and National Musics," 181.

77. McLaughlin and McLoone, "Hybridity and National Musics," 183.

78. McLaughlin and McLoone, "Hybridity and National Musics," 183.

79. McLaughlin and McLoone, "Hybridity and National Musics," 182–83.

80. Jonathyne Briggs, *Sounds French: Globalization, Cultural Communities, and Pop Music, 1958–1980* (Oxford: Oxford University Press, 2015), 110–43.

81. Ken Sweeney, "Dubliners' 50-Year Musical Odyssey," *Independent*, January 11, 2012, https://www.independent.ie/entertainment/music/dubliners-50-year-musical-odyssey-26810023.html. For the Chieftains, see their website at https://www.thechieftains.com/; for Christy Moore, see his website https://www.christymoore.com/.

82. "The Chieftains," *Westpost Festival of Music and Performing Arts*, June 24, 2012, https://web.archive.org/web/20120330194342/http://www.westportfestival.com/the-chieftains/.

83. "Padraig Harrington and Christy Moore Honored at People of the Year Awards," *Rehab*, 2007, https://web.archive.org/web/20080430185857/http://www.rehab.ie/press/article.aspx?id=304.

84. McLaughlin and McLoone, "Hybridity and National Musics," 187.

85. McLaughlin and McLoone, "Hybridity and National Musics," 188.

86. Colm McAuliffe, "Jem Finer of the Pogues: A Millennium in Music," *New Statesman*, October 22, 2015, https://www.newstatesman.com/culture/observations/2015/10/jem-finer-pogues-millennium-music.

87. McAuliffe, "Jem Finer of the Pogues."

88. Nuala O'Connor, *Bringing It All Back Home: The Influence of Irish Music at Home and Overseas* (Dublin: Merlin, 2001), 122.

89. O'Connor, *Bringing It All Back Home*, 123.

90. Quoted in O'Connor, *Bringing It All Back Home*, 123.

91. Darach Ó Séaghdha, "Raft of the Medusa: The Pogues and London Irish Identities." *Motherfoclóir*, no. 120, February 28, 2020, https://www.headstuff.org/motherfocloir/120-raft-of-the-medusa-the-pogues-and-london-irish-identities/.

92. Ed Power, "Celebrating St. Patrick's Day? Don't Do it with the Pogues . . . ," *The Guardian*, March 17, 2010, https://www.theguardian.com/music/musicblog/2010/mar/17/st-patricks-day-pogues.

93. Power, "Celebrating St. Patrick's Day?"

94. Jana Evans Braziel and Anita Mannur, "Nation, Migration, Globalization: Points of Contention in Diaspora Studies," in *Theorizing Diaspora: A Reader*, ed. Jana Evans Braziel and Anita Mannur (Malden, MA: Blackwell, 2003), 1.

95. Braziel and Mannur, "Nation, Migration, Globalization," 3.

96. Braziel and Mannur, "Nation, Migration, Globalization," 6.

97. Piaras Mac Éinrí, "Introduction," in *The Irish Diaspora*, ed. Andy Bielenberg (London: Longman, 2000), 4.

98. Mac Éinrí, "Introduction," 4.

99. Ros Franey, "Guildford Four: Trial and Error," *The Guardian*, October 17, 1989, https://www.theguardian.com/uk/1989/oct/18/guildford-four-northernireland.

100. The Pogues, *If I Should Fall from Grace from God* (Island, 1988).

101. Adam Sweeting, "Philip Chevron Obituary," *The Guardian*, October 9, 2013, https://www.theguardian.com/music/2013/oct/09/philip-chevron.

102. "Giein It Laldy: 80s/90s Scottish Folk-Punk from Nyah Fearties," *WFMU's Beware of the Blog*, November 7, 2012, https://blog.wfmu.org/freeform/2012/11/nyah-fearties-interview.html.

103. "Alistair's Biography," *Folk Icons*, March 4, 2001, https://web.archive.org/web/20060615022312/http://www.folkicons.co.uk/alisbio.htm.

104. Ken Burke, "Dropkick Murphys," in *Contemporary Musicians: Profiles of the People in Music Volume 69*, ed. Tracie Ratiner (Detroit: Gale, 2011), 52.

105. Burke, "Dropkick Murphys," 53.

106. Burke, "Dropkick Murphys," 54.

107. Burke, "Dropkick Murphys," 54.

108. James M. Manheim, "Flogging Molly," in *Contemporary Musicians: Profiles of the People in Music Volume 66*, ed. Tracie Ratiner (Detroit: Gale, 2010), 55.

109. "Band," *Orthodox Celts*, http://www.orthodoxcelts.com/band/ (accessed July 11, 2021).

110. "About Our Music," *Selfish Murphy*, 2021, http://selfishmurphy.com/?page_id=713.

111. Debbie Elliot, "Gogol Bordello: Music from 'Gypsy Punks,'" *NPR Music*, April 29, 2006, https://www.npr.org/templates/story/story.php?storyId=5371385.

112. Hütz and GB, "Gogol Bordello Artist's Statement," *Gogol Bordello*, 2021, http://www.gogolbordello.com/.

113. Christian Hoard, "Gogol a Go-Go," *Village Voice*, May 8–14, 2002, https://web.archive.org/web/20051231065352/http://www.villagevoice.com/news/0219,hoard,34562,1.html.

114. "Band," *Gogol Bordello*, 2021, http://www.gogolbordello.com/.

115. Mat Ward," A Biting Musical Voice for Roma," *Green Left*, August 28, 2010, https://www.greenleft.org.au/content/biting-musical-voice-roma.

116. Kevin E. G. Perry, "Hütz Attacks," *The Collected Works of Kevin EG Perry*, January 30, 2007, https://kevinegperry.com/2007/01/30/eugene-hutz-interview-pied-piper-of-hutzovina/; Pavla Fleischer, *The Pied Piper of Hützovina* (Arts Alliance America, 2008).

117. "DeVotchKa," *LA Phil*, April 2007, https://web.archive.org/web/20120616044837/https://www.laphil.com/philpedia/artist-detail.cfm/?id=3144.

118. "About," *Balkan Beat Box*, 2021, http://www.balkanbeatbox.com/about.

119. Alan Ashton-Smith, "Colonized Culture: The Emergence of a Romani Postcolonialsm," *Journal of Post-Colonial Cultures and Societies*, vol. 1, no. 2 (April 2010): 74.

120. Ashton-Smith, "Colonized Culture," 74.

121. Ashton-Smith, "Colonized Culture," 74.

122. Ashton-Smith, "Colonized Culture," 75.

123. Omar Sacirbey, "The Challenges and Growth of Progressive Muslims," *Alicia Patterson Foundation*, May 5, 2011, https://web.archive.org/web/20121202091957/http://aliciapatterson.org/stories/challenges-and-growth-progressive-muslims.

124. Michael Muhammad Knight, *The Taqwacores* (New York: Soft Skull Press, 2003).

125. Quoted in Christopher Maag, "Young Muslims Build a Subculture on an Underground Book," *New York Times*, December 23, 2008, A16.

126. Eyad Zahra, *The Taqwacores* (Strand Releasing, 2011); Omar Majeed, *Taqwacore: The Birth of Punk Islam* (EyeSteelFilm, 2009).

127. Hisham D. Aidi, *Rebel Music: Race, Empire, and the New Muslim Youth Culture* (New York: Vintage Books, 2014), 109.

128. Aidi, *Rebel Music*, 109.

129. "Alien Kulture: The Story . . . ," *Alien Kulture*, 2010, http://alienkulture.org/index.html.

130. Wendy Fangyu Hsu, "Mapping the Kominas' Sociomusical Transnation: Punk, Diaspora, and Digital Media," *Asian Journal of Communication*, vol. 23, no. 4 (August 2013): 387, http://dx.doi.org/10.1080/01292986.2013.804103.

131. Hsu, "Mapping the Kominas' Sociomusical Transnation," 387.

132. Hsu, "Mapping the Kominas' Sociomusical Transnation," 387.

133. Hsu, "Mapping the Kominas' Sociomusical Transnation," 387.

134. Kun, *Audiotopia*, 2.

135. Eugene D. Genovese, *Roll, Jordan, Roll: The World the Slaves Made* (New York: Pantheon Books, 1974), xv.

136. Genovese, *Roll, Jordan, Roll*, xv.

137. Komozi Woodard, *A Nation within a Nation: Amiri Baraka (Leroi Jones) and Black Power Politics* (Chapel Hill: University of North Carolina Press, 1999), 2.

138. Woodard, *A Nation within a Nation*, 1.

139. Spooner, *Afro-Punk*.

140. Devon Maloney, "Afropunk Started with a Documentary. Two Years, Two Websites, and Eight Festivals Later . . . ," *Village Voice*, August 21, 2013, https://www.villagevoice.com/2013/08/21/afropunk-started-with-a-documentary-ten-years-two-websites-and-eight-festivals-later/.

141. Maloney, "Afropunk Started with a Documentary."

142. Maloney, "Afropunk Started with a Documentary."

143. Brian Josephs, "Is Afropunk Fest No Longer Punk?," *Vice*, August 17, 2015, https://www.vice.com/en/article/qbxjx7/is-the-afropunk-festival-no-longer-punk-813.

144. Josephs, "Is Afropunk Fest No Longer Punk?"

145. Carolyn Keddy, "Movies," *Maximum Rocknroll*, no. 244 (September 2003), 109.

146. Keddy, "Movies," 109.

147. Keddy, "Movies," 109.

148. George B. Sanchez, "Afro-Punk Filmmaker James Spooner," *Punk Planet*, no. 62 (July/August 2004), 65.

149. Sanchez, "Afro-Punk Filmmaker James Spooner," 66.

150. Sanchez, "Afro-Punk Filmmaker James Spooner," 66.

151. "Letters," *Punk Planet*, no. 64 (November/December 2004), 9.

152. "Letters," *Punk Planet*, no. 64 (November/December 2004), 9.

153. "Letters," *Punk Planet*, no. 64 (November/December 2004), 9.

154. Brian Peterson, "Cipher," *Punk Planet*, no. 68 (July/August 2005), 58.

155. Peterson, "Cipher," 58.

156. Peterson, "Cipher," 60.

157. Peterson, "Cipher," 60.

158. "MRR Radio #1310," *Maximum Rocknroll* (August 19, 2012), https://maximumrocknroll.com/radio_show/mrrradio-1310/.

159. Dave O'Dell, "The Early Days of Beijing Punk," *Maximum Rocknroll*, no. 403 (December 2016), 28.

160. O'Dell, "The Early Days of Beijing Punk," 28.

161. O'Dell, "The Early Days of Beijing Punk," 31.

162. Nevin Domer and Leo, "The Current Beijing Scene," *Maximum Rocknroll*, no. 403 (December 2016), 32.

163. Domer and Leo, "The Current Beijing Scene," 32.

164. "Blast from the Past," *Maximum Rocknroll*, no. 403 (December 2016), 71–74.

165. Jonathan DeHart, "Punk in Asia: Rebelling from Burma to Beijing," *The Diplomat*, April 16, 2013, https://thediplomat.com/2013/04/punk-in-asia-rebelling-from-burma-to-beijing/

166. DeHart, "Punk in Asia."

167. Olaf Schuelke, "The Punks of Myanmar," *The Diplomat*, May 12, 2014, https://thediplomat.com/2014/05/the-punks-of-myanmar/.

168. Sandra Hoyn, "The Punk of Burma," *Sandra Hoyn Photography*, https://www.sandrahoyn.de/portfolio/the-punk-of-burma/.

169. Hoyn, "The Punk of Burma."

170. Gunter, "Worldwide Punk Rock," *Maximum Rocknroll*, no. 280 (September 2006), 60.

171. Gunter, "Worldwide Punk Rock," 60.

172. "Myanmar Releases Long-Serving Political Prisoner," *Maximum Rocknroll*, no. 306 (November 2008), 44.

173. Mika Reckinnen, "No U Turn," *Maximum Rocknroll*, no. 412 (September 2017), 38.

174. Reckinnen, "No U Turn," 38.

175. Reckinnen, "No U Turn," 38.

176. Reckinnen, "No U Turn," 41.

177. Quoted in Reckinnen, "No U Turn," 40.

178. Luk Haas, "Column," *Maximum Rocknroll*, no. 184 (September 1998), 54.

179. Flox, "Tam89 Records Interview with Luk Haas," *Profane Existence*, March 5, 2012, https://profanexistence.com/2012/03/05/tam89-records-interview-with-luk-haas/

180. Flox, "Tam89 Records Interview with Luk Haas."

Conclusion

1. Erik J. Egenes, "Muro," *Maximum Rocknroll*, no. 422 (July 2018), 65.

2. Egenes, "Muro," 65.

3. Mike English, "Death Ridge Boys: The Right Side of History," *Maximum Rocknroll*, no. 420 (May 2018), 63.

4. English, "Death Ridge Boys," 64.

5. Grace Elizabeth Hale, *A Nation of Outsiders: How the White Middle Class Fell in Love with Rebellion in Postwar America* (Oxford: Oxford University Press, 2011), 6.

6. Hale, *A Nation of Outsiders*, 280.

7. Megan Barth, "The Outsiders," *Reagan Babe*, September 2, 2015, https://www.reaganbabe.com/national/the-outsiders/.

8. Shermicheal Singleton, "The Rise of the Political Outsider," *The Hill*, September 4, 2015, https://thehill.com/blogs/pundits-blog/presidential-campaign/rise-of-bernie-sanders-the-political-outsiders.

9. Andrew Kaczynski, "David Duke Urges His Supporters to Volunteer and Vote for Trump," *Buzzfeed News*, February 25, 2016, https://www.buzzfeednews.com/article/andrewkaczynski/david-duke-urges-his-supporters-to-volunteer-and-vote-for-tr#.ivQ4dr6l9A.

10. "Ku Klux Klan Newspaper Declares Support for Trump," *Reuters*, November 2, 2016, https://www.reuters.com/article/us-usa-election-trump-kkk-idUSKBN12X2IG.

11. Patrick Strickland, "What Is the Alt-Right and What Does it Stand For?," *Al Jazeera*, March 4, 2017, https://www.aljazeera.com/features/2017/3/4/what-is-the-alt-right-and-what-does-it-stand-for.

12. Strickland, "What Is the Alt-Right and What Does it Stand For?"

13. LastWeekTonight, "Tucker Carlson: Last Week Tonight with John Oliver (HBO)," *YouTube*, March 15, 2021, https://www.youtube.com/watch?v=XMGxxRRtmHc.

14. Adam Serwer, "Conservatives Have a White-Nationalism Problem," *The Atlantic*, August 6, 2019, https://www.theatlantic.com/ideas/archive/2019/08/trump-white-nationalism/595555/.

15. Jaclyn Diaz and Rachel Treisman, "Members of Right-Wing Militias, Extremists Groups Are Latest Charged in Capitol Siege," *NPR*, January 19, 2021, https://www.npr.org/sections/insurrection-at-the-capitol/2021/01/19/958240531/members-of-right-wing-militias-extremist-groups-are-latest-charged-in-capitol-si.

16. Shelby Steele, "Conservative as Counterculture," *National Review*, March 2, 2015, https://www.nationalreview.com/2015/03/conservatism-counterculture/.

17. Greg Jones, "Conservatism Is the New Counterculture," *The Federalist*, October 22, 2018, https://thefederalist.com/2018/10/22/conservatism-new-counterculture/

18. Jones, "Conservatism Is the New Counterculture."

19. Jones, "Conservatism Is the New Counterculture."

20. David Alm, "Alt-Right Street Punk 'Sabo' Calls GOP the New Punks—He's Wrong," *Forbes*, December 29, 2017, https://www.forbes.com/sites/davidalm/2017/12/29/alt-right-street-artist-sabo-calls-gop-the-new-punks-hes-wrong/.

21. David Alm, "Alt-Right Street Punk 'Sabo' Calls GOP the New Punks—He's Wrong." *Forbes*, December 29, 2017, https://www.forbes.com/sites/davidalm/2017/12/29/alt-right-street-artist-sabo-calls-gop-the-new-punks-hes-wrong/.

22. Reggie Ugwu, "How Electronic Music Made by Neo-Nazis Soundtracks the Alt-Right," *Buzzfeed News*, December 13, 2016, https://www.buzzfeednews.com/article/reggieugwu/fashwave.

23. Ugwu, "How Electronic Music Made by Neo-Nazis Soundtracks the Alt-Right."

24. Michelle Goldberg, "Alt-Right Facts," *Slate*, February 23, 2017, https://slate.com/news-and-politics/2017/02/cpac-invented-an-alternate-history-of-the-alt-right.html.

25. Goldberg, "Alt-Right Facts."

26. Jamie Thomson, "How Punk Changed Cities—and Vice Versa," *The Guardian*, March 17, 2017, https://www.theguardian.com/cities/2017/mar/17/how-punk-changed-cities-and-vice-versa.

27. Jamie Thomson, " 'No Fascist USA!,' How Hardcore Punk Fuels the Antifa Movement," *The Guardian*, September 9, 2017, https://www.theguardian.com/music/2017/sep/09/no-fascist-usa-how-hardcore-punk-fuels-the-antifa-movement.

28. Thomson, " 'No Fascist USA!,' How Hardcore Punk Fuels the Antifa Movement."

29. Noel the TrollXSplitter, "Right Wing Politics in the Punk/Hardcore Scene," *BlogXSplitter*, September 17, 2017, https://dukecityhardcorepunk.wordpress.com/2017/09/21/right-wing-politics-in-the-punkhardcore-scene/.

30. "Ebullition: History," *Ebullition Records*, http://www.ebullition.com/catalog.html#5 (accessed August 17, 2021).

31. "The Big Takeover Show," *The Big Takeover*, http://bigtakeover.com/radio.

32. Grace Ambrose, "Bay Area Girls Rock Camp," *Maximum Rocknroll*, no. 429 (May 2018), 29.

33. Ambrose, "Bay Area Girls Rock Camp," 29.

34. Ambrose, "Bay Area Girls Rock Camp," 29.

35. Grace Ambrose, "Little Debbie and the Crusaders," *Maximum Rocknroll*, no. 420 (May 2018), 31.

36. Ambrose, "Little Debbie and the Crusaders," 32.

37. Hannah Ewens, " 'There Are No Rules Now': How Gen Z Reinvented Pop Punk," *The Guardian*, July 23, 2021, https://www.theguardian.com/music/2021/jul/23/there-are-no-rules-now-how-gen-z-reinvented-pop-punk.

38. Ewens, " 'There Are No Rules Now': How Gen Z Reinvented Pop Punk."

39. Ewens, " 'There Are No Rules Now': How Gen Z Reinvented Pop Punk."

40. Jason Friedman, "The Linda Lindas Sign to Epitaph Records," *Paste*, May 27, 2021, https://www.pastemagazine.com/music/the-linda-lindas/the-linda-lindas-sign-epitaph-records/.

41. Jen Chaney, "We Are Lady Parts Rocks Outside the Box," *Vulture*, June 3, 2021, https://www.vulture.com/article/we-are-lady-parts-peacock-series-review.html.

Bibliography

Adorno, Benjamin, and Max Horkheimer. *Dialectics of Enlightenment*. Stanford, CA: Staford University Press, 2002.

Aidi, Hisham D. *Rebel Music: Race, Empire, and the New Muslim Youth Culture*. New York: Vintage Books, 2014.

Anderson, Benedict. *Imagined Communities: Reflections on the Origin of and Spread of Nationalism*. London: Verso, 1983.

Antonia, Nina. *Too Much, Too Soon: The Makeup & Breakup of the New York Dolls*. London: Omnibus Press, 1998.

———. *Johnny Thunders: In Cold Blood*. London: Cherry Red Books, 2000.

Arnold, Gina. *Route 666: On the Road to Nirvana*. New York: St. Martin's Press, 1993.

Ashton-Smith, Alan. "Colonized Culture: The Emergence of a Romani Postcolonialism." *Journal of Post-Colonial Cultures and Societies*, vol. 1, no. 2 (April 2010): 73–90.

Auslander, Phillip. "Watch That Man, David Bowie: Hammersmith Odeon London, July 3, 1973." In *Performance and Popular Music: History, Place, and Time*, ed. Ian Inglis, 70–80. London: Routledge, 2006.

Azerrad, Michael. *Our Band Could Be Your Life: Scenes from the American Indie Underground 1981–1991*. Boston: Little Brown, 2001.

Bag, Alice. *Violence Girl: East LA Rage to Hollywood Stage: A Chicana Punk Story*. Port Townsend, WA: Feral House, 2011.

Baraka, Amiri (LeRoi Jones). *Blues People: Negro Music in White America*. New York: Harper Perennial, 2002.

Baumgarten, Mark. *Love Rock Revolution: K Records and the Rise of Independent Music*. Seattle: Sasquatch Books, 2012.

Beeber, Steven Lee. *The Heebie-Jeebies at CBGB's: A Secret History of Jewish Punk*. Chicago: Chicago Review Press, 2006.

Benjamin, Walter. *The Work of Art in the Age of Mechanical Reproduction*. New York: Schocken, 2005.

Bernays, Edward. *Propaganda*. New York: Routledge, 1928.

Braziel, Jana Evans, and Anita Mannur. "Nation, Migration, Globalization: Points of Contention in Diaspora Studies." In *Theorizing Diaspora: A Reader*, edited by Jana Evans Braziel and Anita Mannur, 1–22. Malden, MA: Blackwell, 2003.

Briggs, Jonathyne. *Sounds French: Globalization, Cultural Communities, and Pop Music, 1958–1980*. Oxford: Oxford University Press, 2015.

Brotton, Jerry. *The Sultan and the Queen: The Untold Story of Elizabeth and Islam*. New York: Viking, 2016.

Brownstein, Carrie. *Hunger Makes Me a Modern Girl: A Memoir*. New York: Riverhead Books, 2015.

Bourdieu, Pierre. *The Field of Cultural Production*. New York: Columbia University Press, 1993.

———. *The Rules of Art: Genesis and Structure of the Literary Field*. Translated by Susan Emanuel. Stanford, CA: Stanford University Press, 1996.

Burke, Ken. "Dropkick Murphys." In *Contemporary Musicians: Profiles of the People in Music Volume 69*, edited by Tracie Ratiner, 52–55. Detroit: Gale, 2011.

Burner, David. *Making Peace with the 60s*. Princeton, NJ: Princeton University Press, 1996.

Burrows, Terry, and Daniel Miller. *Mute: A Visual Document from 1978→Tomorrow*. London: Thames & Hudson, 2007.

Chambers, Iain. *Urban Rhythms: Pop Music and Popular Culture*. New York: St. Martin's Press, 1985.

Chandarlapaty, Raj. *The Beat Generation and Counterculture: Paul Bowles, William S. Burroughs, and Jack Kerouac*. New York: Peter Lang, 2009.

Chang, Jeff. *Can't Stop, Won't Stop: A History of the Hip-Hop Generation*. New York: Picador, 2005.

Chapman, Kathleen, and Michael du Plessis. "Queercore: The Distinct Identities of Subculture." *College Literature*, vol. 24, no. 1 (February 1997): 45–58. https://www.jstor.org/stable/25099625.

Chastagner, Claude. "The Parents' Music Resource Center: From Information to Censorship." *Popular Music*, vol. 18, no. 2 (May 1999): 179–92. https://www.jstor.org/stable/853600.

Chatterton, Tim, and Georgia Newmarch, "The Future is Already Here—It's Just Not Very Evenly Distributed." *ACM Interactions*, vol. 24 (April 2017): 42.

Chomsky, Noam, and Edward Herman. *Manufacturing Consent: The Political Economy of the Mass Media*. New York: Pantheon Books, 1988.

Cobley, Paul. "'Leave the Capitol.'" In *Punk Rock: So What? The Cultural Legacy of Punk*, edited by Roger Sabin, 170–85. London: Routledge, 1999.

Cohen, Lizabeth. *Making a New Deal: Industrial Workers in Chicago, 1919–1939*. Cambridge, MA: Harvard University Press, 1990.

Coon, Caroline. *1988: The New Wave Punk Rock Explosion*. London: Omnibus Press, 1982.

Cooper, Sam. *The Situationist International in Britain: Modernism, Surrealism, and the Avant-Gardes*. London: Routledge, 2017.

Coulson, Robert. "Fandom as a Way of Life." In *Science Fiction Fandom*, edited by Joe Sanders, 11–16. Westport, CT: Greenwood Press, 1994.

Cresap, Kelly M. *Pop Trickster Fool: Warhol Performs Naivete*. Urbana: University of Illinois Press, 2004.

Crosby, Alfred W. *Ecological Imperialism: The Biological Expansion of Europe, 900–1900*. Cambridge: Cambridge University Press, 1986.

———. *The Columbian Exchange: Biological and Culture Consequences of 1492*. Santa Barbara, CA: Praeger, 2003.

Cullen, Dave. *Columbine*. New York: Twelve, 2009.

Cummings, Alex Sayf. *Democracy of Sound: Music Piracy and the Remaking of American Copyright in the Twentieth Century*. Oxford: Oxford University Press, 2013.

Debies-Carl, Jeffery S. *Punk Rock and the Politics of Place: Building a Better Tomorrow*. London: Routledge, 2014.

Debord, Guy. *Society of the Spectacle*. Detroit: Black & Red, 1983.

de Grazia, Victoria. *Irresistible Empire: America's Advance through 20th-Century Europe*. Cambridge, MA: Belknap Press, 2005.

DeRogatis, Jim. *Let It Blurt: The Life and Times of Lester Bangs, America's Greatest Rock Critic*. New York: Broadway Books, 2000.

Dick, Philip K. *Do Androids Dream of Electric Sheep?* New York: Doubleday, 1968.

Doggett, Peter. *There's a Riot Going On: Revolutionaries, Rock Stars, and the Rise and Fall of the '60s*. Edinburgh: Canongate, 2007.

Du Bois, W. E. B. *The Souls of Black Folk*. Oxford: Oxford University Press, 2007.

Duncombe, Stephen. "One White Riot?" In *White Riot: Punk Rock and the Politics of Race*, edited by Stephen Duncombe and Maxwell Tremblay, 1–17. London: Verso, 2011.

Éinrí, Piaras Mac. "Introduction." In *The Irish Diaspora*, edited by Andy Bielenberg, 1–15. London: Longman, 2000.

Eisenberg, Evan. *The Recording Angel: Music, Records, and Culture form Aristotle to Zappa*. New Haven, CT: Yale University Press, 2005).

Farren, Mick. "Introduction." In *Bomp!: Saving the World One Record at a Time*, edited by Mick Farren and Suzy Shaw, 1–25. Los Angeles: American Modern Books, 2007.

Forbes, Robert, and Eddie Stampton. *The White Nationalist Skinhead Movement: UK & USA 1979–1993*. Port Townsend, WA: Feral House, 2015.

Frank, Thomas. *The Conquest of Cool: Business Culture, Counterculture, and the Rise of Hip Consumerism*. Chicago: University of Chicago Press, 1997.

Friedman, Ken (ed.). *The Fluxus Reader*. West Sussex, UK: Academy Edition, 1998.

Gaiman, Neil. "How to Talk to Girls at Parties." In *Fragile Things*, 255–70. New York: William Morrow, 2006. Garofalo, Reebee. *Rockin' Out: Popular Music in the USA*. Boston: Allyn and Bacon, 1997.

Genovese, Eugene D. *Roll, Jordan, Roll: The World the Slaves Made*. New York: Pantheon Books, 1974.

Ginoli, Jon. *Deflowered: My Life in Pansy Division*. San Francisco: Cleis Press, 2009.

Glasper, Ian. *Burning Britain: The History of UK Punk 1980–1984*. Oakland, CA: PM Press, 2014.

Goffman, Daniel. *The Ottoman Empire and Early Modern Europe*. Cambridge: Cambridge University Press, 2002.

Gonzales, Michelle Cruz. *The Spitboy Rule: Tales of a Xicana in a Female Punk Band*. Oakland, CA: PM Press, 2016.

Gorman, Paul. *The Life and Times of Malcolm McLaren: The Biography*. London: Constable, 2020.

Gramsci, Antonio. *An Antonio Gramsci Reader: Selected Writings 1916–1935*. Edited by David Gorgacs. New York: Schocken Books, 1988.

Gray, Marcus. *The Clash: The Return of the Last Gang in Town*. Winnona, MN: Hal Leonard, 2004.

Greenblatt, David. *The Ball Is Round: A Global History of Soccer*. New York: Riverhead Books, 2006.

Greenfield, Robert. *The Last Sultan: The Life and Times of Ahmet Ertegen*. New York: Simon & Schuster, 2011.

Hale, Grace Elizabeth. *A Nation of Outsiders: How the White Middle Class Fell in Love with Rebellion in Postwar America*. Oxford: Oxford University Press, 2011.

———. *Cool Town: How Athens, Georgia, Launched Alternative Music and Changed American Culture*. Chapel Hill: University of North Carolina Press, 2020.

Hebdige, Dick. *Subculture: The Meaning of Style*. London: Routledge, 1979.

———. "The Meaning of Mod." In *Resistance through Rituals: Youth Subcultures in Post-War Britain*, edited by Stuart Hall and Tony Jefferson,71–79. London: Routledge, 1993.

———."Reggea, Rastas, and Rudies." In *Resistance through Rituals: Youth Subcultures in Post-War Britain*, edited by Stuart Hall and Tony Jefferson, 113–28. London: Routledge, 1993.

Herzog, Dagmar. *Sex after Fascism: Memory and Morality in Twentieth-Century Germany*. Oxford: Oxford University Press, 2003.

Hesmondhalgh, David. "Post-Punk's Attempt to Democratize the Music Industry: The Success and Failure of Rough Trade." *Popular Music*, vol. 16, no. 3 (October 1997): 255–74. http://www.jstor.com/stable/853045.

Heylin, Clinton. *Public Image Limited: Rise/Fall*. London: Omnibus Press, 1989.

———. *From the Velvets to the Voidoids: A Pre-Punk History for a Post-Punk World*. New York: Penguin Books, 1993.

Higgins, Hannah. *Fluxus Experience*. Berkeley: University of California Press, 2002.

Hobsbawm, Eric. *The Age of Revolution, 1789–1848*. New York: Vintage Books, 1962.

Hobsbawm, Eric, and Terrence Ranger (eds.). *The Invention of Tradition*. Cambridge, MA: Cambridge University Press, 1983.

Horn, Gerd-Rainer. *The Spirit of '68: Rebellion in Western Europe and North America, 1956–1976*. Oxford: Oxford University Press, 2007.

Hsu, Bill. "Spew: The Queer Punk Convention." *Postmodern Culture*, vol. 2, no. 1 (September 1991): 1–3. https://www.proquest.com/scholarly-journals/spew-queer-punk-convention/docview/1425513036/se-2?accountid=11226.

Hsu, Wendy Fangyu. "Mapping the Kominas' Sociomusical Transnation: Punk, Diaspora, and Digital Media." *Asian Journal of Communication*, vol. 23, no. 4 (August 2013): 386–402. http://dx.doi.org/10.1080/01292986.2013.804103.

James, C. L. R. *The Black Jacobins: Toussaint L'Ouverture and the San Domingo Revolution.* New York: Vintage Books, 1963.

Johnson, G. *The Story of Oi!: A View from the Dead-End of the Street.* Manchester: Babylon Books, 1988.

Kalinnovsky, Artemy James Mark, and Steffi Marung (eds.). *Alternative Globalizations: Eastern Europe and the Postcolonial World.* Bloomington: Indiana University Press, 2020.

Kallen, Stuart. *The History of Alternative Music.* Detroit: Lucent, 2012.

Kasson, John F. *Amusing the Million: Coney Island at the Turn of the Century.* New York: Hill & Wang, 1978.

Katsiaficas, Georgy. *The Subversion of Politics: European Autonomous Social Movements and the Decolonization of Everyday Life.* Oakland, CA: AK Press, 2006.

Knight, Michael Muhammad. *The Taqwacores.* New York: Soft Skull Press, 2003.

Kramer, Michael J. *The Republic of Rock: Music and Citizenship in the Sixties Counterculture.* Oxford: Oxford University Press, 2013.

Kun, Josh. *Audiotopia: Music, Race, and America.* Berkeley: University of California Press, 2005.

Lampe, John R. *Yugoslavia as History: Twice There Was a Country.* Cambridge: Cambridge University Press, 1996.

Langman, Peter. *Why Kids Kill: Inside the Minds of School Shooters.* New York: Palgrave Macmillan, 2009.

Leach, William. *Land of Desire: Merchants, Power, and the Rise of a New American Culture.* New York: Vintage Books, 1993.

LeBlanc, Lauraine. *Pretty in Punk: Girl's Gender Resistance in a Boy's Subculture.* New Brunswick, NJ: Rutgers University Press, 1999.

Lenig, Stuart. *The Twisted Tale of Glam Rock.* Santa Barbara, CA: Praeger, 2010.

Letts, Don. *Culture Clash: Dread Meets Punk Rockers.* London: SAF, 2007.

Leveritt, Mara. *Devil's Knot: The True Story of the West Memphis Three.* London: Simon & Schuster, 2002.

Lippman, Walter. *Public Opinion.* New York: Harcourt, Brace, 1922.

Lord, Julian. *Teddy Boys: A Concise History.* London: Milo Books, 2012.

Lydon, John. *Rotten: No Irish, No Blacks, No Dogs.* London: Hodder & Stoughton, 1993.

MacLeod, Dewar. "'Social Distortion': The Rise of Suburban Punk Rock in Los Angeles." In *America under Construction: Boundaries and Identities in Popular*

Culture, edited by Kristi Long and Matthew Nadelhaft, 123–48. New York: Garland, 1997.

———. *Kids of the Black Hole: Punk Rock in Postsuburban California*. Norman: University of Oklahoma Press, 2010.

Mailer, Norman. *The White Negro*. San Francisco: City Lights Books, 1957.

Manheim, James M. "Flogging Molly." In *Contemporary Musicians: Profiles of the People in Music Volume 66*, ed. Tracie Ratiner, 54–56. Detroit: Gale, 2010.

Mann, Charles C. *1493: Uncovering the New World Columbus Created*. New York: Vintage Books, 2001.

Marcade, Phil. *Punk Avenue: Inside New York City Underground 1972–1982*. New York: Three Rooms Press, 2017.

Marcus, Greil. *Lipstick Traces: A Secret History of the Twentieth Century*. Cambridge, MA: Harvard University Press, 1989.

———. *Ranters & Crowd Pleasers: Punk in Pop Music, 1977–92*. New York: Doubleday, 1993.

Marks, Craig, and Rob Tannenbaum. *I Want My MTV: The Uncensored Story of the Music Video Revolution*. New York: Dutton, 2011.

Marsh, Nicholas. *Phillip Larkin: The Poems*. New York: Palgrave Macmillan, 2007.

Mason, Robert, and Iwan Morgan (eds.). *The Liberal Consensus Reconsidered: American Politics and Society in the Postwar Era*. Oxford: Oxford University Press, 2017.

Mattson, Kevin. *We're Not Here to Entertain: Punk Rock, Ronald Reagan, and the Real Culture Wars of the 1980s*. Oxford: Oxford University Press, 2020.

McLaughlin, Noel, and Martin McLoone. "Hybridity and National Musics: The Case of Irish Rock Music." *Popular Music*, vol. 19, no. 2 (April 2000): 181–99. https://www.jstor.org/stable/853667.

McMillian, John. *Smoking Typewriters: The Sixties Underground Press and the Rise of Alternative Media in America*. Oxford: Oxford University Press, 2011.

McNeil, Legs, and Gillian McCain. *Please Kill Me: The Uncensored Oral History of Punk*. New York: Grove Press, 1996.

Melnick, Monte, and Frank Meyer. *On the Road with the Ramones*. London: Sanctuary Publishing, 2003.

Mintz, Sidney W. *Sweetness and Power: The Place of Sugar in Modern History*. New York: Penguin Books, 1985.

Mohr, Tim. *Burning Down the Haus: Punk Rock, Revolution, and the Fall of the Berlin Wall*. Chapel Hill, NC: Algonquin Books, 2019.

Monroe, Alexei. *Interrogation Machine: Laibach and NSK*. Cambridge, MA: MIT Press, 2005.

Morrell, Brad. *Nirvana and the Sound of Seattle*. London: Omnibus Press, 1993.

Moynihan, Michael, and Didrik Søderlind. *Lords of Chaos: The Bloody Rise of the Satanic Metal Underground*. Port Townsend, WA: Feral House, 2003.

Mullen, Brendan, and Marc Spitz. *We Got the Neutron Bomb: The Untold Story of LA Punk*. New York: Three Rivers Press, 2001.

Murphy, Gareth. *Cowboys and Indies: The Epic History of the Record Industry*. New York: Thomas Dunne Books, 2014.

Nadler, Ben. *Punk in NYC's Lower East Side 1981–1991*. Portland, OR: Microcosm Publishing, 2014.

Nguyen, Mimi Thi. "Preface." In Michelle Cruz Gonzales, *The Spitboy Rule: Tales of a Xicana in a Female Punk Band*, xv–xviii. Oakland, CA: PM Press, 2016.

O'Connor, Alan. *Punk Record Labels and the Struggle for Autonomy: The Emergence of DIY*. Lanham, MD: Lexington Books, 2008.

O'Connor, Nuala. *Bringing It All Back Home: The Influence of Irish Music at Home and Overseas*. Dublin: Merlin, 2001.

Palmer, Amanda. *The Art of Asking or How I Learned to Stop Worrying and Let People Help*. New York: Grand Central, 2014.

Perl, Jed. *New Art City*. New York: Knopf, 2005.

Perry, Mark. *Sniffin' Glue: The Essential Punk Accessory*. Lanham, MD: Sanctuary, 2000.

Poiger, Uta G. *Jazz, Rock, and Rebels: Cold War Politics and American Culture in a Divided Germany*. Berkeley: University of California Press, 2000.

Polanyi, Karl. *The Great Transformation: Origins of Our Times*. New York: Farrar & Rinehart, 1944.

Pratchett, Terry. *The Globe: The Science of Discworld II*. New York: Random House, 2002.

Quatro, Suzi. *Unzipped*. London: Hodder & Stoughton, 2007.

Radway, Janice. "Girl Zine Networks, Underground Itineraries, and Riot Grrrl History: Making Sense of the Struggle for New Social Forms in the 1990s and Beyond." *Journal of American Studies*, vol. 50 (2016): 1–30. doi:10.1017/S0021875815002625.

Ramet, Sabrina. "Shake, Rattle and Self-Management." In *Kazaam! Splat! Ploof!: The American Impact on European Popular Culture since 1945*, edited by Gordana P. Crnković and Sabrina Ramet. Lanham, MD: Rowan & Littlefield, 2003.

Ramone, Marky. *Punk Rock Blitzkrieg*. New York: Touchstone, 2015.

Reynolds, Simon. *Rip it Up and Start Again: Postpunk 1978–1984*. London: Penguin Books, 2005.

Robb, John. *Punk Rock: An Oral History*. Oakland, CA: PM Press, 2012.

Said, Edward. *Orientalism*. New York: Pantheon Books, 1978.

Saunders, Frances Stonor. *The Cultural Cold War: The CIA and the World of Arts and Letters*. New York: New Press, 2013.

Savage, Jon. *England's Dreaming: Anarchy, Sex Pistols, Punk Rock, and Beyond*. New York: St. Martin's Griffin, 2001.

———. *Teenage: The Prehistory of Youth Culture, 1875–1945*. New York: Penguin, 2007.

———. *The Searing Light, the Sun, and Everything Else: Joy Division—the Oral History*. London: Faber & Faber, 2019.

Schulman, Sarah. *The Gentrification of the Mind: Witness to a Lost Imagination.* Berkeley: University of California Press, 2013.

Sewall Ruskin, Yvonne. *High on Rebellion: Inside the Underground at Max's Kansas City.* New York: Thunder's Mouth Press, 1998.

Sinker, Daniel. *We Owe You Nothing: Punk Planet the Collected Interviews.* Chicago: Punk Planet Books, 2008.

Smith, Patti. *Just Kids.* New York: Harper Collins, 2010.

Spooner, James. "Foreword." In *White Riot: Punk Rock and the Politics of Race*, edited by Stephen Duncombe and Maxwell Tremblay, xiii–xvii. London: Verso, 2011.

Stitziel, Judd. "Shopping, Sewing, Networking, Complaining: Consumer Culture and the Relationship Between State and Society in the GDR." In *Socialist Modern: East German Everyday Culture and Politics*, edited by Katherine Pence and Paul Betts, 253–86. Ann Arbor: University of Michigan Press, 2008.

Sugrue, Thomas J. *The Origins of the Urban Crisis: Race and Inequality in Postwar Detroit.* Princeton, NJ: Princeton University Press, 1996.

Suisman, David. *Selling Sounds: The Commercial Revolution in American Music.* Cambridge, MA: Harvard University Press, 2009.

Sunderland, Sam. *Perfect Youth: The Birth of Canadian Punk.* Toronto: ECW, 2012.

Thompson, Dave. *Depeche Mode: Some Great Reward.* London: Sidgwick & Jackson, 1995.

Thompson, E. P. *The Making of the English Working Class.* New York: Vintage Books, 1966.

"Throbbing Gristle." In *Industrial Culture Handbook*, edited by V. Vale and Andrea Juno, 11. San Francisco: RE/Search 1983.

Troitsky, Artemy. *Back in the USSR: The True Story of Rock in Russia.* London: Omnibus Press, 1987.

Turner, Fred. *From Counterculture to Cyberculture: Stewart Brand, the Whole Earth Network, and the Rise of Digital Utopianism.* Chicago: University of Chicago Press, 2008.

Tutti, Cosey Fanni. *Art, Sex, Music.* London: Faber & Faber, 2017.

Vale, V., and Andrea Juno (eds.). *Search and Destroy #1–6: The Complete Reprint.* San Francisco: V/Search, 1996.

———. *Search and Destroy #7–11: The Complete Reprint.* San Francisco: V/Search, 1997.

Von Eschen, Penny M. *Satchmo Blows Up the World: Jazz Ambassadors Play the Cold War.* Cambridge, MA: Harvard University Press, 2004.

von Strandmann, Hartmut Pogge. "1848–1849: A European Revolution?" In *The Revolutions in Europe 1848–1849: From Reform to Reaction*, edited by R. J. W. Evans an dHartmut Pogge von Strandmann, 1–8. Oxford: Oxford University Press, 2000).

Wachtel, Andrew Baruch. *Making a Nation, Breaking a Nation: Literature and Cultural Politics in Yugoslavia.* Stanford, CA: Stanford University Press, 1998.

Wald, Elijah. *Escaping the Delta: Robert Johnson and the Invention of the Blues.* New York: Amistad, 2004.

———. *How the Beatles Destroyed Rock 'n' Roll: An Alternative History of American Popular Music.* Oxford: Oxford University Press, 2009.

Walker, John A. "Cross-Overs, Art into Pop, Pop into Art." In *Sound & Vision*, edited by Luca Beatrice, 22–32. Bologna: Damiani, 2007.

Wall, Mick. *John Peel: A Tribute to the Much-Loved DJ and Broadcaster.* London: Orion, 2004.

———. *Lou Reed: The Life.* London: Orion House, 2013.

Weber, Max. *The Protestant Ethic and the Spirit of Capitalism.* New York: Norton, 2008.

Weir, Allison. *Henry VIII: The King and His Court.* New York: Ballantine Books, 2001.

Weisbard, Eric. *Spin Alternative Record Guide.* New York: Vintage Books, 1995.

White, Emily. "Revolution Girl Style Now." In *Rock She Wrote: Women Write about Rock, Pop, and Rap*, edited by Evenlyn McDonnell and Ann Powers, 396–408. New York: Delta, 1995.

Williams, Kieran. *The Prague Spring and its Aftermath: Czechoslovak Politics, 1968–1970.* Cambridge: Cambridge University Press, 2011.

Wolfe, Tom. *The Electric Kool-Aid Acid Test.* New York: Farrar Straus Giroux, 1968.

Woodard, Komozi. *A Nation within a Nation: Amiri Baraka (Leroi Jones) and Black Power Politics.* Chapel Hill: University of North Carolina Press, 1999.

Zinn, Howard. *The People's History of the United States, 1492–Present.* New York: Harper Collins, 2003.

Zolov, Eric. *Refried Elvis: The Rise of the Mexican Counterculture.* Berkeley: University of Berkeley Press, 1999.

Discography

Alien Kulture. "Asian Youth / Culture Crossover." RARecords. 1979.

Bad Brains. *Bad Brains.* Reach Out Records. 1982.

Bad Religion. *Generator.* Epitaph. 1992.

Bikini Kill. *Pussy Whipped.* Kill Rock Stars. 1993.

Billy Bragg. *Don't Try This at Home.* Go! Discs. 1991.

Black Flag. *Damaged.* SST. 1981.

Blondie. *X Offender.* Private Stock. 1976.

———. *Blondie.* Private Stock. 1976.

Captain Beefheart & His Magic Band. *Trout Mask Replica.* Warner Bros. 1969.

The Damned. *Damned Damned Damned.* Stiff Records. 1977.

Death. "Politicians in My Eyes b/w Keep on Knocking." Tryangle Records. 1976.

———. *. . . For the Whole World to See.* Drag City. 2008.

———. *Spiritual Mental * Physical.* Drag City. 2011.

———. *III*. Drag City. 2014.

Death Ridge Boys. *Right Side of History*. Death Ridge Boys. 2017.

Destructors. *Exorcise the Demons of Youth*. Illuminated Records. 1982.

DJ Danger Mouse. *The Grey Album*. Danger Mouse. 2004.

Ejected. *A Touch of Class*. Riot City. 1982.

Elvis Costello. *My Aim Is True*. Stiff Records. 1977.

Fear. *The Record*. Slash. 1982.

Ghost Rider / The Ants. *Anthology of Myanmar Punk-Rock Vol. 1*. Tian An Men 89. 2000.

G.L.O.S.S. *Trans Day of Revenge*. Nervous Nelly Records. 2015.

Gogol Bordello. *Trans-Continental Hustle*. American Recordings. 2010.

Green Day. *American Idiot*. Reprise. 2004.

Guttermouth. *Puke*. Dr. Strange Records. 1991.

Hüsker Dü. *Zen Arcade*. SST. 1984.

———. *WareHouse: Song and Stories*. Warner Bros. 1987.

The Kominas. *Wild Nights in Guantanamo Bay*. The Kominas. 2008.

Max's Kansas City: New York New Wave. CBS. 1978.

Miles Davis. *Kind of Blue*. Columbia. 1959.

Nirvana. *Live Concert—10-31-91 Seattle*. DGC. 1991.

———. *Nevermind*. DGC. 1991.

No New York. Antilles. 1978.

Offspring. "Come Out and Play." Epitaph. 1994.

Pankrti. *Dolgcatj*. ŠKUC. 1980.

Patti Smith. *Horses*. Arista. 1976.

———. *Live in London at the Roundhouse in May 1976*. Smilin' Ears. 1977.

The Pogues. *Rum Sodomy & the Lash*. Stiff. 1985.

———. *If I Should Fall from Grace from God*. Island. 1988.

Prince Buster. *Madness*. 1963.

Ramones. *Ramones*. Sire. 1976.

Rancid. *Let's Go*. Epitaph. 1994.

Rise Above: 24 Black Flag Songs to Benefit the West Memphis Three. Sanctuary Records. 2002.

Rumors from the Air-Conditioned Tiger Pit. Rotten House Records. 1997.

Sex Pistols. *Never Mind the Bollocks, Here's the Sex Pistols*. Virgin. 1977.

Spitboy. *Mi cuerpo es mio*. Allied. 1994.

Strike Under. *Immediate Action*. Wax Trax! Records. 1981.

Subhumans. *Rats*. Bluurg Records. 1984.

Suicidal Tendencies. *Suicidal Tendencies*. Frontier. 1983.

Suicide. *Suicide*. Red Star. 1977.

Talking Heads. *Talking Heads:77*. Sire. 1977.

Teriyaki Asthma. C/Z. 1989.

Velvet Underground. *Velvet Underground and Nico*. Verve. 1967.
X. *Los Angeles*. Slash. 1980.

Filmography

Adler, Lou. *Ladies and Gentlemen, The Fabulous Stains*. Paramount, 2008.

Brooks, Jameson. *Bomb City*. 3rd Identity Films, 2017.

Covino, Mark Christopher, and Jeff Howlett. *A Band Called Death*. Drafthouse Films, 2012.

Curtis, Adam. *Century of the Self*. BBC 2, 2002.

Dynner, Susan. *Punk's Not Dead*. Punk's Not Dead Production, 2007.

Fleischer, Pavla. *The Pied Piper of Hützovina*. Arts Alliance America, 2008.

Hardy, Don. *Theory of Obscurity: A Film About the Residents*. KTF Films, 2015.

Hoppe, Jörg, Heiko Lange, and Klaus Maeck. *B-Movie: Lust & Sound in West Berlin 1979–1989*. DEF Media, 2015.

Jarman, Derek. *Jubilee*. Megalovision, 1978.

Kerslake, Kevin. *Joan Jett: Bad Reputation*. Magnolia Pictures, 2018.

Kral, Ivan, and Amos Poe. *The Blank Generation*. Poe Production, 1976.

Letts, Don. *The Punk Rock Movie*. Punk Rock Films, 1978.

Losurdo, Joe, and Kristina Tillman. *You Weren't There: A History of Chicago Punk 1977–1984*. Regressive Films, 2007.

Majeed, Omar. *Taqwacore: The Birth of Punk Islam*. EyeSteel Film, 2009.

Merendino, James. *SLC Punk!* Sony Pictures Classics, 1998.

Scott, Ridley. *Blade Runner*. Warner Bros., 1982.

Sng, Paul. *Poly Styrene: I Am a Cliché*. Skyart, 2021.

Spooner, James. *Afro-Punk*. Afro-Punk, 2003.

Wright, Geoffrey. *Romper Stomper*. Film Victoria, 1992.

Zahra, Eyad. *The Taqwacores*. Strand Releasing, 2011.

Index

CPSIA information can be obtained
at www.ICGtesting.com
Printed in the USA
BVHW071112250722
642940BV00001B/149